Women of Fes

CONTEMPORARY ETHNOGRAPHY
Kirin Narayan, Series Editor

A complete list of books in the series is available from the publisher.

Women of Fes

Ambiguities of Urban Life in Morocco

RACHEL NEWCOMB

PENN

University of Pennsylvania Press

Philadelphia

Published by
University of Pennsylvania Press
Philadelphia, Pennsylvania 19104-4112

Printed in the United States of America on acid-free paper

10 9 8 7 6 5 4 3 2 1

Library of Congress Cataloging-in-Publication Data
ISBN 978-0-8122-4124-2

*To my parents,
and to Noureddine and Sofia*

Contents

Notes on Transliteration

Moroccan Arabic *darija* is a dialectic form of Arabic that varies from region to region. For words common in Modern Standard Arabic, (such as those referring to standard Islamic practice), I have followed the *International Journal of Middle East Studies*. In reporting expressions and dialogue of Moroccan dialect, I have consulted Heath 1987 and Harrell 1962 for transliteration of *darija* terms. Where there are standard spellings for words that appear in English texts, such as *Alaoui* or *tagine*, I have retained the anglicized version. The glossary contains the Arabic words with fuller diacritics, but in the text I have simplified them to make them accessible to the English-speaking reader. Phonemes whose equivalents do not exist in English include the following:

hamza, ', a glottal stop
ayn, ', a voiced pharyngeal fricative
gh, a voiced uvular fricative
kh, a voiceless uvular fricative, as in "Bach."

Chapter 1
Introduction: Women of Fes and the Territories of Ideology

5:00 a.m.

   Before dawn Huriya wakes up, rising from the velvet-covered sofa in the salon to wash and perform the first prayers of the day. She is careful not to rouse her two-year-old grandson, who fell asleep next to her the night before, or his mother, both visiting from their home in northern Morocco. After praying, Huriya walks quietly through the darkened family room, where her two sons, Rachid and Ali, are sleeping soundly. From the refrigerator she takes out meat, vegetables, and onions she has chopped the night before to prepare a stew, lighting the gas burner for the small, two-burner stove. In a pressure cooker she starts to simmer a rich tagine while she gets ready for her job at the court where she has worked ever since her husband's death more than twenty years ago. Over her dress she throws on a long, embroidered Moroccan djellaba, carefully fastening a silk scarf under her chin, a present from another daughter, who lives in Europe. Before leaving the house she makes coffee and toast, preparing a breakfast tray for her adult children. She switches off the pressure cooker, which her daughter will heat up in time for lunch, when the city of Fes will shut down and everyone will come home for the largest meal of the day, and perhaps a siesta. Then Huriya will regale everyone with tales of the day's indictments and courtroom intrigue, and she will catch a bit of the neighborhood news: the marriages and jobs, births and illnesses, emigrations and returns that map out the shifting constellations of life in this neighborhood of old "Fassi" families whose lives have been connected for generations.[1]

9:00 a.m.

   Naima parks her hand-controlled car outside the café closest to the courthouse, reaching into the back seat for her crutches. The café is large and clean, a welcoming place for both male and female customers, and the

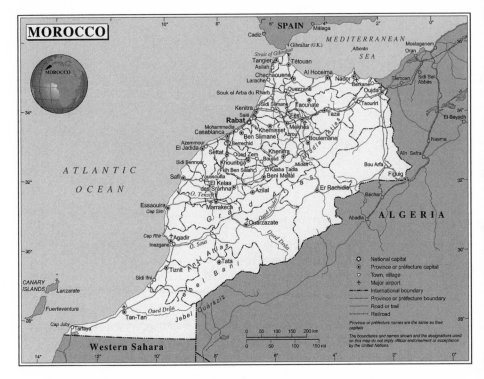

Figure 1. Morocco. Cartographic section, UN Department of Peacekeeping Operations.

waiters know her by name. On her way to the table where Ibtisam and Alia are waiting, Naima greets other lawyers she knows from her work. Like Naima, Ibtisam is also a lawyer, while Alia is a professor at the University of Fes. What brings them together is their interest in women's rights and activism, and together they run the Najia Belghazi Center, a women's nongovernmental organization (NGO) that offers legal advice, job training, and domestic violence counseling, among other services. Over café au lait and pain au chocolat, they discuss the latest national developments in the struggle to reform the mudawana, *the legal codes that govern a woman's rights in marriage and divorce. Conversation drifts to the Center, and they speculate on whether the Belgian government will give them the grant they have applied for, or whether the generous Fassi factory owner who gave them money last year might support their plans to open a shelter for abused women. They consider which of the Center's volunteers they might send to an event the following weekend in Meknes, a training session dedi-*

cated to handling the issues of domestic violence they are faced with every week at the Center.

Glancing at her watch, Naima realizes it is time to leave: she has a client at ten o'clock. She kisses her friends on the cheek and promises to stop by the Center late in the afternoon. It will be a long day, with a brief respite for lunch with her family, followed by a trip to the cyber café, where she will exchange emails with virtual "pen pals" as well as activist contacts in France and throughout Morocco. Aside from her small group in Fes, her email friends reinforce her sense that there are many women out there who share a vision of a better life for Moroccan women, and for women everywhere.

Noon

Across town Layla sleeps until noon in a small room in the Hotel Samir, a grand, five-star hotel whose occupancy has dwindled considerably since the terrorist attacks of September 11, 2001. The night before, she sang until two in the morning to a mostly empty piano bar, waiting for a group of Italian tourists who never materialized. One of them, Paolo, had watched her sing two nights before and promised to come back. He was transfixed by her beauty, he told her: the way the light caught the reddish glints of henna in her long, dark hair, her expressive, heavily lashed eyes. Deep down she was flattered, though she knew from experience that his comments were meaningless, and his failure to return the following night proved it. Instead she had performed her usual mix of nightclub standards and Arabic classics for a small audience that consisted of her American anthropologist friend and two of her girlfriends, who left before nine to avoid having to walk home late at night by themselves. Later, a few Moroccan businessmen stumbled in after drinking for hours at the cheaper bar next door. She avoided their leering eyes and kept focused on her hope that the Italians would arrive, since only foreigners, it seemed, understood her. At the end of the night she hid her disappointment from her accompanist, Massoud, kissing him on both cheeks and leaving for her room before anyone could follow her. In the bathroom mirror she peered at the dark circles under her eyes, wondering if the late hours and the strain of holding on to her dream were aging her, and if she had grown too old to make it as a singer. Lying in the dark of the hotel room, her thoughts grew still darker, and she lay awake for what seemed like hours until she was finally able to sleep.

At this moment in history, when images of veiled and "oppressed" Muslim women crowd the television and are used in support of policy initiatives ranging from economic development to war, public understanding, particularly in the United States, of what it means to be a Muslim woman is limited at best. The "Muslim woman" remains an essentialized entity, a hooded figure imagined to be subjected to a vindictive, patriarchal religion, tribal mores, and certain abuse from her husband. Sensationalized stories of honor killings, female circumcision, and women singled out for improper dress by the Taliban and brutally attacked, capture the public imagination and lead to the widespread impression that the Muslim world is a singular place where the lot of all women is appalling. There is little awareness that the women of the "Muslim world," which stretches from Morocco to Indonesia, are not a monolithic group, and that there is as much diversity along regional, national, urban/rural, class, and ethnic lines as there is among women in the "West." There is also almost no sense that the difficulties women in the Muslim world experience may not be due to "Islam," but to poverty, resulting from seemingly abstract forces such as globalization, structural adjustment programs, and uneven modernization.

Particularly at this time, nuanced portrayals of women in Muslim countries are needed more than ever, if for no other reason than to highlight the complexities of their lives and to underscore the fact that they are not waiting to be "saved" by the West.[2] My ethnographic work attempts to do this by sharing one anthropologist's experiences in a particular community of urban, middle-class women in the city of Fes, Morocco, at the beginning of the millennium. By examining the tactics women employ in negotiating the conflicts of living in a modern world, I hope to evoke as much as possible of the lived experience of a particular group of "Muslim women." In a proliferation of urban spaces, ranging from exercise clubs to women's NGOs, from the streets to the cyber cafés, women tangle with competing ideologies as they attempt to define who they are. Ideologies of the past, such as kinship networks and patronage, continue to have resonance in the present, and I explore how form and content are manipulated to mold them to current situations. Similarly, women crafting new forms of identity face the choice of drawing on more recent ideologies, such as Islamism, nationalism, modernization, and human rights.

Huriya, Naima, and Layla were the women I knew best in the city of Fes, and their stories demonstrate many of the themes of life for urban, middle-class women who are attempting to carve out new spaces for women in Moroccan society. First there was Huriya, who, after her husband's death, went out to work to support her five children, all under the age of ten. Because of her middle-class status and family connections, and because she could read and write, she was able to find viable employment. With the help of other family members who lived in the same family-owned apartment building, there was always someone to watch the children when she was working.

Huriya had not always faced an easy road, yet many of the resources she was able to draw on would not have been available to women of a different social class. I encountered many of those women through Naima, a lawyer and founding member of the first NGO in Fes dedicated to women with legal issues related to divorce, women who had frequently been abandoned by men. Naima herself had struggled to prove to Fassi society that being handicapped did not make her incapable of succeeding in society as a lawyer and advocate. The obstacles she faced, I often speculated, must have led her to identify with the marginalized women who came to her for help.

Finally there was Layla, who was determined to pursue a career as a singer without being perceived as a prostitute. Fassi women might sing at home to the radio, or dance modestly at a wedding when a potential suitor (or his mother) was watching, but the act of singing and dancing in public for paying customers gave the profession associations with prostitution.[3] Layla loved to sing, and she had undeniable talent, but was Fassi society willing to accept her work as respectable?

What the future holds is uncertain for those mavericks who attempt to strike out into new territory. A single person cannot alter an entire society. Or can she? The currents of Moroccan culture may exhibit dramatic surface changes, wrought by processes such as modernization, structural adjustment programs, massive rural-urban migration, and emigration, yet underneath, the waters are still and unyielding. Among the middle class of Fes there is a resistance, an insistence that change can only be accommodated insofar as one maintains a distinctive identity and sense of self. The outliers succeed when they are able to translate their actions into idioms comprehensible to others who would be quick to reject innovations perceived as completely foreign to Moroccan culture. In other words, working within the existing structures of power to gain acceptance for something new was often absolutely necessary.

A visitor to Fes, or to any large city in Morocco, will see more women than ever in the public space, going from home to work, from school to market, always active, moving, dynamic. There are schoolgirls in their white lycée smocks walking down the tree-lined Avenue Mohammed V, gazing in the windows of shops selling teapots and jewelry, Bata shoes, and shiny plastic novelties from China. Couples stroll hand in hand, admiring the new washing machines and televisions on display in the housewares store. A mother steers her child, ice cream cone in his hand, away from the beggars stationed outside the ice cream shops, while a girl darts downstairs from her apartment building to purchase flour or boullion cubes at the nearest convenience store. New spaces, such as cybercafés, are always packed with men and women browsing the Internet. However, the ways women experience the public space are still culturally distinctive, the ethics of shame and hospitality guiding them as they argue over how to present themselves to the world.

Middle-class women's roles, not only in the public space but also in the family, also contain ideas of the old mixed with the new. The debates surrounding the reform of the *mudawana* played themselves out in Fassi households in discussions about the roles women assume in their families, and what should happen to a woman in the event of a divorce. From the time the government proposed reforming the *mudawana* in 2000 until the king announced the laws would be changed in 2003, the issue of *mudawana* reform was constantly in the news. Those in favor of the reforms, which included raising the age of marriage from fifteen to eighteen and giving women the right to a judicial divorce, argued that, although Morocco had signed the Convention on the Elimination of All Forms of Discrimination Against Women (CEDAW) in 1993, Moroccan laws still discriminated against women.[4] Moroccans against the reform felt that the proposed changes both went against Islam and relied on concepts of human rights imported from the West. Based on the Maliki school of Islamic law, unlike Morocco's other criminal and civil codes, the *mudawana* favors a vision of extended patrilineal control over resources and women. Again, class colors everything, and the middle-class Fassis who seemed the most vocal about maintaining the laws rarely felt the full brunt of the law's negative effects.

The continued influence of patrilineal power structures is evident as women manipulate concepts that once applied primarily to men, such as patron-client relations. Women's networks, far from being limited just to other women, can extend beyond the family to entwine numerous people in a web of possible resources. Favors lead to commerce, and a better deal for the person who originally granted the favor, but also to a newly established business relationship for the client. While patron-client relations may be uneven, indicative of inherent societal inequalities, these relations are, at least, something to depend on in an otherwise uncertain world. For the middle-class women involved, their position at the center of these networks is new and different, even if the style of networks is not.

The ethnographic focus of this book is situated in the newer quarters of a particularly historic and ancient city, a place with a strong sense not only of its own identity and importance but also of having been slighted, bypassed as a global city. What does it mean to be *of* Fes, to be Fassi, a member of a group claiming origins in the great Muslim empire of Andalusia, stereotyped across Morocco for shrewd business sense and a strong sense of religiosity? Since their independence from the French in 1956, Fassis have been prominent in the halls of power in Rabat and Casablanca, the political and economic capitals of Morocco. But what has happened to the ones who chose to remain behind? The city and its past glories are essential to the identities of its inhabitants.

This book is an ethnography of women in urban space, moving through uncertain, uncharted territories of ideology, using (and sometimes discarding) maps drawn by custom and tradition. What people assert about themselves is often far from the truth, or the many contradictory truths of existence in Fes. Fassis construct a world through talk and discussion, and they also attempt to create and define idealized visions of women through various discourses. But it is more interesting to observe how women themselves respond to the expectations of others, where they demonstrate agency, and where they grapple with the indeterminacy of the modern condition. We can see these processes in everyday life; in arguments over how space should be used and how men and women should relate to one another; and in the different ways that women can be simultaneously modern, Fassi, Moroccan, and Muslim. Fassis, male and female, frequently make assertions about who "they" are. But frequently these assertions belie reality. As an ethnographer, I do not claim access to this reality. Rather, my attempt is to mark out and analyze that subtle area between what I witnessed and what people told me, the only space to which the ethnographer can legitimately lay claim.

Middle-Class Moroccan Women and the Territories of Ideology

Although the status of Muslim women—legal, social, economic, and otherwise—has been a popular topic for anthropologists since the 1970s, it was particularly relevant during the first summer I spent in Fes, just months after Moroccan prime minister Abderrahmane Youssoufi had announced the government's intentions to reform the *mudawana* family laws. In March 2000, competing demonstrations were organized both in support of and against the reforms, and the question of whether women's legal status had kept pace with their advancements in Moroccan society was suddenly on everyone's lips. Women's rights, women in Islam, women in the public sphere, and women and the nation state were topics constantly batted about in the media, at conferences and seminars, on university campuses, and in NGOs.[5] But what did all this mean for everyday life in a provincial city like Fes, the nation's religious heart, home to the oldest university in the world, al-Qariwiyin, which was, ironically enough, said to have been founded by a woman?

In Fes, as in other urban areas around Morocco, the agitation of large numbers of women for changes in the personal status code (*mudawana*) has reflected not only the increased visibility of women in the public sphere but also women's insistence on having a voice in legal, political, and economic realms. Since the 1960s, Moroccan society has witnessed the creation of a substantial middle class, and within that class, significant numbers of women have left the home to pursue educational and economic opportunities. Although women are still expected to shoulder the burden of domestic chores, a fundamental shift in the division of labor has occurred such that women are now in economic positions that were once the privilege of men only.

There has also been a change in kinship and marriage patterns, due to economic development, education, urbanization, and population demographics. According to official statistics, 69.7 percent of households in Fes are now nuclear, with 30.3 percent extended, revealing an increase in nuclear households during the past few decades (Guerraoui 1996: 166). Even in the official statistics, women play a significant economic role in their families. Among families who work in civil service and commercial occupations, in one out of three households the wife's income serves as the primary means of familial support.[6]

As wage earners and heads of households, middle-class women are increasingly forming social networks that are visible in the public sphere and extend beyond the family itself. Some networks are modeled on previously existing social patterns that anthropologists have long noted for men in Moroccan society, most notably the "patron-client" relationship, but other networks reflect newer forms of association in society. These include NGOs that bring together women of different social classes whose common agenda is forged through their interactions, and not determined a priori by their encounters with one another.

Since women's social roles, economic positions, and networks are changing, it is not surprising that some Moroccans feel threatened. In debates over the revision of the *mudawana*, some claim that changing the laws would be an affront to Islam, to Morocco, and to Moroccan culture and tradition. Others, however, declare that the existing laws fail to acknowledge the fundamental transformation of women's roles in Moroccan society, and that the current laws are contradictory to human rights documents that Morocco has signed. Arguments over these issues frequently raise questions about acceptable relationships between men and women in a modern, integrated Islamic society, as well as about the very meaning of community itself.

As different factions assert competing visions for the identity of the Moroccan state, the status of women is frequently invoked as a barometer for the country's "progress." Larger socioeconomic issues play themselves out in local struggles to define not only the proper place for women in society but also an identity capable of responding to the challenges of globalization. I was interested in pursuing these local struggles in public spheres outside cities like Rabat and Casablanca, but also in learning how individuals in cities marginal to operations of power conceive of women's roles in Moroccan society. In my fieldwork, I sought out "ways of operating," the everyday practices through which Fassis make use of spaces designated for them by others (de Certeau 1984: xiv). Fassi Moroccans maneuver both in social space and in what I have termed the "territories of ideology" to create their own distinctive identities, and to define new spaces for women in Moroccan society. These territories of ideology include all those assertions made by others about the proper place for women in society. Power designates strategies for how a place is to be used, but as de Certeau has shown, the less powerful also have their tactics, their ways to make use of the strong.

Conceptualizations of power in Morocco must take into account first and foremost the monarchy, which wields a charismatic hold over individual imaginations as it attempts to further its own authority (Miller and Bourquia 1999: 5). Recent anthropological writings on Morocco, such as Abdellah Hammoudi's *Master and Disciple*, seek in cultural forms clues to the current regime's longevity. A collection of essays edited by Miller and Bourquia, *In the Shadow of the Sultan: Culture, Power and Politics in Morocco*, reflects a more general shift in Moroccan anthropology, influenced by Foucault and Weber, toward studies that explore the strength of the monarchy through the relationship between discourse and power, religious legitimacy and ritual, nationalism and the postcolonial condition (Crawford 2001: 8).

In the current study, power is also seen to emanate from those controlling the terms of the *mudawana* debate, which often became polarized into binaries: the government versus the Islamists, for instance. But power also comes from outside, in the form of ideologies imported from elsewhere, ideas and images beamed from the satellite and into Moroccan households from the Middle East, from Europe, and from North America. Programs from the Middle East, such as those of the charismatic Egyptian preacher Amr Khaled, profess to give a true vision of Islam, laying out a way that pious Muslim women should live. Fassis also receive images from Europe, visions of an elsewhere that many find appealing, promising an existence abroad full of economic opportunities and stylish, modern lifestyles, unobstructed by daily bureaucratic worries, unemployment, or the pressures of familial expectations. These ideological territories offer not only a recipe for personal conduct but also a particular vision for social space. They aim to construct the utopian space of an ideal Islamic society, or of a successful and modern postcolonial nation. The particular positioning of women is essential to carrying out these visions, and so it sometimes seems that those concerned with defining Moroccan identity are obsessed with women:

where they are, how they occupy space, and whether their position in a particular space is permitted or forbidden.

Territories of ideology, then, attempt to delimit women's participation in the public sphere. The way that women respond to these ideologies, manipulating them to give meaning to the urban spaces they occupy, is largely the subject of my ethnographic study. De Certeau associates strategies with those who hold power, and tactics with the weak, arguing that "the actual order of things is precisely what 'popular' tactics turn to their own ends, without any illusion that it will change any time soon" (1984: 26). I ask what makes ideologies representing "patriarchy," "Islamism," or "modernity" appealing or unappealing to Fassis depending on their social positions. I am concerned here with how space is gendered, and how women succeed or fail at manipulating ideologies and transforming the public sphere.[7] But occasionally in this ethnography, a narrative creeps in through which something quite different is expressed in relation to power. In studying the middle class of Fes, I am also attentive to power as an object lost, stemming from the sense of many of the Fassis I knew that the world has passed them by.[8]

Entries

We enter Fes in the back of a recent model Peugeot, constructed in Morocco, after a three-hour drive on the newly paved *autoroute* from Rabat. Our car slices through vineyards and olive groves on a toll road almost empty of cars. Outside the city sprawls a giant rest stop with fake waterfalls and a café, featuring tea, pizza, kabobs, *tagine* stews, and even crackled Berber flatbread. The rest station is owned by a French company, and the employees are not locals.

After leaving the last toll booth behind, we circle a *rond-point* and are in the Ville Nouvelle, the New City, whose core was built by the French but whose recently constructed spokes radiate out from the city in all directions, covered with identical four-story apartment buildings and housing projects, neighborhoods that seem to have mushroomed overnight. From here it is less than ten minutes to the city center, and our car passes villas and apartment buildings, towering white high-rises, two supermarket chains, a palatial police headquarters, and another chaotic *rond-point* from which several streams of cars all seem to converge without method.

Coming down the wide, palm tree-lined Hassan II Boulevard the buildings are older, a testament to the French presence from 1912 to 1956: dilapidated art deco apartments and cafés on the left, and on the right the courthouse, the *Bureau des Tabacs*, and the old post office. For the sake of scenery we turn right, onto Avenue Mohammed V, the main street of commerce in the Ville, dominated by photo labs, shoe stores, and pharmacies. Café goers spill out onto sidewalks; waiters running between tables balance trays of coffee and pastries. On street corners sit female beggars, some with one or two children playing beside them, or breastfeeding as their mothers reach up to implore passersby for a dirham.

Passing the immense central market, bursts of color radiate from the flower and vegetable stands, the produce marking the passage of time through the seasons of availability: pomegranates and figs in the fall, buttery avocados and mandarin oranges in early spring, succulent, cloying melons in the summer. We drive past newer buildings that have not had time to gather the dirt of the years, as we glimpse storefronts filled with chic women's clothes, patisseries and cafés with neon signs. Farther out on the Rue de Immouzer the villas begin, villas inhabited by the wealthiest residents of Fes, while a few of the villas are available to be rented out for middle-class weddings.

Then we turn our car around and head back to the city center, pulling down an alley off Chefchaouni Street. The Lux neighborhood is an older one, named for a cinema that has since been torn down to make way for a high-rise. To our right, behind arcades held up by concrete columns, three-story French-built apartment buildings extend all the way down the street, in the shadow of new high-rises going up around them. There is almost no vegetation except for a small grassy area with two palm trees and several concrete benches. A few children—the infamous *shemker*, runaways and orphans who sniff fumes to get high—lounge in tattered clothes on the ground.

The shops on the ground floors of the apartment buildings in this neighborhood are all different from the ones that stood here ten years before. A *téléboutique* stands where previously a carpenter worked. A leather shop has become a music store. The last Jewish shopkeeper on this street, an elderly man who sold men's formal wear, is gone, his building torn down for yet another high-rise. A family-owned gourmet supermarket that sold Dutch oatmeal and pure honey has been replaced by the two new chain supermarkets on the road leading out of town. Only the tailor is still in his place, a wizened old man crouched on a stool, sewing buttons onto a silk caftan as we pass by.

The Lux neighborhood was where I lived during the eighteen-month period of my fieldwork from February 2001 to July 2002. Along with an NGO, an exercise club, cyber cafés, offices, and households in other parts of Fes, the Lux neighborhood was one of my primary fieldsites. My husband and I rented an apartment there in one of the high-rises, built ten years before, with views of the ancient *medina* or old city in the background, framed by mountains. By the time we left, a nicer, newer building had been erected next to ours, one so tall that we could no longer see the *medina*. All over town it was a familiar story. There was a building boom going on, and everywhere people were tearing down the art deco structures built by the French and putting up new buildings whose apartments most Fassis could not afford.

I had never expected to end up in Fes. My infatuation with Morocco began with the Moroccan Pavilion at Disney World's Epcot Center.[9] As a child I was entranced by the miniature replicas of *casbahs*, the delicious food, the belly dancers, and the Aladdin-like costuming. An idea of Morocco began to take shape in my mind, a land of veiled women, sumptuous carpets, and luxuriant excess overlaid by my knowledge of the 1960s hippie paradise lauded in songs like Crosby, Stills & Nash's "Marrakesh Express." After taking a class in Islamic history during college, I decided to find out if the real Morocco bore any resemblance to the country of my imagination. Morocco seemed the ideal place to experience the Muslim world: westernized enough that I could feel comfortable as a nineteen-year-old with very little travel experience, but exotic enough that it would literally be the most earthshaking thing that had ever happened to me.

Although the real Morocco was not quite like Epcot, it did not disappoint me. The stereotypes of excellent food and hospitable people are largely true, although rather than slipper-clad pashas on camels, in the city of Rabat I found people who dressed like I did, simply going about the business of everyday life, in office buildings, markets, and schools. For one semester I took classes in history, culture, and Arabic and lived with a host family in the working class neighborhood of Youssoufia. My final month studying in Morocco left the biggest impression. For the month-long independent research project required by the program, I traveled to the town of Taznakht in southern Morocco to study carpet weaving. Accompanied by a friend, I went to Taznakht and met my first "informant," an erudite scholar of Roland Barthes with an MA in linguistics, who had returned home to run a not-very-profitable family carpet shop. From Mohammed I learned my first lesson of fieldwork: that the best sources for information are often those people who feel estranged in some way from their own culture and want to reflect on it with other outsiders, with people who remind them of elsewheres, of other existences in which they may have dabbled. I also learned that the Moroccan government had a hand in everything, even in the seemingly innocuous business of women's weavings. The government had created cooperatives where they hoped women would weave for a wage; they had published design books and encouraged those patterns and colors that would sell with tourists. But the women of Taznakht resisted, still preferring to make the carpets at home, surrounded by their kin. I interrogated the women through Mohammed, wanting to know about the meaning of symbols and particular designs, but the answers I got seemed more about survival. Often the entire family income for months depended on the whims of the tourist industry, and on whether a carpet brought to the Sunday market might catch the eye of a middleman from Marrakech, who would then sell the carpet for a price much higher than what the family had been paid.

The daily struggle to put food on the table, to deal with government interference, and to raise a family were ultimately compelling. My interactions with Mohammed and the women of Taznakht destroyed the romanticized notion I had had of bohemian carpet weavers who practiced art for art's sake, with an uncompromising sense of integrity about their materials. I would never look at another carpet the same way again. When the semester ended and I boarded a plane back to America with my American classmates, my first reaction was despair that I might never see Morocco again, but my second thought was how to make Morocco a part of my life.

I returned again several times over the following years, first as a traveler and then later as a graduate student of anthropology. In the summer of 2000, searching for a field site, I came to Fes to study Arabic. The American Language Institute in Fes would be the place where I would learn to transform my command of the formal, unspoken Modern Standard Arabic (MSA) into Moroccan *darija*. I would also meet my future husband, whose family would welcome me as if I were a daughter. Middle-class Fassis themselves and residents of the Lux neighborhood, his family introduced me to their entire network of relatives, friends, and business acquaintances, which made some of the initial work of finding people to interview easy. Because of these connections, I decided to make Fes the site of my fieldwork.

I had always been interested in gender issues, and I was also impressed with the way that so many of the Moroccan women I met destroyed all the stereotypes of the passive, oppressed Muslim woman. I sought a project that would provide a point of comparison to anthropological work on Morocco that I admired,[10] but I decided to focus on urban, middle-class women, a topic that had not been studied in depth. Women, and their position in Fassi society, constantly came up as a subject in discussions, and it seemed that even in everyday life, women had become a trope for anxieties about what it meant to be a modern, Muslim nation-state in the twenty-first century.[11]

Fes as an Object of Nostalgia

Do things change but their forms, sounds, and impressions remain? Or does space remain but time passes and changes to express its presence in other forms and feelings?

It is as though we always recall time-space at the expense of an uncertain present. . . . It is as though what happens now has happened in an area lying between
what is lived and what is fancied, between the palpable and the imaginary. Everything is possible, and the journey of life can begin again with the same enthusiasm, if it were not for the weight of experience and the axe of time!
Does the city lie? Does Fez lie? (Berrada 1996: 109)

The city of Fes itself is an implicit character in my narrative, particularly the relationship between new and old, between the ancient Arab
quarters, the French-built sections, and the results of postcolonial efforts
to tear down the remnants of French colonial history in Morocco. How
middle-class Fassis interact with the built environment is significant,
since with new forms of space come questions about how these spaces
might be gendered. The places of the past where Fassis locate their history and sense of belonging evoke strong sentiments of memory and
nostalgia, power and belonging, even as the Fassis experience a distance
from the physical spaces themselves. Those middle-class Fassis who claim
ancient origins in Fes (*min asl Fes*) I refer to throughout this book as
"original" Fassis.[12]

The section of Fes that is now known as the *medina* was founded in
808 by Sultan Idriss II, shortly after the Islamic conquest of Morocco.[13]
One of the great imperial cities of Morocco, Fes was renowned for its
merchants and artisans and famous as a center of Islamic learning.
Although Moulay Rachid designated it as the first capital for the current
'Alaoui dynasty (1666), by the sixteenth century, Fes had begun to
decline.[14] Under the French Protectorate in 1912, the capital was moved
to Rabat. The *medina* of Fes has long been a favorite topic for Orientalist
historians, who asserted that the city embodied the essence of the
"Islamic city," but who paid little attention to actual social organization
(J. Abu-Lughod 1987: 157). What characterizes the "Islamic city" is a
topic too large to be addressed here, but a few basic features that historians have described are the division of space according to trades, the
legal status of various groups (such as religious minorities), and Islamic
attitudes toward gender. Early Orientalist scholarship set the tone for
later interpretations by erecting certain themes said to be characteristic
of the "Islamic City," which would continue to dominate the scholarship.[15] These themes include Islam as an "urban religion"; the city as
seen through institutions such as bazaar, public bath, and mosque; and
a lack of municipal organization. This practice of repeating the same
themes and descriptions comprises what Edward Said has described as
the Orientalist tendency toward citationary practices, in which new representations were built on the foundations of the old and "the actuali-
ties of the modern Orient were systematically excluded" (Said 1978:
177).

Yet the French built the Ville Nouvelle after the Protectorate began in 1912. The French practice of separating *medinas* from Villes Nouvelles in Morocco, which Janet Abu-Lughod has elsewhere called "urban apartheid," was a new strategy befitting Morocco's status as what the French termed a "protectorate" (rather than a colony), designed to protect native customs and simultaneously to create a modern city of order and administration. As Timothy Mitchell has shown, colonization inscribes on individuals "a new conception of space," encouraging "new forms of personhood" (1988: ix). Within colonial administrations, power became dispersed through the social system to operate internally and productively, producing institutions characteristic of the modern nation-state but also individual subjects who could be constituted as "modern" (xi). Such disciplining accompanied the development of capitalism and its spread to the non-European parts of the world.

The Villes Nouvelles of Morocco demonstrate how French disciplinary techniques organized society into manageable units, creating the effect of a transparent reality; structures that almost seemed to run themselves; and systems that gave the illusion of order, openness, and truth.[16] Literature has echoed these illusions. The main character of Mohamed Berrada's novel *The Game of Forgetting*, for example, moving between childhood in Fes and adulthood in the administrative capital of Morocco, Rabat, describes Rabat's Ville Nouvelle as "an open city without secrets or surprises, its streets were wide and straight, its houses low and not heavily covered with mosaic tiles of plaster decorations" (Berrada 1996: 45). By contrast, the old city of Fes is misunderstood by the French, who are ignorant of the social processes taking place along its narrow, winding streets. Of his neighborhood in the Fes *medina*, Berrada's narrator says, "It is almost a blind alley, but actually it is a thoroughfare" (16). While Orientalists may have seen a blind alleyway, going nowhere, or at most conjured up a rigid barrier between domestic privacy and public life, these alleys served as fluid boundaries, mediating between house and street.

In the case of Fes, academic research has ignored the Ville Nouvelle in favor of studies of the ancient *medina* as a site for religious learning and a place where "traditional" trades and professions are still practiced. The Ville Nouvelle possesses its own substantial population of modern city dwellers, virtually ignored in the literature. How do individuals in Fes, particularly women, consider their relationship to the built environment? How do local and global discourses interact in the gendering of modern Muslim cities? More importantly, which discourses are most salient to women as they determine the "rules" for occupying new urban spaces? Attention to these questions sheds light on the ways in

Figure 2. Lux neighborhood, Ville Nouvelle. A new high-rise is being constructed at the center right.

which national and global processes play themselves out in specific local settings.

Privileging the old *medina* as somehow characteristic of a timeless, essentialized Fes, and disparaging the Ville Nouvelle as that which has been corrupted, is false, and the lie, alluded to in the earlier quotation from Berrada, rests in the belief that places can remain static. The Ville Nouvelle is no less "Islamic," despite the history of its construction. As Robert Rotenberg writes, "to isolate a single moment and privilege it as somehow truer than other moments is misleading. Spatial meanings must be seen in this light. They are historically contingent" (Rotenberg and McDonogh 1993: xiv).

Writing about Fes in the twenty-first century, Driss Guerraoui has spoken of a rupture between the old city and the new, between heritage and conservation and the demands of a burgeoning population, especially for housing (1996: 159). A strong tension exists between modern, functional habitats and the precarious living conditions of others. *Medina* districts have become overpopulated due to rural-to-urban migration, and shantytowns are scattered liberally at the outskirts of most Moroccan cities. The old *medina* of Fes now boasts a population density of more than 1,000 inhabitants per hectare, and although UNESCO declared the city a world heritage site in 1980, very little has been accomplished in the way of renovations. The economy of Fes has remained largely unindustrialized, with the majority of workers employed in artisanal, commerce, and civil service positions. Official unemployment statistics place Fes at 20 percent, four percentage points higher than the rest of the country (161).

Among the Fassis I know, the *medina* serves as an object of nostalgia, as a symbol of the former apogee of Moroccan civilization, and as a place over which they feel proprietary even if they no longer own property in its districts.[17] My friends in the Ville Nouvelle only venture out to the *medina* occasionally, to shop for jewelry or household goods (such as wool or traditional wooden furniture) in the neighborhood of Fes Djedid, or to visit friends or relatives. However, some of the old Fassi families still own houses there. In many cases, they rent them out, room by room, to migrants from the countryside, or else they keep them empty in the hopes that a foreigner might be interested in buying and renovating them. A few members of the "original" Fassi families I knew still lived in their *medina* homes, but very few.

Middle-class Fassis asserted that the *medina* was dirty, overcrowded, overrun by people from the countryside, and the opposite of what a modern city ought to be. They recognized that the *medina* was interesting to tourists but were somewhat embarrassed that visitors to Fes would receive the impression that all Fassis live "medieval" lives, using donkeys as transportation and enduring insufficient plumbing. By contrast, these Fassis were very proud of the Ville Nouvelle, and of its tall high-rises, wide boulevards, gleaming cafés, and modern administrative buildings. They were less interested in the French-built art deco structures, which, as I mentioned earlier, were being torn down one by one to make way for new high-rises. Although in other Moroccan cities, attempts were under way to preserve the colonial architecture, in Fes there was a definite preference for modernity as constructed by Moroccans, in which French presence was rapidly being erased from the urban residential landscape. The Lux neighborhood where I lived was originally a Jewish quarter, and there were still a few older Jewish residents left. After Independence in 1956, Fassis leaving the *medina* purchased the buildings one by one, and the Jewish families gradually left, most of them heading to Israel, Canada, or France. Families speculated that one day soon, they might sell their property to a developer from Casablanca, taking the money and moving out to a newer suburb.

Many Fassis claim to trace their origins back hundreds of years and consider their family lineage to have played a significant part in the history of Morocco. Any studies of power in the Moroccan context will encounter assertions of Fassi influence, as Fassis are always assumed to be working hand-in-hand with the government, receiving favors, and occupying prominent positions in business and politics. Yet although the Fassis in this book bore the prominent names and social origins of those who had gone elsewhere and reaped the benefits of influence and proximity, they themselves had stayed behind to make the most of life in Fes. True, some had inherited family businesses or civil service positions, but others were unemployed and had no immediate prospects. The wealth of a great-grandfather who had the ear of a sultan was now considerably dissipated among heirs, and in some cases only remained as a distant memory that fewer and fewer of the living could claim to have shared.

The dream of recovering their past influence, but more practically, the need to find viable employment, led some of these Fassis to emigrate, though for the most part they seemed conflicted about leaving. Many thought that emigration was for the lower classes and sought to distance themselves from the Moroccans they met abroad. The assertion that emigration was only a temporary strategy was one way of doing this. Some spoke of raising enough capital to come back, start a business and revitalize the city's economy. However, particularly among young men, the longing for "elsewhere" frequently appeared in their conversations. "Elsewhere" could be tied up with feelings of nostalgia for the old Fes *medina*, other Moroccan cities such as Casablanca or Agadir, or nations with better economic prospects, such as Sweden or Canada. Although all of the people mentioned in this ethnography lived in Fes, some had designs on elsewhere, while others had been there, been disappointed, and had returned home. The identities of the Fassis under discussion here are solidly linked to the city itself, and Fes is a significant part of their self-definition.

"When I went to Sweden in the early '90s," Mehdi, a man in his mid-thirties who now owned a small business, told me, "I was living in a room with several other guys, because that was the only way we could afford it. It was very cold, and I worked all the time. At night, nothing was going on, the streets were deserted. Everything was cold, the people, the weather. And I was nobody there." This sense of being "somebody" is recoverable only in Fes, where family names indicate one's position in a social network whose roots run deep into the city's culture.

Some of the Moroccans who appear in these pages were not "original Fassis," and their narratives are significant for the perspective they bring to Fassi identity practices and hegemonic attempts by the "original Fassis" to control and define social space in Fes. I also encountered lower-income women whom I met through Naima at the local NGO; *medina* residents whom I met through other social connections; and people from other social groups, including the upper-class clients of my husband's sound and recording business; and the small Jewish population of Fes. Those Fassis who do not trace their origins back to Muslim Spain resent the insularity of the "original" Fassis and do not feel there is any significant difference between the two groups in the present. Even people who have lived in the city for a long time or were born in Fes still identify with their own or their parents' natal region. Many were successful, industrious members of the middle class, although their families had reached this social position relatively recently. In contrast, the "original Fassis" who still projected a certain sense of noblesse oblige, had, by virtue of their economic status, fallen into the middle class.[18]

The growth of a substantial middle class in Middle Eastern societies is a relatively recent phenomenon, stemming from economic development in the region (Moghadam 1993: 17). After Independence, Moroccans benefited from new opportunities for education and employment in the public sector, in addition to a rising standard of living (Cohen 2003: 171). Early descriptions of this new middle class in the Middle East and North Africa characterized them as a salaried class dedicated to creating economic opportunities for all, and "committed ideologically to nationalism and social reform" (Halpern 1965: 53).[19] Many benefited from new educational opportunities created by colonialism, and it was hoped they would eventually overthrow the existing power structures and ruling families to create dynamic new economies built on skills and not privilege. Economic development and nation building were part of the same endeavor, and individuals were encouraged to conceive of themselves as citizens of the nation-state. The creation of a "modern middle class," in the words of André Adam, was a product of this postcolonial project of modernization, as the Moroccan economy experienced moderate economic growth and a minimal trade deficit. A modern middle class would be more inclined to support nationalist modernization projects than an entrenched bourgeoisie that had been accustomed to reaping the benefits of social position (Adam 1968: 730).

In the 1970s, through loans and phosphate mining profits, the Moroccan government created civil service professions, developed industries, and expanded the education sector. Economic crises in the 1970s, along with the adoption of structural adjustment polices in the 1980s, led to calls from the monarchy for the development of the private sector, and newly educated Moroccans began to seek work in growing industries such as marketing, tourism, education, and media. Morocco's entry into the global market has led to high rates of unemployment, with unemployment statistics hovering around 30 percent of the active labor force (*Activité, Emploi, et Chomage* 2000). In these circumstances, power manifests itself in the psychic toll on individuals unable to find work, receive credit, or travel abroad (Cohen 2004: 17).

Dale Eickelman has written that education erodes "intellectual and physical boundaries" and enables "connections to be made across formerly impenetrable boundaries of class, locality, language, and ethnic group" (Eickelman 2001: 97). While this may be true in some contexts, in Fes, social class still frequently determines occupational possibilities, creating resentment among those who are educated but unable to find work. Further, those without any education at all (whose numbers are suggested by the country's 50 percent illiteracy rate) are unable to participate in debates that may take place within new forms of media such as the Internet. Eickelman notes this disparity, stating that while globalization has led to increased mobility among the elite, it "increases polarities with the more localized rest" (103).

Within the middle class, there is differentiation, from "traditional" groups of longer standing such as entrepreneurs and shopkeepers to more recently created categories, such as civil service employees, or private sector employees like administrators, secretaries, health professionals, and lawyers (Moghadam 1993: 17). Sociologist Shana Cohen divides the Moroccan middle class into three categories: "the unemployed and exploited service workers, traditional public sector occupations of the modern middle-class and small-level entrepreneurs, and those businessmen and women and entrepreneurs benefiting directly from trade and direct foreign investment" (Cohen 2003: 176). Cohen proposes a new social category, the "detached middle," comprised of unemployed university graduates who lack social connections and feel no attachment to the nation-state. This detached middle "no longer takes center stage as a nation's achievement or, similarly, no longer acts to defend its own continuity and stability" (2003: 180). Those within the "detached middle" include entrepreneurs who do benefit from social influences, especially Fassis, but who ultimately come up against other types of obstacles. Cohen writes that "managers and entrepreneurs . . . tend to be of Fassi origin" (2003: 177) and have advantages over their peers in terms of education and social connections. But despite some advantages over other middle-class Moroccans, Fassis share anxiety about Morocco's position in the global market as well as a sense of uncertainty about the future. A sense of melancholy, "the psychic imprint of the lost ideal of human and national potential," is pervasive (2003: 181). However, unlike the middle-class Casablancans that Cohen describes, who have set their sites beyond the nation-state and toward "the nonlocated social space of the globe" (Cohen 2004: 108) the Fassis in my study continued to believe that the city of Fes would provide—economically, socially, and politically.

Casablanca is a global city, while Fes has lost its former centrality to world markets and important political events. Similar to Cohen's Casablancans, many younger Fassis between the ages of twenty and thirty-five did exhibit a cynicism toward the projects and aims of the nation-state. Yet instead of floating away as part of what Cohen calls the "detached middle," looking toward transnational opportunities and globalization, many Fassis were more likely to identify with the city itself, whose history seems to offer a vision of continuity and stability, albeit an illusory one.

Mounia Bennani-Chraïbi (1994) has argued that scholarly works on Moroccan history and sociology have been concerned with elite political movements and the monarchy, thus ignoring the concerns of the middle and lower classes. This ethnography is concerned with the everyday life and social connectedness that helped to create a sense of stability for the middle class of Fes; it takes into account how people's responses to events happening elsewhere, particularly those concerning women, affect the construction of social life.

Everyday Practices Within Territories of Ideology

A focus on "everyday practices," or on individual efforts to contest or manipulate discourses of power, enables a shift away from framing this inquiry as a study of the ways "traditional" people deal with "modern" spaces and ideologies. The reified nature of this construction is limiting, as it continues to associate tradition with all that is "native," while modernity implies something imposed from above, usually from the West. Moving away from considering colonial and postcolonial space solely in terms of issues of representation and reception, it is more useful to consider those individual tactics that insinuate, manipulate, and finally reappropriate social space in order to highlight human agency in response to powerful ideologies. Thus, in describing a gendered city, I am interested in how individuals respond to the ideologies that attempt to order the city according to conceptualizations of appropriate spaces for men and women.

Everyday practices consist of those small, sometimes fragmentary tactics that represent "the ingenious ways in which the weak make use of the strong" (de Certeau 1984: xvii). In Fes, women give meaning to urban social spaces by using their own cultural categories to shape space in a way that reflects the construction of a female, Moroccan, and Fassi identity. This is not a neutral process, however. Through the ways in which people contest urban social space, more is at stake than just the creation of an individual identity. In defining the meanings and uses of new spaces, Moroccans are also making a claim for a collective vision of gendered identity and relations between men and women. Everyday practices, rather than being mere individual tactics, are profoundly social. In this case, gendered everyday practices assert an individual's idea of the proper place for women while simultaneously responding to and transforming various ideologies about women's position in Moroccan society.

What, then, are these ideologies, and how does each attempt to lay out a specific map for women's practices? On the surface these ideologies often appear as binary opposites, although the reality is much more complex. The meanings Fassis attach to the concept of "modernity" are significant. Some Fassis do experience "modernity" as an export from the global North that countries of the global South are struggling to follow. This sense of inadequacy is often blamed on the nation and then internalized. However, others express no self-consciousness about asserting a modern identity in distinctive local idioms. For Naima, for example, the freedom to go to cafés, agitate for changes in women's rights through her NGO, and travel alone to other cities (and even to Europe) for conferences did not threaten her sense of identity or propriety, and her family accepted her actions. Relocating the specific and the local within this hegemonizing discourse allows us to learn more about how individuals experience modernity from within particular cultural frameworks.

With confusion over current local and national strategies for achieving "modernity," Fassis often questioned whether they might return to their own "traditions," and this was a hotly debated topic, particularly where it concerned women and women's rights.[20] Some felt that revising the *mudawana* to give women more control over their marriages and divorces was tantamount to abandoning Moroccan culture, which was then collapsed with Islam and the legitimacy of patriarchal control of women. Others feared that they were being asked to embrace the projects of a Eurocentric "modernity," and to abandon the uniqueness of Moroccan culture.[21] The Islamist discourse responds to this fear by claiming that in the slavish desire to follow European ways, Moroccans have lost their religion and their principles, and that the apparent chaos of Moroccan society is a direct result of Muslims forgetting to live by God's laws.

"Islamism" is another ideology that was gaining currency between 2000 and 2002, and the term carries a negative or positive valence depending on context and speaker. Fassis variously referred to Islamists as *mutatarifin, muhafidin, ikhwaniyin,* and, in French, *les intégristes,* but I take "Islamism" as the idea that religion should interpenetrate all areas of life, collapsing boundaries between sacred and temporal (Ruedy 1994: xv). Islamism in North Africa is frequently considered in opposition to secularism, a term that has come to be associated with Western society, colonialism, and anticolonial nationalism (xvi). The secular pro-

grams promoted by elites after Independence have not reached a majority of the population, and thus people often consider secularism an
imported discourse that has fostered corruption and an unequal distribution of wealth. Islam is often used as an irrefutable critique of government practices believed to diverge too much from religious ideals.
However, those Fassis who hold a more secular self-positioning strongly
disapprove of Islamist ideologies. In times of great political stress, Islamists are blamed for importing ideas that disrupt the social order and
threaten local and national stability.[22]

It has become commonplace among academics to speak of many
"Islams" rather than a single, unified vision, and practices loosely associated with Islam in Morocco are numerous. Throughout the country,
white-domed tombs commemorating holy figures revered for their piety
or miracles are everywhere, and Sufi brotherhoods have been present in
Morocco since the thirteenth century.[23] The diverse local practices not
directly sanctioned by the Islamic scholars representing the state (*ulama*)
are often termed as "popular" Islam, but a third variant of Islamism has
become visible in recent years that positions itself in opposition to both
popular practices as well as the state-supported *ulama*. This is nothing
new, as Salafi Islam, the reformist movement that argues Muslims should
follow the example of the Prophet Muhammad and return to Islam as it
was practiced in its earliest days, first appeared in Morocco in the nineteenth century. Later, Salafi doctrine became a part of nationalist ideology in the movement for Moroccan independence.[24] Yet under the reign
of King Hassan II, Islamism was encouraged as a counterweight to socialism, and since the 1970s, numerous Islamist organizations, both nonvio-
lent and militant, have sprung up. Some Moroccans perceive Islamists as
importing incorrect Saudi doctrines, while others argue that Islamism is
merely a return to the "fundamentals" of the faith, and to an ideology
that promotes Islamic ideals of fairness and justice.

Scholars have long noted the appeal of an Islamist ideology to the poor
who have emigrated to the cities and been unable to make ends meet.
But Islamism has found a foothold in other areas of society as well,
among the educated but disenchanted young men who have been unable
to find jobs, among those critical of corruption and government excess,
and even among those who consider themselves politically neutral. Co-
opting discourses from the Moroccan women's rights movement, Islamists draw attention to the fact that women's entry in the public sphere
leads them to be overworked both at home and at work (Benkirane 2002:
83). In an interview with the French language women's magazine *Femmes
du Maroc*, Abdelilah Benkirane, leader of the religiously oriented Party of
Justice and Development, argues that Moroccans are becoming more and
more like Europeans, and that equality between men and women might

ultimately lead to men insisting on never marrying, and fewer children being born (83). Other Islamists in Morocco, most notably Abd al-Salam Yassine and his daughter Nadia, leaders of the banned Association for Justice and Charity (al 'Adl wa'l-Ihsan), have been critical of the legitimacy of the monarchy and questioned its Islamic credentials. Responding to their arguments, many Fassis accept that an unproblematic return to authentic sources of Islamic piety would provide an ideal means for liberating the masses. This quest to regain cultural authenticity "expresses a critical resistance to the assimilative strategies and homogenizing practices of modernity" (Göle 2002: 187).

While Islam is used as a justification for women's status in Muslim societies and as an argument for returning to supposedly more "authentic" Islamic forms of behavior, excessive focus on the subject of religion can mask other factors that also contribute to the position of women.[25] An overemphasis on religion leads to neglect of other social issues, as well as to a sense of overdeterminism that the position of women in Islamic societies can never change because the religion will not allow it (Erturk 1991: 318).

Where does the state stand in all this? The Moroccan government, which proposed the controversial changes to the *mudawana* in 2000, tries to play to all sides at once, although its agenda appears to be more on the side of the secular modernists. From 1999 to 2003 a statement of the government's position could be found on a government-sponsored website dedicated to the promotion of the (singular) Moroccan Woman.[26] The Moroccan Woman "enjoys the guarantee of her rights and has very strong expectations for the future." Yet the Moroccan Woman is "ambivalent." Her role is to be "the guardian of Moroccan cultural values at home and the proponent of modernity outside her house." Through organizations and education she seeks to create a "space of liberty" and fights for her rights in previously male-dominated spheres. Yet she "is still ambiguous; she has poor knowledge of the law, she also has the paradox of female self-censorship and insufficient education, especially in rural areas."[27]

From the founding of Morocco in the eleventh century to its independence in 1956, women are said to have played a significant part—aiding rulers in ministering to the state in the role of royal wives to signing manifestos seeking independence from the French. According to the Moroccan constitution, the Moroccan woman has "the same political rights as man, but she is discreetly present, she is a trade unionist who does not give speeches, but who works behind the scenes in order to obtain her full rights and manages to establish rights of the active woman." Politics and woman are "not necessarily incompatible, it is just a matter of faith."

The website mentions the committee that formed to revise the *muda-wana*, in order to "bring the condition of women closer to the ideals of the United Nations." Women of the twenty-first century want to "live with their time and be free of social dichotomies and various kinds of negli-gence which have been condemned by the United Nations conventions on the banning of all forms of discrimination against women (1979)." The *mudawana* reform issues are described as "religion and social conser-vatism clashing with the urgency of change." While women have the right to education and employment, and equal protection in matters of work according to Morocco's signing of the International Treaty on Economic, Social, and Cultural rights, the site admits significant inequalities in mat-ters of marriage. "Recourse to tradition" is the reason for a sexual divi-sion of labor as well as the husband's role as head of the family. The website then lists the many rights women have in the Qur'an.

The decline of illiteracy since 1989 and women's presence in the eco-nomic world are then noted. Not only are women working in the sci-ences, but they are also novelists, artists, and singers. They are "security agents, insurers, architects, bus drivers, physicians, judges, notaries, engineers, business managers, business women travelling all around the world in search of markets, film-makers, parachutists, NASA interns, computer scientists, electronics engineers, co-pilots and pilots, and the list grows longer!"[28] Lest we forget, women are also active in rural areas where they "represent the majority of laborers." Finally, the site con-cludes:

Moroccan woman as mother is a true keeper of traditions. She is the nourishing mother and the educator, thus occupying a dominant place in society and espe-cially within the family. She perpetuates life, cements identity, and keeps tradi-tions. She is also valued by social powers, still, in a patriarchal society, she comes second to the father or the husband. . . . [She] finds her strength in doing many tasks; she keeps the upper hand over her home (housekeeper) but she also per-forms other tasks outside home.

The government website highlights multiple possibilities for women, and yet suggests that women occupy all these positions at once: modern and traditional, vocal yet silent, present yet somehow absent. The image is of the Moroccan Woman as fragmentary, scattered—caught in an intermediate space between numerous binarisms and expected to inhabit all categories with ease. In government valorizations, women appear as "a nameless and faceless mass and as a generic, passive and reactive people, who are present in history, but never as agents who initi-ate historical processes" (Kozma 2003: 127).

For three years after mass demonstrations took place in March of 2000 over the proposed changes to the *mudawana*, the government remained largely silent about the issue. For three years, both sides endlessly debated the issue in the press, giving the impression of a society irreparably divided by different value systems. Finally, on October 13, 2003, King Mohamed VI ruled on the issue, widening the grounds on which women can petition for divorce, raising the age of marriage, and placing restrictions on polygamy, while not completely outlawing it.[29]

It should be clear, then, that the identity of Moroccan women is inextricably connected to the way Moroccans imagine their nation. How urban, middle-class Fassis, particularly women, construct their identities and gender space in response to ideologies is largely the subject of this book. Chapter 2 paints a broad picture of Fassi identity by focusing on rumors, on stories Fassis repeated that highlighted anxieties about gender, patriarchy, poverty, and Islamism, while simultaneously asserting a vision of Fassi identity and critiquing the nation state. In Chapter 3, I examine the proposed *mudawana* reforms through the lens of social class, showing how the advantages of patriarchal ideologies still benefit the middle class while limiting the possibilities of engagement for other women who lack the resources offered by patriarchal society.

Not all middle-class Fassis were unconcerned with the inequitable distribution of resources in society, and Chapter 4 highlights the efforts of one NGO, the Najia Belghazi Center, to offer new resources for Fassi women who had experienced the *mudawana*'s negative effects. I show how women like Naima worked tirelessly to provide legal advocacy, domestic violence counseling, job and literacy training, health seminars, and other services to a population who generally had the least to benefit from divorce. However, the center's effectiveness was hampered by a number of factors, and efforts to establish links across social classes that might have led to larger structural changes improving the status of women often failed. Here, the ideologies of nation-state, internationalist human rights discourses, and local conceptualizations of tradition and women's rights often collided. I draw attention to the Moroccan government's encouragement of the formation of NGOs in an era in which the state itself had evaded many of its responsibilities for suffering brought on by cuts in government spending (as a result of structural adjustment programs) and by government laws that legitimate discrimination against women. The failure to achieve solidarity across social classes is but a byproduct of this tension.

Chapter 5 examines kinship as a form of patriarchal ideology, focusing particularly on the patron-client relationship and how middle-class women have adopted this model as a framework for forging their own networks that extend beyond the family. Huriya was an example of how women with the advantages of social position and income are able to adopt a model of interaction previously restricted to men, one that enhances women's power and influence in the community. While this is not necessary a positive development in terms of providing equitable resources to all Moroccans, it is an accepted (if hierarchical) way of getting things done in Moroccan society, and the public power of women that is visible in kinship networks is a notable development.

In Chapter 6 I look more generally at the issue of public space, and how women gender both old and new forms of space in urban Moroccan society. New spaces such as NGOs, exercise clubs, or cyber cafés complicate the divisions of public and private, and the rules users employ to navigate women's positions were particularly intriguing to me. Local notions of hospitality and shame are invoked to legitimate women's presence or argue for a particular way of perceiving space, but in the process, women transform space into something new and unique. Finally, in Chapter 7 I return to the story of Layla, a case in which space was not transformed. As a nightclub singer, Layla was unable to create a new position and identity for herself outside the safe confines of acceptable spaces for women. Detailing Layla's social biography is a way of showing the limits of everyday practices when confronted with ideologies that are simply too powerful to contravene.

Much of this research was conducted through participant observation, but also through formal and informal interviews, mapping, surveys, and genealogies. Living in the Lux neighborhood, as the wife of a man who had grown up there, I was able to spend much of my time involved in activities of everyday Fassi life, but I also attended numerous events such as weddings, naming ceremonies, circumcision parties, and funerals. Daily lunches with my in-laws provided a window into the happenings of the neighborhood, and participating in household tasks and visiting rituals enabled me to get to know other networks of middle-class Fassis. I also spent time with Fassis I met in other circumstances: through the American Language Institute in Fes, academic contacts, my membership in an exercise club, visits to the NGO, and other chance meetings that developed into friendships, such as my relationship with Layla, whom I met on the street through a mutual friend.

The resulting ethnography is an attempt to recreate the unique world that emerged from my own particular positioning: observing a new middle class and wondering about the prospects for its continuity, living in an urban setting where history is still relevant for the way individuals interpret the world, and experiencing those spaces in which women navigate conflicting ideologies as they simply make their way through life. What emerges is a portrait that can perhaps be compared not just to the situation of women in other Muslim countries but also to any place where humans negotiate conflicting territories of ideology as they struggle to make meaning of the spaces in which they live.

Chapter 2

Rumors: Constructing Fes

> *We all raise memories like trees*
> *to live under their shadows,*
> *to be sheltered by their magnificent,*
> *leaking roofs.*
>
> —*Khaled Mattawa, "Letter to Ibrahim"*

It is early June in 2002, and Scheherezade and I have come to an elegant café near the old French racetracks for an afternoon coffee before she has to return to work. The café is bright and immaculate, the walls covered with smooth, beige marble. As always, Scheherezade is impeccably groomed, wearing a charcoal gray pantsuit and an aubergine blouse, her long fingernails painted to match the color of her shirt. She is constantly on a diet, her weight vacillating between Rubenesque plumpness and flat-out heaviness, but she knows how to make herself look attractive, and the men stare at her as she passes. I see her returning the gazes of some, refusing to meet the eyes of others—and not for the first time, I think there is some kind of unwritten code here that I do not understand, some way she has of projecting power and sexuality that I have not yet learned. We take a table near a group of young students, both male and female, who are studying together for their upcoming exams. Nearby, two professional women in suits share a pot of tea.

I call her Scheherezade because of her ability to enchant with stories, particularly of the life she has crafted for herself here in Fes. If our tendency as humans is to constantly create our selves through narrative, the identity that Scheherezade presents is one of a woman often in conflict with her city, and with the narrow-minded social mores that she associates with "original" Fassis. Our journey into the heart of Fes starts with someone born here whose roots (*asl*) are elsewhere, which makes her a thoughtful observer of Fassi social life. Somehow she is in this world but not entirely of it, as the Sufis say. Although she will be the first to admit the humbleness of her roots, Scheherezade has used her cleverness to rise above her family's poverty, and she is proud of this. It is not an easy feat, particularly in a city where many decent jobs are only open for the briefest moment before they are snapped up through family connections. Somehow Scheherezade made her way through the educational system and managed to find a position as a secretary in a local travel agency. Her boss treats her well and the job is a secure one, and over time she has saved enough money to buy her own apartment.

When she tells me about her life, everything seems perfectly ordered: a balance between work and responsibility to family on the one hand and a life of independence and fun on the other, one in which she refuses to bow to local standards of propriety. Scheherezade likes to go out to parties at friends' houses or for dinner at the nicest local restaurants, of which there are not many. There are men she speaks elusively of knowing, silver-haired businessmen in suits who send her drinks when we are out together, powerful government functionaries who bow to kiss her hand when they pass our table at the cafés. At these moments I shoot her a puzzled look, wondering what it all means, but she says men are good for nothing, and she insists she does not get too close to any of them. I am constantly aware that I am seeing only the facet of her self she chooses to show me.[1]

That does not stop her from telling stories, not only about her own life but also about the misdeeds of others. Although she socializes with influential Fassis, she chides them for their hypocrisy, for showing a pious face to the world while engaging in all manner of debauchery behind closed doors. Fassis, she says, believe themselves to be superior to everyone; they are the most religious, the best businesspeople, the finest scholars. They pride themselves on their bloodlines, claiming to trace their ancestry back to Andalusian Spain, back to the conquering Arab warriors who crossed the desert in the seventh century, back to the Prophet Mohammed himself. Scheherezade lights a long, thin cigarette as she talks, the smoke circling languorously above her manicured hands. Although Scheherezade seems confident in her assertions, there is the slightest trace of resentment in her words, the resentment of someone who has worked hard for what she has but nonetheless is accustomed to feeling scrutinized, or judged. As we talk, she seems to have all the time in the world, and I hang onto her every word. But she has a knack for stopping her narratives just at the point when I have ceased to note the passage of time, the stories dropping off abruptly, lacking closure. Then she picks up the thread to another narrative just as I am longing to have the last one resolved, and we are off again.

Her words weave a tapestry about the underside of Fassi social life, and today she is telling me a story that demonstrates the hypocrisy of Fassis, and their concern with appearances. Something about a pious judge, always in the mosque, and his wild teenage daughters, who are seen riding in cars with boys and coming home with whiskey on their breath. In contrast, she portrays the straightforwardness of her own behavior, paralleling events that are both sacred and profane. Last night, she says, rubbing her eyes, she returned home at dawn from an all-night session of Sufi chanting only to run into her judgmental neighbor, up for morning prayers.

"Another night I came home early," she says, "and nobody noticed, even though this time I had been at a party where everything had taken place: important men were there with women who were not their wives, there was alcohol, sex, everything. . . . But when I was out praying all night, my nosy neighbor assumed the worst. For this reason, I don't care what people say about me, because they don't know what really goes on in my life. There is no escaping people's gossip (*klam dyal nas*)."

Through Scheherezade, Fassi social hegemony is the first territory of ideology that we encounter. Fassis, she says, desperately want to uphold the city's image as the spiritual capital of the nation, the ancient center for religious learning, and they believe themselves to be the most spiritual, the first true Moroccans. The appearance of piety is everything. Yet in terms of actual behavior, she continues, Fassis are on the same level as everyone else in Morocco, they just hide their sins and then criticize others. Fassis are famous for this.

"The camel looked at the other camel and made fun of his hump," she says, laughing.[2] She always presents Fassi Islam this way, as a hypocritical struggle to maintain the façade of piety, and a judgment of those who do not. The theme of her narratives is frequently religion, and bad faith. In contrast to the Fassis in the stories she tells, Scheherezade believes that Islam and a Western-inspired modernity can coexist amicably. She follows the religion but also traffics with the world of *jnun*, or spirits. The existence of *jnun* are acknowledged in Islam, but according to orthodox belief, only prayer and piety should be invoked to keep them away.[3] Those who go further, as Scheherezade does, are treading on potentially heretical territory. She speaks frankly of her own spirits, which are quiet during Ramadan. Sometimes they demand she wear red and have her hands painted with henna, other times they want to hear *shikhat* music, and there is one, a Jewish spirit, who likes alcohol. She has a good job, her own money, and she tells me that she does not have to answer to anybody.

Usually Scheherezade has an ally, her best friend Hanane, a woman also in her thirties, who hosts alcohol-soaked soirées but is equally comfortable at all-night possession ceremonies where women dance to appease their personal spirits with the help of musicians who call them up. But today she tells me that Hanane has begun to wear the veil, stopped using makeup, and announced that all parties are illicit (*haram*), not only the parties with alcohol but also those for bringing out the *jnun*. Hanane listens obsessively to cassettes of an Egyptian cleric, Amr Khaled, who professes to be "modern" and has recently become all the rage among young women in Fes.

"He refuses to shake women's hands unless their heads are covered. He's not like the others, he claims, who won't shake a woman's hand at all, but he claims to be modern, and he says, 'You come to me wearing the headscarf (*hijab*), Allah will be pleased, and then I will be happy to shake your hand.' And this he calls modern?"

She trails off, and for the first time since I have known her, seems at a loss for words. But then she continues, on a related note. Have I heard, she asks me, about the religious extremists who have been attacking women for not being Muslim enough? I note the connection she has suddenly made: between the modern Islamist and the violent extremist.

"They're terrible," she says, lighting another cigarette. "A friend of someone I know was in a car with his wife, who was wearing a tank top. At an intersection they came up to the window and demanded his wife cover up. He told them to mind their own business, that she was his wife and the way she dressed pleased him, and they pulled him out of the car and began beating him. Oh, it is really terrible."

"I heard," I add, familiar with this story, "that they were also out in the popular neighborhoods, beating up drunks."

"Yes," Scheherezade affirms. "They beat up anyone. There is no stopping them. If they see a woman and she is not covered up, or if she smokes, it is terrible. They follow the Taliban. Believe me, there are Taliban here in Morocco."

"And this Amr Khaled," I say, steering the conversation back to the religious figure. "Does he have anything to do with it?"

"Hanane has been brainwashed. I don't understand it. Her family is puzzled, too." She lights another cigarette. "But I am afraid because things are getting bad, worse than they have been in years. They want to force us all to wear veils. They want this country to be like Algeria. It is very bad for Fes. We don't need someone to tell us how to practice our religion. In Fes, we have always been strong in our religion."

The Persistence of Rumors

I was struck by how suddenly Scheherezade's "they" (other Fassis) became a "we." Under challenge by two competing forms of religiosity, Islamism and fundamentalism, Fassi religiosity became an ideology that Scheherezade now identified with. Because she chose to defy local codes of propriety, and because she was a self-made individual who did not coast on a sense of noblesse oblige, Scheherezade normally distanced herself from Fassis through her narratives. Her stories were usually personal, reflecting her struggles against Fassi ideologies that questioned her religiosity and attempted to limit a woman's freedom for the sake of appearances. Scheherezade could expect me, as a foreign anthropologist and an outsider to Fassi social life, to respond in a way that acknowledged her autonomy and recognized her self-presentation as legitimate.[4] However, when it came to rumors, she was quick to define herself as a citizen of Fes, fighting against the shadowy threat of extremism. She was not alone in relating this story of the misdeeds of the extremists. There were other versions: variations on the tale of the girl in the tank top with a cigarette, or the knife-wielding fundamentalists lying in wait for drunks stumbling home from the bars, or religious figures invading beaches, making demonstrative prayers, and demanding the women cover themselves up.

Rumors were everywhere during my fieldwork, and they did not just concern religious fundamentalism. A forum for communication that is similar to gossip, rumors can delineate the boundaries of a particular social group (Haviland 1977), marginalize external threats, and serve as a repository of a community's fears.[5] But while gossip frequently addresses a known figure in the community, rumors do not, nor do they seem, like Scheherezade's *klam dyal nas,* to be concerned with commenting on or constraining the behavior of a single individual. In Fassi discourse, rumors are characterized by repetition and arise at moments of insecurity. They are significant for what they reveal about people's efforts to assert a singular Fassi identity, and hence to circumscribe reality. Whenever conversations grow tense or infused with too much of the "wrong" kind of reality, Fassis often repeat these rumors. Through rumor, a competing claim of identity is presented, only to be undercut, demolished by a reassertion of a "true" Fassi identity which renders all other ways of being "outside."

Fassi rumors offer stories asserted as truth, of individuals or groups, always known at a remove: "those people," "a friend of someone I know," "it happened to a cousin." This sense of a threatening "other" is also a feature of urban or contemporary legends, but unlike contemporary legends, rumors generally lack a developed plotline (Brunvand 2001). Seldom are they verifiable as news items, although rumors are sometimes based in historical events. Here, however, I note the rumor but attend more to the context: when were such stories told, and why? The contexts in which these stories came up were often moments where the teller had just revealed insecurity about some other issue. Here, it was Scheherezade's sense that her best friend had changed. Hanane's newfound religiosity had removed her from a friendship that had been characterized by less rigid forms of sociality, a friendship in which the secular, the orthodox, and the spirit world coexisted easily with one another. Yet Hanane had become judgmental, and the judgment came from somewhere outside: an imported ideology that was directly threatening to the way Scheherezade had constructed her own identity.

Disparate in subject matter, Fassi rumors insist on one outcome: the verbal assertion of Fassi solidarity over obstacles, outsiders, and adversaries. Yet while the stories themselves often contain a resolution, rumors are borne of uneasiness, and on another level reflect incommensurable positions, moments of indeterminacy, and loss. They convey nostalgia for an imagined era of social cohesion; they represent power as an object lost. Asserting a singular vision of reality, rumors simultaneously undercut Fassi unity by highlighting ideological conflicts that lie at the heart of Moroccan social organization. These conflicts include shifting ideas about the status of women, poverty, the disenfranchisement of young men, and the rising influence of imported religious practices. Locating the contexts in which these rumors appear reveals much about the fissures that lie beneath the foundations of Fassi society, and also about people's shared unease concerning whether overreaching ideologies such as Islamism or nationalism provide legitimate schemas for the future.

In this chapter I track several rumors that circulated in Fes from 2000 to 2002. Along with the aforementioned rumor of the marauding Islamists, there were others. One story, concerning shantytown residents and their wealth, offered a confusing commentary on poverty and, in one case, gender. Another rumor highlights the anomie of disenfranchised young men by critiquing patriarchal forms of social organization that obstruct efforts to craft new models for identity and relationships. Finally, often in conjunction with this narrative of male disenfranchisement, I heard the success story, the tale of the successful Fassi émigré.

These stories position middle-class Fassis vis-à-vis others: poor urban migrants who cling to the margins of the city; fundamentalists and Algerians; a patriarchal system favoring older, employed Moroccan men; and Westerners. Through speech, an ideology of Fassi unity and identity is asserted. "Communion with others," write Elinor Ochs and Lisa Capps, "elusive and fleeting though it may be, constitutes the greatest potentiality of narrative" (1996: 31).

Context is crucial to social utterances, and controlling the discourse about outsiders is an attempt to control and manage reality. I attend here to the literal territory of rumor, to the setting and the conversational surroundings that accompany a rumor's utterance. Rumors cannot exist in a vacuum but are intimately related to other utterances, and so they reflect Mikhail Bakhtin's description of social communication.

Bakhtin writes that "the very boundaries of the utterance are determined by a change of speech subjects. Utterances are not indifferent to one another, and are not self sufficient; they are aware of and mutually reflect one another. These mutual reflections determine their character. Each utterance is filled with echoes and reverberations of other utterances to which it is related by the communality of the sphere of speech communications" (1986: 91).

There is a distance between the settings in which rumors are told (a house, a café, a train compartment), and an "outside" where the story takes place, beyond the known, shared world of the teller and his or her audience. Imagined others float on the periphery, threatening chaos (*fitna*) and an upheaval of the social order, should Fassis lose sight of proper cultural ideals and values. In stories, these others appear like ghosts, circulating as words or images that can provoke fear, while commenting on Fassi resilience in facing the specter of threats from outside.

The identities of most of the Fassis under discussion here are solidly linked with the city, and Fes remains a significant part of their self-definition. Rather than affirming an identification with any overarching ideology, including that of the nation-state, Fassis are more likely to identify with the city itself. Being Fassi, I argue, is an ideology in itself, here made visible within the discourse of rumor, and entailing a specific set of beliefs about how the world should be. Even Scheherezade, who was the least likely of anyone I knew to assert solidarity with other Fassis, drew on this unified sense of belonging to Fes, especially when forces more powerful than the Fassis who criticized her seemed to hover beyond the gates. In moments of uncertainty and instability, Fassis, like all human beings, employ narrative tactics to recreate a social world capable of dispelling anxiety. Rumor as narrative draws on the hope that the ideal can transcend what is actually taking place (K. Burke 1969). Through rumor, Fassis construct and reconstruct Fassi identity at the same time that they question other aspects of existence.

Rumors of Wealth amid Poverty

The Sunday afternoon train from Casablanca to Fes was packed with weekend travelers returning home, weighed down with baggage. Children played in the aisles, and smokers positioned themselves near open windows, puffing on Marlboros and staring pensively at the desiccated wheat fields, yellowed in the late spring. In one second-class compartment, Si Mohammed and Ibrahim were traveling with their wives and their adult daughters. Acquainted with one another through government jobs from which they were now retired, the two old men talked for most of the journey. For over three hours I listened to their conversation, amazed that even though they knew each other and shared news of mutual friends and acquaintances, they somehow managed to retell much of their biographies to one another during the course of the train ride. Their life narratives paralleled one another, and whether it was a case of one-upmanship or merely each wanting to convince the other that his life had taken the proper course, I was not certain. Aside from exchanging a few smiles and polite words, I did not insert myself into the two men's conversation. From time to time a ticket taker stepped into the cabin, and both men flashed special government passes. The ticket takers bowed deferentially and wished them a nice trip.

Si Mohammed and Ibrahim wore respectable, nondescript suits, their wives *djellabas* and silk headscarves. They spoke Arabic, mixed with a few words of French. Si Mohammed was returning from a weekend at his beach villa in the town of Mohammedia, while Ibrahim had been visiting family in an upscale Rabat neighborhood. Both agreed that retirement was a nice state of affairs. Ibrahim announced proudly that his son had taken over his civil service position. They discussed their children, comparing the two adult daughters in the car. Ibrahim's daughter, her head covered, was slim and neat in a tailored beige overcoat and matching slacks. She had married well, Ibrahim said, casually mentioning her husband's illustrious family name. Her young son sat obediently and quietly in her lap, a plump and serious baby with docile brown eyes.

Si Mohammed reported that his daughter had not yet married. His daughter, who seemed to be in her late thirties, cast her eyes downward, visibly uncomfortable. She did not wear a headscarf, but was dressed more casually, in a loose T-shirt and sweatpants.

"But it's nice to have children who can take care of you in your old age," Ibrahim asserted.

"She is a great help around the house," said her father.

"If it's fated, she will marry, God willing," her mother announced. The other women nodded. Si Mohammed's daughter looked out the window, crossing her arms. With the confidence of a woman assured of her social position, the married daughter leaned over and patted her on the arm.

"God willing, you will marry. There is still time."

Everyone looked out the window, and a silence, the first in two hours, passed over the car. We had crossed the low mountain ranges of the Middle Atlas, past vineyards and wheat fields, and were approaching the city of Meknes. Uniform government apartment buildings perched atop ravines filled with trash. Close to the railway, shanties sprawled everywhere, their tin roofs leaning inward, a few chickens pecking in the dirt. Children kicked a soccer ball among old tires scattered around the makeshift huts.

"I'll tell you something," Ibrahim said, eager to change the subject. "Some of those people own four television sets!" He gestured out the window at the shantytown, where one could, in fact, see a few white satellite dishes dotting the metal rooftops.

"The wealth in those places!" Si Mohammed agreed. "Those people could afford to live in villas if they wanted, but they hoard their money."

"There are rich men in there, hiding so they don't have to pay their taxes, sending their kids into the city to beg and coming home with hundreds of *dirhams* each day. They make more money than you and I both."

"It's shameful. Gives a bad look to the cities. They're country people (*'arubi*), they don't care if they live like animals."

"But the money? Unbelievable. Tremendous amounts of money hidden in there," Ibrahim emphasized.

"W'li, w'li w'li," exclaimed Si Mohammed.

Riding in the same second-class compartment with these middle-class Fassi travelers, I noted how, yet again, the topic of the shantytowns had been raised. In the company of other middle-class Fassis I heard the same story, told by lawyers and schoolteachers, secretaries and doctors, sales clerks and waiters. The plot was always the same: poverty was only a façade, with great wealth lying beneath, and the shantytown dwellers were outsiders from the countryside who "chose" to live that way. The condition of their poverty was debatable. What, then, did this story reveal about the Fassis who told it?

Fassi Rumors as Narratives of Identity

Anthropologists working on the Middle East and North Africa, particularly since the 1980s, have focused on the possibilities that social texts (such as poetry, folk tales, personal narratives, oral histories, and allegories) can reveal hidden aspects of social organization.[6] In *The Poetics of Military Occupation*, Smadar Lavie argues that allegories are private narratives that represent the collectivity. With allegories, Mzeini Bedouins transform the paradoxes of their lives, using stories to assert cultural values of autonomy and freedom that have been lost under military occupation. For Lavie, allegories are self-critical and fragmentary; they lament a disappearing past and reflect an ultimate paradox: "that [the Mzeini] could not maintain an independent Bedouin identity beyond the fragments incarnated in allegory, because they were disenfranchised on their own land by continual military occupations" (Lavie 1990: 39).

Rumors in Fassi discourse function in much the same way. Individuals use rumor to comment on aspects of social life that are changing rapidly or are threatened by the presence of alternative ideologies. Rumors often contain a complicated commentary on reality; although they place Fassis at the center of social life, battling a clear external threat, a subtle thread of criticism simultaneously suggests that blame for social ills might lie elsewhere. While the apparent enemy of rumor might be Islamists, "country" people, or, as we shall see, entrenched patriarchies, rumors also critique the nation-state for failing to control social chaos and uncertainty. Finally, they lead one to question whether this "failure" is accidental or deliberate.

Rumors might not express events that are historically verifiable, but they possess what Jean-Noel Kapferer calls "the raw facts." They do not twist what is true but rather "seek out the truth" (Kapferer 1990: 3). Whether or not Fassi rumors are true, the momentary agreement among those who hear a rumor creates an elusive sense of community among listeners and teller, which in turn suggests that Fassi identity is incorruptible. Fassi rumors might be said to adhere to what Ochs and Capps call the "fundamentalistic" tendency of narratives, which "lends consistency to otherwise fragmented experiences" while also creating community and assuming that others share a similar viewpoint (1992: 32). The literal truth of rumors is not the issue; more important is the creation of solidarity. As Luise White has written, the very falseness of rumors "is what gives them meaning; they are a way of talking that encourages a reassessment of everyday experience to address the workings of power and knowledge and how regimes use them" (White 2000: 45).

Through rumor, Fassis actively construct reality. Listeners do not passively absorb the stories but contribute to the conversation, offering opinions and bits of evidence gathered from their own experiences and other conversations. Rumors serve as a means of "collective problem solving," enabling people to resolve uncertainties and to "construe a meaningful interpretation . . . by pooling their intellectual resources" (Shibutani 1966: 18).

Fassi rumors are narratives of identity, although they reveal disjunctures between a vision of the world asserted in story and the world as it truly exists. Like the Mzeini Bedouins, through stories Fassis resolve contradictions inherent in self-presentation and attempt to reconcile the presence of competing ideologies. Yet the resolution of conflict through rumor is a temporary and partial strategy, unable to solve the larger problems that capture the public imagination.

The "true Fassi" depicted in rumor always occupies a solid cultural position, besieged but ultimately fending off challenges from outside. Although, under normal circumstances, status disparities among middle-class Fassis might have led some, such as Scheherezade, to distinguish themselves from others, some external threats are perceived as so menacing that differences are temporarily effaced. In repeating rumors, Fassi Moroccans grapple with adversaries but ultimately never lose sight of who they are. Yet the contexts of these rumors, and the stories they relate, reveal insecurity about identity and social position. In the story, the outcome is never in doubt. But the outsiders hover at the margins, gathering strength.

Disorganized Shantytowns

In the story above, two older Fassi men of similar social positions subtly compared their lives. They discussed retirement and the possessions they had acquired; they mentioned family and the successes of their children, particularly a son taking over a father's position at work, a sign of the continued importance of family connections within a patriarchal family unit. The conversation stopped when Si Mohammed announced that his daughter, who was past marriageable age, had not found a husband. After a few moments of silence, Ibrahim offered a new topic for discussion: the questionable existence of poverty in the shantytowns.

Most large cities in Morocco have shantytowns (*berrarak* or *bidonvilles*), huddled along the city limits. Whether or not the shantytown dwellers, who often do not have access to fresh water, are "rich" is debatable, although a few shantytowns have turned into makeshift markets, where people sell clothes and household goods, as well as the latest electronics, videos, compact discs, and mobile phones. These shantytowns of commerce are distinguishable from those used primarily for living. *Berrarak* such as the one we passed in the train are residences, and, aside from the satellite dishes, which have become common at all socioeconomic levels, show little evidence of wealth.

My interest lies not in whether wealth was actually present in these shantytowns. What is significant is that I often heard variations on this story repeated by middle-class Fassis in a variety of circumstances. There was no real poverty in the shantytowns, they all said, but only wealth, and for some reason *those people* "just preferred to live that way."

The discussion of the older, unmarried daughter provided the only visible moment of tension in the discussion; otherwise, both men presented their lives in a linear progression from career to family to retirement. Ibrahim's married daughter, who sat smugly with her baby, followed the socially desirable pattern; her parents had fulfilled their duty by marrying their daughter to a man from another prominent family. The unmarried daughter of the other couple, already in her late thirties, had not achieved what was expected.[7] Silence ensued, and then Ibrahim made an effort to find a new topic of conversation, one that would again reassert the status quo and the comfortable feeling that had prevailed earlier. The wealth of the shantytowns could be agreed on, and true poverty did not exist in Morocco. The shantytown dwellers were different, their motives for living in ramshackle huts irrational, attributable to their status as country people who had moved to the city. Furthermore, they did not pay their taxes, and were thus unlike these men, former government employees and law-abiding citizens now enjoying the fruits of their retirement (including special permits that allowed them to ride the trains for free).

In Moroccan society, ideally every able-bodied adult should marry. Quoting a popular tradition (*hadith*) of the Prophet, Fassis say that "marriage fulfills half the duty of religion," and there is particular pressure on women in their twenties to marry. Unmarried men and women are considered capable of provoking societal chaos or *fitna*, as sexuality is a powerful and potentially dark force that needs to be legitimated by marriage (Mernissi 1987). Unmarried men and women are still a threat to the social order.

Expectations for the age of first marriage differ according to gender and class. Among the lower classes in Fes, girls marry as young as fifteen, although recent revisions to the personal status code (finally changed in October 2003) have raised the minimum age to eighteen. Among middle-class Fassis, people feel that a woman should be married by her mid-twenties, which reflects the national average age of marriage for women.[8] Young women pursuing an advanced degree or a career can delay their marriages for a few years, but parents often pressure daughters to marry as soon as possible, preferably to a spouse who will be amenable to their career plans.

Most men also expect to marry, but men marry much later across all social classes. This is due to the length of time it takes for men to find work, build their careers, and afford an apartment. While in the past, new brides moved into the husband's family home, many middle-class couples now prefer to start their married lives independently, and families of young women often demand a separate apartment away from extended family in marriage negotiations. Because of high unemployment, young men, even with education and skills, are frequently unable to find work. Unmarried men in their forties are not perceived as an anomaly, and families do not place pressure on men to live on their own or marry before they are ready. Men come and go freely from their parents' homes, are given pocket money for coffee and cigarettes, and are generally not expected to contribute to the upkeep of the household.

The inability to find work can be emasculating, but families understand the economic conditions and are forgiving in the case of sons. This seems less true with respect to unmarried daughters. Although families do not reject older, unmarried daughters, families often speak of them with a sense of disappointment that I never heard regarding sons. Intense societal pressure to marry still falls hardest on women, and whenever an unmarried woman in her late twenties or older is present at intimate family gatherings, the discussion always turns toward her problematic status. Women with careers can shake off some of this scrutiny, insisting that they have their work and their "economic independence," as Scheherezade often told me. Marriage is, of course, not impossible after age thirty, but because men usually marry younger women, a woman in her thirties is often not considered a desirable marriage partner and in some cases will marry a much older man who is widowed or divorced.

In the past forty years, demographic factors have led to an increase in the age of first marriage for both men and women. Unemployment and a faltering economy have contributed to an imbalance of young brides and older husbands, with young men and older women often left in the cold. An unmarried older daughter can be a source of embarrassment for a family, as marriage is still a family affair, offering proof that parents have provided for their children. While many marriages are no longer arranged as they were in the past, parents still network to find potential spouses and carry the informal right to approve their children's choices. For the two old men in the train, then, Si Mohammed's unmarried daughter was a sign of failure. While everything is ultimately up to divine will (people will marry if it is "written," or *maktub*), human agency is partially to blame.

The rumor of the shantytowns directed attention elsewhere, at matters on which all could agree. However, this rumor serves as social critique as well. Massive, unchecked rural-to-urban migration has contributed to the rapid construction of vast shantytowns on the outskirts of Moroccan cities. An increasingly mechanized agricultural sector and subsequent loss of economic opportunities for rural Moroccans have led to a disappearing peasantry who migrate to the cities and outside Morocco in search of viable employment.[9] While the speaker and his audience rejected any identification with the people "outside" the train window, the story points at aspects of the social landscape that do not make sense. Shantytowns represent social chaos, and their inhabitants are considered incapable of living their lives with "order," as one Moroccan told me. Their presence threatens Fassi ideas of the city as comprised of relatively homogenous social groups. Rumor is thus a way to order reality through narrative, when visible evidence is often to the contrary.

The subject of the *bidonvilles* was frequently raised during my fieldwork and is not unique to Fes, nor are the rumors of wealth hidden in the shantytowns. Middle-class Fassis refused to admit the visible evidence of poverty and instead attested to what remained hidden. One man offered an analogy with the construction of traditional houses in the old *medina*, stating that you could never tell the wealth of a person from looking at his door. The modest, outer aspects of houses do not reveal the secrets contained within. By assuming that *bidonville* dwellers follow the same "rules" as urban Fassis for concealing their wealth behind plain and even dilapidated façades, Fassis delineate "inner" and "outer" realities.

Shantytown residents are *'arubi*, or from the countryside. Calling someone *'arubi* is an insult, and the term connotes country people who fail to understand civilized, urban ways. Fassis attribute different value systems to the *'arubi* shantytown dwellers, and offer as evidence the fact that "they" send their children to beg in the streets of the Ville Nouvelle, a violation of human rights. Human rights (*huquq al-insan*) are prominent in Fassi conversations about the "new" Morocco ushered in by King Mohammed VI since his ascension to the throne in 1999. Conceptualizations of human rights and modernity enable Fassis to distinguish themselves from others, according to standards that are variously believed to have been set out by the European Union, the United States, or more generally, the West. People speak about "human rights" as if they were a concrete list of rules a country could follow, guaranteeing its modernity. "In human rights, children should not work," Alia, a university professor, told me. "Children should be in school, learning to read. Until practices of child labor are stopped, we will not fully have human rights here."

While using children to beg is believed to be a human rights violation, begging by adults is considered a low-status profession. A corollary to the shantytown rumor was one that insisted that the female panhandlers who clustered around the central market of the Ville Nouvelle rode the buses back to the shantytowns at night with their skirts heavy with coins, making as much as two or three hundred *dirhams* per day (around twenty to thirty U.S. dollars in 2001).

Fassi discourses about poverty thus assert Fassi superiority in matters of human rights, insisting that "true" Fassis earn money honestly and do not send their children to beg. The rumor about the shantytown dweller often devolves into a denunciation of the living habits of *'arubi* people in the old *medina*, once the orderly and aristocratic domain of old Fes. The "country people" have taken over the ancient Fes *medina*, people say: they crowd ten families into formerly opulent villas, have too many children, and live "like animals," unable to control themselves. Discussions of poverty among "original" Fassis frequently turn to the way "they" are destroying the *medina*, piling too many families into houses once meant for one extended family alone. Nostalgia and ambivalence about the past once again come into play, with the *medina* revered as historical evidence of Fassi greatness, even though many Fassi landlords have allowed their ancestral homes to deteriorate, renting out rooms but not participating significantly in the old buildings' overall upkeep. The poor are blamed for letting the *medina* fall apart, and the *medina* becomes a landscape on which middle-class Fassi nostalgia for the past and anxieties about modernity are projected. The *medina* here represents what Gold and Gold have termed a "landscape of regret," a historically significant place reminding people of the existence of a lost Golden Age that may, somehow, be reclaimed in the future (2003).

Rumors attribute discourses of contagion to the *'arubi*, but the migrants themselves are not solely to blame.[10] While ostensibly deriding migrants from the countryside, these discourses also contain implicit criticisms of uncontrolled rural-to-urban migration, a byproduct of national policy. Migration has been exacerbated by governmental structural adjustment programs taken on in the 1980s, whereby the conditions for receiving international loans required the Moroccan government to privatize, cut public-sector jobs and services, and endure a supposedly temporary rise in unemployment. These programs are, to many Fassis, still without visible benefit.[11]

Disorderly Fundamentalists

The rumor of the fundamentalists attacking people in the streets, especially women, additionally concerns anxieties over gender, but its timing reveals collective insecurities about the future. At the time of my conversation with Scheherezade in June 2002, the country was preparing for parliamentary elections in September, and tales of the misdeeds of extremists were in constant circulation. While such rumors are always present, they travel more frequently at times of political stress. Some middle-class Fassis expressed their fears that religious parties would sweep the election, resulting in the kind of civil war that had afflicted neighboring Algeria for over a decade. The collapsing of Islamism here with extremism is noteworthy, as a number of people, including Scheherezade, told me that even the moderate Islamist parties were closet extremists waiting to gain power so that they could implement a brutal, Saudi-style version of Islamic law.

There were other moments during my fieldwork when Fassis repeated variations on this tale of fundamentalist excess. It was on everyone's lips when the United States began bombing Afghanistan, stemming from a fear that Morocco's support of America might one day lead to attacks on Morocco from al-Qaeda.[12] I also heard this story when Moroccans held a large, government-sponsored demonstration in Rabat to assert solidarity with Palestinians and protest the Israeli refusal of a United Nations inquiry into the Jenin massacre.

The pan-Arab news network al-Jazeera, which many Fassis watched on satellite television, had fed the furor over Jenin. Broadcast out of London, al-Jazeera was reporting on news events all over the Arab world, often including events that were censored by state media coverage. The contrast between al-Jazeera's no-holds-barred reporting and Morocco's own newscasts, featuring lengthy segments dedicated to the king's ceremonial visits to Moroccan cities, where he was often shown cutting a ribbon to inaugurate development projects, was striking. Al-Jazeera's broadcasts contributed to a sense of identification among Moroccans against oppression of Muslims elsewhere.

Fassis in one of the popular neighborhoods (*hay shabi*) on the outskirts of town formed their own demonstrations in response to the Jenin incident, before the government had announced an official protest. These loosely organized demonstrations turned into small-scale rioting without any discernible target, during which rioters were said to have torched a city bus, and the army was called out to halt the demonstrators. Some said the demonstrators were only groups of angry youth (*shebab*) who were frustrated over the lack of job opportunities. Others speculated that the Islamists were associated with the demonstration and were planning to attack various targets in Fes, and friends reported seeing men with beards standing on each street corner, silently awaiting orders to mobilize. The usual rumors floated about, of brigades of fundamentalists attacking drunken youth, throwing acid on the legs of women wearing miniskirts, or pulling women from cars and demanding they cover up.

However, that night the national news mentioned nothing. My Fassi friends had been in a state of near panic the entire day, and many stayed home from work and urged me to remain in my apartment "just in case." Some repeated stories of the riots of 1990, in which the military had, people claimed, shot student demonstrators at the university and in which many demonstrators had simply disappeared, again with little media documentation.[13] Although I had observed a general sense of unease, the presence of army in full riot gear, and the military trucks parked on every block, I did not witness the riots, nor could I find any newspaper reports of the unofficial demonstration the next day. I began to wonder, had all of this been a rumor too? If so, who started it, and who was responsible for creating the atmosphere of fear that permeated everything? Rumors appeared again to comment on the government's tenuous control over the populace, yet the reports over who was demonstrating suggested action rather than simply guarded dissent. It was unsettling to experience reality in a way that made me constantly question it, particularly when the news media could not be counted on to confirm that any event had taken place at all.[14] How, then, could rumors ever be verified, if it was in the interest of the powerful to suppress what might have happened?

Huriya, who worked in the courthouse, said the "rioters" had been brought in the next day. They were mostly young men, she reported, with no "beards" (or fundamentalists) in their midst. For several days afterward, military trucks filled with soldiers remained parked all over the city. The government subsequently organized a demonstration in Rabat in support of the Palestinians, and offered free train travel for all who wished to take part. It was a way to channel the hunger for a protest, as well as to direct the anger of street youth into one unified, peaceful, government-sanctioned rally.

Many of my friends insisted that "the fundamentalists" were behind it all, and that the illegal demonstration was part of a larger campaign led by Algerian extremists who wanted to create discord among Moroccans. It was rumored that a shadowy, Algerian-backed group of "fundamentalists" were living in the poorer neighborhoods of Fes, from which they plotted demonstrations and attacked individuals. One person told me the fundamentalists were planning to storm the bar at the Sheraton, usually packed with Fassi businessmen during happy hour. Others repeated the story of the assaults on young, drunk men, knifed for carrying bottles of whiskey. But many of the rumors described attacks on women who were not properly covered, or who were otherwise flaunting the dictates of what the fundamentalists considered "appropriate" Islamic behavior.

Whether the rumors of the extremists can be verified as truth is unimportant compared with their significance in local imaginations. Related as social facts, these rumors affect the way Fassis perceive themselves, their religiosity, and the "outsiders" in their midst. In rumors, Islamist behavior is portrayed as a threat to middle-class Fassi culture and practices. Ironically, Scheherezade, who was born in one of the popular, working class neighborhoods of Fes and had her roots (*asl*) elsewhere, aligned herself with Fassis when the topic came around to the threat presented by the fundamentalists. Her self-positioning depended on the context, but most of the time she situated herself as an outsider. In describing her identity, when I asked her once if she was Berber, she told me,

"No, I'm not Berber, but I'm not really Arab either. Who is? Fassis are hypocrites, wanting to pretend they are pure Arabs, as if that makes them more Muslim than the rest of us. Do you think, after a thousand years of mixing, that anyone is pure in this country?" With her shrewdness and intelligence, she had managed to raise her income and social status, but she had no illusions about her membership in the crowd of "original Fassis" who traced their origins back to the Andalusians. In decrying the religious hypocrisy of Fassis, she disavowed her identification with Fassi religious practices. But when describing the fundamentalists, she spoke of a "we": Fassis as a unitary social body, defending their way of life against imported ideologies.

The importance of gender in this matter is also noteworthy. The fundamentalists of rumor pursue either intoxicated men or women whose dress and behavior are signs of insufficient piety according to conservative Islamist ideologies. Women serve as signifiers for modernity, national identity, or religiosity, not as actual beings with agency but as representatives of competing ideologies. To some Fassis, proof of the country's modernity means that women have the freedom to dress as they like, and to elect whether or not to wear the headscarf (*hijab*). The first king after independence, Mohammed V, had even publicly unveiled his daughters, an act many older Fassis remember and speak of as a sign of women's liberation. Privately, some people express confusion over media images from the Middle East that convey the message that to be truly religious, women must cover their hair. However, many continue to assert that the *hijab* should not be a matter of public control but of personal conscience.

Assaulting uncovered women was an attack on middle-class Fassi religiosity. When she discussed Islamist influence in Morocco, Scheherezade suggested that if the fundamentalists had already made inroads by subtly convincing women to veil, the next step might be a demand for the entire country to be ruled by Islamic law (*shari'a*).[15] Her sense that Islamists and extremists were pursuing the same ends led her to collapse distinctions between the two in narrative.

The rumor of the reputed attacks in the "popular" or lower-middle-class neighborhoods implied that the government did not have effective control over the populace. The Fassis who related these stories to me are unanimous in criticizing the extremists. They depend on the government's ability to keep peace and protect its citizens, but there is some speculation as to whether King Mohammed VI is up to the task.

"Under his father, there were no human rights," a Fassi man in his forties, Younes, told me. "Now we have human rights, and it does us no good. The police can't discipline the prisoners anymore, so we have more crime. People can say anything they want now, which isn't a good thing, because people are ignorant, and they do not realize the problems they cause with their opinions. *Especially people from the countryside.* Morocco is not ready for democracy. Certainly, Hassan II [the former king] was harsh, but at least we were safe. Nobody dared to commit a crime because they knew they would be punished. With human rights, people can get away with anything."

Here, "human rights" resulted in the government's inability to maintain order. Younes's critique was echoed by many, and it is significant that he blamed outsiders for the misunderstanding of human rights. His words reflect an entrenched paternalism, which likens Moroccans of other social classes and rural migrants to children, in need of different laws and harsher discipline. Furthermore, this discourse also implicitly criticizes the king for allowing wayward elements to threaten Morocco's stability. The presence of the fundamentalists reveals that pockets of chaos (*fitna*) exist outside the new regime's control.

While pointing at the government's inability to control the population, these rumors also reflect ambivalence about religiosity, and about the relationship between religion and modernity. Occasionally some of my friends would blame colonialism, stating that French influence has watered down Islamic tenets and caused Moroccans to "forget" a true, essentialized Islamic self. Those who keep abreast of media reports from other Muslim countries sense that the entire Muslim world is returning to its roots, expelling foreign influence and finding the true faith. An authentic, original form of Islam, untainted by fourteen hundred years of history or by French occupation, is perceived by some Fassis as the solution to social ills. This, essentially, is a goal of moderate Islamists as well, yet it was not a contradiction in other conversations for middle-class Fassis to argue for the same principles. However, when expounded by outsiders, these ideas became threatening and, particularly in light of the experience of Algeria, seemed as if they would inevitably be linked with violence. Even the most religious Fassis would tell the story of the extremists attacking the women and the drinkers, as this was a tale with a moral all could agree on. Violence and intolerance are antithetical to middle-class Fassi self-images.

Disenfranchised Young Men

Rumors are also the provenance of the disenfranchised. Other sites for the production of rumors are those settings in which young Fassi men gather to discuss life and the world outside Morocco. I witnessed many such conversations at a music store in the center of Fes owned by my husband's family, which at the time sold recordings of American and European popular music, as well as the latest hits from the Middle East and the CDs of Algerian raï stars such as Khaled and Cheb Mami. Customers were a mix of mostly middle-class Fassis younger than forty, both male and female, but also foreign employees of the French consulate, and students and teachers from the Spanish and American language centers. Some of the wealthier Moroccan clients spent their summers in Europe, drove fancy sports cars, and owed their situations, employed or not, to their fathers, who were well connected and extremely wealthy. But also in this mix were the neighborhood's unemployed young men, who often stopped by to hang out and exchange gossip.

Commodities and words were in constant circulation at this shop, the commodities selling an elsewhere, a vision of the world projected on the television screen above our heads, which was always tuned to MTV Europe. The young men kept up with the latest musical releases and were conversant with trivia about movie stars and pop singers. Many expressed ambitions to go to Europe and had given up on the possibility of finding work in Morocco.[16]

One day at the shop, one of the young men, Taoufik, told a story about a friend of his. Faris was a twenty-two-year-old high school graduate, enrolled in computer classes at a local technical school, preparing for a profession in which there was some hope of finding work.[17] From his parents, who paid for his classes, he had enough pocket money to buy cassettes and clothes, and he was handsome and likeable. He also had a girlfriend of two years, Karima, who attended the local university. They managed to see each other or talk on their cell phones every day. Faris, his friend said, was in love with Karima, and would have done anything for her, but at this age, marriage was not an option. Without steady employment, it would be years before he could support a wife. For now, Faris was content to be involved with a girl he cared about.

But one day Karima refused to see him. Stunned, Faris tried calling her, but her cell phone had been disconnected. He went to the university to meet her after her classes but could not find her. Finally, he heard from one of Karima's girlfriends that she was engaged.

Karima's parents had convinced her to marry a forty-five-year-old pharmacist, who had money and belonged to a well-known Fes lineage. Persuading her that money and security were more important than love, her family told her that she might never again have opportunities as good as this one. The pharmacist respected her education; he would allow her to finish university before expecting her to have children. She would not have to work, if she wanted to stay at home.

Faris was from a good family and was a "child of Fes" (*wlid Fes*) from an "original" Fassi family, but so was the pharmacist. Unable to talk to Karima, Faris became depressed, and began skipping his classes, sleeping all morning, and smoking a lot of hashish. His friends at the music store shrugged their shoulders. It was sad, but these kinds of things happen. Maybe in ten years they would finally have work and be able to get married. It certainly was not in the realm of possibility for now.

To the young men who hung out at the music shop, Faris's experience was emasculating: losing his modern relationship with a girlfriend his own age through her marriage to someone else. After hearing the story, everyone remained silent, until our attention was distracted by the television set flickering above us, showing a music video by a popular American rap group in which scantily clad women were draped around a man in the back of a limousine.

"Is it really like this?" someone asked, gesturing at the video's images of endless parties.

"In Europe?" Taoufik responded. "Of course! Do you know how much money Fassis have made there?"

And so another story began, segueing from a rumor of disappointment to one of success. This rumor always followed the same pattern. So-and-so had emigrated to Spain/France/America several years before. He got there by overstaying a tourist visa/marrying an American Peace Corps worker/paying a smuggler to hide him on a fishing boat. Once there, he started working as a waiter/taxi driver/businessman. He was so wily and cunning that he soon owned a restaurant and a fleet of limousines. One voice, that of Mehdi, who was a few years older than Taoufik and his friends and had lived outside Morocco, rose in protest above the others.

"What about the Moroccans cleaning the streets of Paris, doing the dirty work the French refuse to do? Or breaking their backs to pick vegetables for the Spanish, even when they would never work in the fields here? And the racism. There have been attacks."

Taoufik and his friends exchanged glances, but it was as if Mehdi had never spoken at all. They continued to narrate the exploits of successful émigrés, repeating if only, if only, if only they themselves could go to Europe, they would come back with more money than you could find in one of the king's palaces.

The story about Faris flourished in a setting where young men went to gaze on the "elsewhere" provided by the music videos, and to talk about their own disappointments. The future is often bleak for young men, even for university graduates, who find they still need connections to get a job. Businesses remain in families, with sons inheriting the work of their fathers, and brothers passing opportunities on to brothers. In Fes, unemployment rates are four percentage points higher than in the rest of Morocco (Guerraoui 1996: 157). Rather than take work they consider to be low status, many middle-class Fassi men wait passively for some outside intervention to change their situation. Although Faris was not a university student, he was attempting to follow a more practical path: educating himself in a new industry, computer programming, where there were rumored opportunities. However, over a period of several years in the early part of the millennium, I watched what happened to the men I knew who became skilled programmers. Several of them found internships with corporations, a few in cities like Casablanca and Rabat. The internships would pay, according to one young man, "just enough for cigarettes and coffee," with the promise of turning into a permanent job. Without fail, after several months, the young men were fired and more new interns took their place. Permanent work, they told me, usually went to a university graduate with a degree from Europe or America, or to someone with connections. The young men moved from internship to internship, always hopeful that something would turn into real work, but after several years, many are in exactly the same place that they were when the conversation about Faris took place in the music store.

In an ideal world, studying would lead to employment, and the modern relationship would lead to marriage. Yet when Karima broke up with Faris, it demonstrated that her loyalty was ultimately not to him but to traditional ideals of marriage. Her decision also cast into doubt the possibility that Faris would be employed any time soon. In a society where patriarchal ideologies are still strong, young men often lose out to older men of higher status. Marriage, while encouraged, requires capital, and for those who have nothing, it remains out of reach.

Fredric Jameson has written that the story of the private individual struggle is an allegory for developing nations (1986: 65). The men in the record store spoke freely; what happened to Faris showed that Morocco was "upside down," one unemployed man told me. "We are only half modernized; it is an incomplete process. People make choices in one direction and then they change their minds and go in a different one. Everyone is uncertain. There are no clear paths." Because of this, many were stuck in the middle. A "traditional" Fassi way of life had fallen away, but rather than replacing it with clear opportunities, modernity presented only chaos (*fitna*) and incompleteness.

It is not surprising, then, that young men's stories of failure often appear with rumors of achievement on an international stage. The tale of Faris's defeat exemplifies the disappointments of those who have never left Fes, and who bear witness to the endless dead time spent waiting for the future to present itself. In contrast, the rumor of the émigré represents possibility, and is also a testimony to Fassi cleverness. Such rumors are numerous, and have some basis in reality, although success stories tend to be exaggerated. Immigrants to the United States or Europe speak of feeling pressure to return to their homeland presenting visible proof of their achievements. Despite modest incomes, they return home laden down with gifts, presenting themselves as full participants in the illusory dream of the commodified world outside. In summer, and on various religious holidays, young men return to Fes, showing off their sport utility vehicles and their chic foreign girlfriends or wives. Tales of their accomplishments circulate, growing larger in their absence, and even if the émigré is only a driver of a limousine, in the rumors, the limousine swells into a private jet.

Conclusion

Middle-class Fassi rumors exemplify the human tendency across cultures to employ narratives to resolve insecurities and make statements about the world. Through rumor, people assert the strength of Fassi values and identities in opposition to other ways of being. Competing ideologies are numerous, threatening to take over the city, and to upset middle-class Fassi hegemony, while people are looking the other way. The examples in this chapter have shown how rumors position particular groups against outsiders: poor rural migrants, fundamentalists, other social classes of Fassis, or foreigners. Outsiders present alternative ideologies that are in conflict with Fassis' sense of themselves. In rumors, competing claims to identity are presented and then dismissed. Yet the very presence of these "others" demonstrates that identity is unstable, and that the resolution through narrative does not smooth over the uncertainties of social life.

Fassi rumors arise at moments of danger, when an ideally unitary, cultural self is perceived to be under threat, and they reassert a unified, harmonious condition. These narratives seek closure and attempt to heal "the gap between the present and the disappearing past, which without interpretation, would be otherwise irretrievable and foreclosed" (Fineman 1981: 29). Paradoxically, rumors are infused with a sense of loss, nostalgia for a city that was once governed by rules that everyone agreed on. They reflect a "landscape of regret" for a territory belonging to Fassis alone, even as such a world no longer exists (and may never have).

Because rumors respond to changes and conflicts in the social environment, on another level they criticize a world that is no longer as it should be, a world where everything is "upside down." They reveal social tension about subjects as disparate as gender, poverty, religion, and emigration. Fassi rumors contain an implicit critique of a government that cannot quite control the disruptive social forces in its midst. The imagined chaos (*fitna*) represented by disorganized shantytown dwellers and disorderly fundamentalists must be kept in check by a government capable of enforcing laws and protecting its citizens.

Defining a Fassi Moroccan identity through an ideology of "Fassiness" is a project in which many disparate groups have a stake, and each resolution through rumor offers a singular fantasy about what the

Moroccan nation should consist of, to the exclusion of all other claims. On the surface, rumors provide the illusion of cultural solidarity, as well as a resolution for otherwise messy, indeterminate situations. With words, these narratives construct an orderly world in which everyone plays by the same set of rules, and those who do not are dismissed from the game. But a temporary resolution through narrative is paradoxical, as reality is much more conflict-filled and open-ended. The contexts of rumors reveal unresolved social tensions, and their repetition points to the impossibility of an ordered social world. As propositions about the unitary nature of Fassi Moroccan culture, rumors are just as transitory and unstable as the shantytowns they criticize. The stories middle-class Fassis tell about themselves, and others, set the stage for a particular way of being-in-the-world that women, in the following chapters, will have to contend with as they attempt to make new places for themselves in Moroccan society. Territories of ideology are laid out through discourse, and keeping in mind what Fassis say about who they are, we turn to other stories to observe women as they come to terms with ideology in occupying new spaces in the Fassi urban milieu.

Chapter 3

Mudawana Reform and the Persistence of Patriarchy

Malika burst into the Najia Belghazi Center, holding one of her two small children by one hand, carrying a bag of hot doughnuts in the other. She greeted the volunteers with kisses and a charming, dimpled smile, pulled her scarf off her red hair and sat down at the large conference table, where a session on women's reproductive health was about to begin. I could see from her relaxed demeanor how comfortable she was here. She treated the space of the NGO as the volunteers wished all the women would, not only as a resource but also as a place where women could gather and learn from their shared experiences with the law, with men, or with life in general.

For the women who volunteered at the only NGO in Fes dedicated to legal and domestic violence issues, Malika was one of the most notable success stories. She was a constant presence at the Najia Belghazi Center, eager to dispense advice to other women who were going through problems with marriage and divorce. At the time of my initial fieldwork from 2001 to 2002, activists in Moroccan society were debating the proposed reforms to the *mudawana* family code that governs a woman's rights in marriage and divorce, and Malika's experiences illustrated many negative effects of the *mudawana* that activists sought to change. A number of issues coalesced in Malika's life history: an early marriage forced by her parents to a man many years her senior, unsuccessful attempts to get a divorce from the abusive husband, and finally, a failure to find viable employment and a turn to prostitution. With the help of the volunteers at the Najia Belghazi Center, Malika managed to overcome most of her difficulties. For the volunteers, she had become something of a poster child for *mudawana* reform, as well as for the Center's efforts to help women successfully pursue their cases through the legal system.

But not everyone was in agreement that Malika's was a story of triumph. Khadija, a young lawyer in her late twenties, was firmly against the proposed *mudawana* reforms, and she saw Malika as a "country person" (*'arubi*), incapable of living an ordered life. The urbanized, middle-class Khadija told me she "understood the mentality" of people like Malika, which was simple, childlike, and unreformable. The existing *mudawana* laws were there to protect Malika, and any alteration of those laws represented a direct critique of God's immutable design. Khadija's opinions represented those of many other middle-class Fassis I knew, and her perspective was further informed by her direct experience with the legal profession. However, Khadija's views reflect more than mere class prejudice or resistance to change. Shared by many, they represent an ideology associated with a patriarchal social structure. This ideology impedes the breakdown of traditional hierarchies and the cooperation necessary to tackle larger issues such as entrenched poverty or violence against women. In this chapter, I examine how one woman's lived experience of the *mudawana* made her an advocate of reform, while another woman's resistance stemmed from her own adherence to an ideological system that was more likely to benefit women of her position and social class.

Malika

I had met Malika many times, hearing versions of her story from the other volunteers long before she told it to me herself. At the Najia Belghazi Center, Malika was a vivacious, smiling presence, eager to encourage other women to pursue their legal battles or take literacy classes. Although she had spent only a few years in school, her sharp common sense and forthrightness suggested a profound intelligence, one that had served her well in negotiating the legal system. When I met her she had recently remarried, and with her husband's blessing she spent many hours at the Center.

Originally from a village not far outside Fes, Malika had been married off at fourteen to a man fifty years her senior. The *mudawana* laws at that time required the bride to be at least fifteen, and she suspected her family of forging her birth certificate to make her older than she was. Her bride price (*sdaq*), which by rights should have belonged to her as "insurance" in the event of a divorce, was a gift of land offered by the husband, which her father subsequently intercepted. Malika told me: "My first marriage? I hardly even knew I was married until after it happened. I didn't know that I had to agree to the marriage until I came here [to the NGO]. That was what I told the judge [when she argued for her divorce]. Also I was only fourteen. I had no idea my family was planning this. They signed the act without me, then told me I was married. Then they did the henna so I knew.[1] I wasn't happy. I knew the old man had asked to marry me but I didn't know my family had agreed. He was such an old man!"

As we talked, sipping cups of Nescafé at the large conference table in the main room of the Center, Malika's children sat on the floor coloring on handouts from a health lecture. Malika clearly relished telling her story to someone new. "Make sure you put that down," she would say from time to time, when she gave me a detail she considered particularly important. Her delight in having her words recorded was a contrast from the legal advice sessions I attended every Friday at the Center, in which I avoided taking notes until after women left the room. In those circumstances, my lawyer friend Naima had told me, women resented note taking, which reminded them of bureaucratic encounters where authorities recorded observations they could not read before dismissing the women outright. But Malika had had successes and was encouraged by the praise of the Center's volunteers.

Malika's first husband was a widower, with adult children who no longer lived in the village; thus, Malika felt the primary reason he had wanted to remarry was to gain a caretaker and a maid.

"There was no understanding between us. . . . Sometimes he would hit me, even though he was so old. I never told anybody. Who would I tell? People would say, 'You deserved it, you must have been bad.' I couldn't go to my family. They would have been angry. They said, 'Look, your husband is a rich man. You will never find someone young who can marry you.' The young ones don't work. Or else they're working abroad." Migration had reduced the number of marriageable men in Malika's village.

During the day, Malika's only job was to cook and take care of the house while her husband was gone. He spent most of his time in the mosque or in the village café with his friends, coming home for lunches that they ate in silence before he left again in the afternoon. These were lonely times for the young woman, whose family refused to visit her after she tried to run away once to her father's house. She became resentful, sometimes testing her husband by refusing to prepare his lunch. Often he would respond by beating her, other times by not coming home at all.

Still childless, Malika decided to run away. She was vague about the circumstances of her arrival in Fes, saying only that someone from her village had helped her to get to the city.

"I worked when I could, cleaning houses, but everything was difficult," she told me. "What could I do? There was no work. But going back would have been worse." I knew from the other volunteers that the person who had "helped" Malika move to the city had pushed her into prostitution, but she seemed uncomfortable with this part of her story, so I did not press her.

"Then I met my [second] husband," she said, her face brightening.

"We loved each other. We tried to get the old man to release me, but he refused. Finally I came here [to the Center] when someone told me about this place, and they helped me. They taught me that if a girl doesn't agree, she can't be married. I told this to the judge. I told him how nobody had asked me. I told him I didn't even know about *sdaq* (bride price), and wasn't I supposed to receive this?"

For months, Malika worked to amass evidence and follow her case carefully through the legal system, and finally she managed to get the divorce.

"So many things were illegal, and I never knew it," she told me. "My age. That I never agreed to the marriage. My father taking the *sdaq* that was supposed to be mine. My husband mistreating me. Finally he agreed to the divorce, when he saw that I knew my rights."

Many of the proposed *mudawana* reforms would have affected Malika's case directly. I asked her how she felt about the proposal to raise the marriage age from fifteen to eighteen.

"Raising the age of marriage is a good idea," Malika said. "Because then it will be harder to force a girl to be married while she's still young. It still happens, you know. Maybe with education, it will not happen so much. But if there is a law . . . [then the] people will know about it. They will tell us on the radio, or the news, that the laws have changed. It won't be like before. If a girl is too young, people decide for her. When she is older, she sees more, hears more. Look at me, I am older now, and I chose my husband. With the first, I wasn't ready. I wasn't expecting to be married. I was still a child. Now I have chosen my husband, and I'm going to school."

"There's also," I said, "the issue of whether a girl can get married without her father giving her away. What do you think about this idea?"

"When I wanted to marry my [second] husband, the judge gave us permission," Malika said. "Because my father, my family—they wanted nothing to do with me. My new husband declared that he had children with me, and that we were already married in the eyes of the religion, and that we had agreed between us to be married, and we had twelve witnesses, and the judge allowed it."

Malika believed a woman should have the right to marry without the male guardian's permission.

"A father doesn't always have his daughter's best interests in mind," she said. "Look at my father. He just wanted to get his hands on the land. So if a girl meets someone she really loves, she should have the right to choose him herself. Like I did."

Malika turned and looked out the window, where the sun was just beginning to set behind the high walls surrounding the Center. Calling to her two children to gather their belongings, she pushed the chair back from the table.

"It's getting late," she said. "My husband," and here I could hear the pride in her voice, "will be waiting for me."

Legal Contexts

On March 12, 2000, less than a year after King Mohammed VI ascended the throne, thousands of Moroccans took to the streets of Rabat and Casablanca, demonstrating both for and against a government proposal to augment women's rights within the *mudawana*, the personal status code legislating the rights of women in marriage and divorce. Demonstrators in Casablanca, many of them veiled and marching separately from the men, argued that the plan was anti-Islamic. In Rabat, however, marchers from various women's and human rights groups rallied in its favor.

Estimates of the number of demonstrators varied, depending on the source. The newspaper *Asharq al-awsat* reported 500,000 in Casablanca and 100,000 in Rabat. The radio channel Médi1 reported an even 200,000 in each city, while *al-Ittihad Ishtiraqi*, the newspaper of the government majority USFP political party, announced that 700,000 marchers in Rabat had supported the plan. *L'Économiste* (Casablanca) reported a conservative guess of 60,000 in Casablanca. Given the vast disparities, the estimates themselves are unreliable, but they do hint at some of the underlying conflicts that make discussion of women's rights in Morocco such a heated issue.

Titled "the integration of women in development," the proposed reforms would have altered the existing *mudawana* in several areas. The proposal aimed to remove the restriction that women needed the consent of a male guardian in order to marry. Along with raising the age of marriage, the plan gave women the right to a judicial divorce, and removed men's unilateral freedom to repudiate their wives. It also proposed to outlaw polygamy. Finally, under the existing laws, a divorced woman had the right to retain custody of her children only should she remain unmarried; if she remarried, the father of the children could remove them from her custody. Reformers wanted to grant the mother primary custody, even in the event of remarriage.

As the contradictory estimates of the number of demonstrators show, Moroccans were polarized over the reforms. *L'Économiste* called those who would impede the reforms "les rétrogrades, les obscurantistes ou les fascistes" (*L'Économiste*, March 13, 2000). Those opposing the plan stated that it went against the dictates of the Qur'an and the Sunna, and was therefore not only anti-Islamic but willfully neglectful of Morocco's cultural foundations in Islam. Abouzid Al-Mokri Al-Idrissi, the parliamentary deputy of the Islamist political party of Justice and Development (PJD), denounced the plan as full of imported occidental ideas, stating that a revision of the *mudawana* needed to be in harmony both with the principles of Islam and the needs of Moroccan society.

The reforms, proposed by then-prime minister Abderrahmane Youssoufi, were quickly suspended. Youssoufi announced that the plan would not be implemented as proposed, yet he promised supporters that it would not be abandoned entirely. The king appointed a committee of *ulama* to debate the matter, where it languished for the next three years. Invoking the specter of Islam and the Qur'an (despite the fact that the laws were derived *from* those sources in the eighth century), those against the plan questioned the legitimacy of a government in a Muslim country that would propose civil laws in an area so clearly legislated by religion. Few on the other side seemed willing to call for a new interpretation of the Islamic jurisprudence, or to point out that in all other areas of criminal law, Morocco does not follow Islamic law (*shari'a*). Rather, they argued that the laws denied women their basic human rights and violated the 1979 Convention on the Elimination of All Forms of Discrimination Against Women, which Morocco had signed.

In the press, the issue was often distilled into two presumably opposing ideologies: one represented by Islam as a system interpenetrating all aspects of social life and the other by the ideals of internationalist human rights, which opponents argued were imported concepts. Representatives of both sides were intent on proving that their point of view incorporated Islamic principles. As Turkish scholar Deniz Kandiyoti has noted, women's rights debates in Muslim countries always come back to a reified notion of Islam that is both essentialist and imaginary, especially given the numerous "Islams" that actually exist (Kandiyoti 2001: 53). To insist, as opponents to the plan did, that the existing *mudawana* is unchangeable because it is Islamic, effaces the law's rootedness in Moroccan culture, and ignores other deeply held cultural ideologies, not solely in the areas of law and religion, that led to the creation of the *mudawana* in the first place. Supporters appeal to universalist notions of modernity and human rights as if they were easily applicable in all situations, while also overlooking the patriarchal underpinnings that still affect many facets of Moroccan social life.

During my fieldwork in Fes in 2001–2002, the national debates resonated in discussions I took part in at local universities, in conferences I attended on civil society, and at NGOs such as the Najia Belghazi Center. The national positions were mirrored on a local level by political parties, groups and organizations that made their own positions a prominent part of their mission statements. When Fassis spoke of the controversies in the abstract, the same oppositions formed along the lines of the national debates, and talk came to an impasse. But locally, when faced with situations related to the actual implementation of the laws, the terms of the argument sometimes shifted in unexpected ways.

Malika and Khadija came from different social classes and had vastly disparate levels of education, but both were firm when it came to their opposing perspectives on *mudawana* reform. Their views were informed by experience and by education, but also by what both stood to lose or gain under a different system. Their opinions were representative of the viewpoints I heard expressed in numerous Fassi conversations in 2001–2002, and I contrast them here, not only for what they reveal about social position but also for some of the other, hidden ideologies that were not always obvious in the national arguments. In local discussions about the *mudawana*, Islam was sometimes in the background, while the influence of family, patriarchy, and social class figured prominently in local imaginations. A focus solely on the national debates obscures other issues involved in the application of the *mudawana*, most notably the way the laws benefit the interests of patriarchal social organization. Interpreting the demonstrations of March 2000 as simply a battle over Islam and women's rights obfuscates other operations of power that are also at work. The ideology representative of a patriarchal social system is relevant in understanding not only the workings of the *mudawana* but also the social inequalities in Moroccan society. Women tread lightly in attempting to challenge territories of ideology that lay claim to "Islam," or to the "Moroccan way of life."

Examining specific cases demonstrates how extralegal aspects of Moroccan social life have come to bear on the workings of the laws themselves. The very same patriarchal qualities operative in the original formation of the laws can work to people's advantage or disadvantage, depending on social position. Just as rumors position Fassis against outsiders, an attempt to maintain a conservative *mudawana* reflects similar efforts to represent certain "others" as irrational. The *mudawana* is said to uphold traditional norms for behavior in order to prevent these "others" from producing social chaos. An investigation of some of these controversial proposed revisions, such as raising the age of marriage, eliminating the need for a male guardian (*wali*) to approve a woman's marriage, and ending polygamy, sheds light on how different groups benefit from or are disadvantaged by the laws as they stand now.

Discussions of the *mudawana* often reflect a kind of paternalism, not only with the idea of men looking after women but also one social class looking after the interests of another. Initially I could not understand why many middle-class Fassis spoke as if the laws were meant for some other group, stating that they protected those who had no protectors, or who had not "advanced" to the point where access to education, employment, and other resources made the laws moot. Yet this paternalistic rendering of others masked the fact that the existing laws supplemented resources the middle class had always had, while often hurting those who had the most at stake. But if the laws were there to protect those "others" of a different social class, another argument against changing them emphasized the inherent connection of the *mudawana* with Moroccan culture. By this formulation, changing the laws was the first step on a slippery slope toward the total abandonment of Moroccan culture—which, as usual, fell on the shoulders of women as its principal bearers.

"Changing the *mudawana* would destroy our culture," said Driss, a professor at Sidi Mohamed Ben Abdellah University in Fes. "They're part of our tradition. Would the reformers have us abandon our traditions? If this happens, we will be lost." Other middle-class Fassis echoed Driss's opinions. "Tradition" and "modernity," however, present a false dichotomy that conceals some of the very real social inequalities that the laws do nothing to alleviate. Middle-class Fassis believe the "other" Fes—poor, underclass, disadvantaged—are the true target of laws which, though perhaps outdated, are said to be necessary to safeguard a traditional way of life that "modern" Fassis claim no longer to follow.

In practice, however, the laws do apply to everybody.[2] Often it is not until a dispute arises that people become aware that the laws continue to privilege strong, male-headed familial networks. The *mudawana* favors male control over a woman's ability to marry or divorce. True, middle- and upper-class women frequently have strong family networks, access to resources, education, and a prominent social position from which to negotiate in the event of a marital dispute. However, these resources are often due to the grace of a male relative, such as an uncle who provides a job connection, a father who allows his daughter to choose her own husband, or an inheritance. The laws depend on a man's benevolence, but they permit male intervention in situations where a woman's choices conflict with male self-interest. Middle- and upper-class women could assert their independence in other contexts, such as employment or level of education, while a façade of "modernity" obscures the operations of patriarchy still prevalent on all levels of society.[3] As this chapter will show, members of any social class could face the brick wall of patriarchal ideology that continues to promote the interests of one group over others.

Patriarchy

A familial, hierarchical system of inequality characterized by domination by senior males, patriarchy in North Africa infuses all aspects of social life (Waltz 1995: 41).[4] In the past, individual identity was subsumed into that of the group, and the family served as the primary economic, political, and social unit. Typically, family members were identified by their relationship to others within the family, as mothers, sisters, or brothers (Zerdoumi 1970: 42). As I will show in Chapter 5, there are more recent variations on this model due to women's entry into the public sphere; subsequently, in some prominent families in Fes, women exercised more economic and social power than their male siblings. Yet the model continues to exert a hold, manifesting itself in subtle ways throughout all levels of society.

In traditional patriarchal social organization, the head of the family, usually a father or grandfather, organizes production within the family unit, controls property, assigns work, and deals with outsiders.[5] Within this unit, the father or grandfather is located at the top of the hierarchy, with younger males deferring to older siblings, women to men. "To avail itself of a force sufficient to impress others," writes Abdellah Hammoudi, "the family submits itself to uncontested discipline, laying the foundation for power through obedience and work under the leadership of a patriarch who must be feared by everyone" (Hammoudi 1997: 78).

In this traditional model, young brides, leaving the protection of their families to live with their in-laws, face numerous hardships. Control by the mother-in-law over the new bride asserts the authority of an elder female while also threatening nascent bonds of affection between the son and his new wife. The mother's affective bonds with her son lead not only to her resentment of her daughter-in-law but also to the son's stunted relationship with his new wife.[6] Women achieve status in the family only toward the end of their childbearing years, when they themselves are able to dominate daughters-in-law and others now below them in the hierarchy.

Today, many of the original functions of patriarchy as a form of economic production are outmoded. Salaried workers now maintain employment outside the family, and couples increasingly no longer live with their parents. Yet the patriarchal model remains, not only within the family but also in the relations individuals form within society. The patrilineage serves as the basic political unit in rural communities and as "the structural model for larger political groupings" (Zghal 1971: 20). In social relations, the concept of "idiomatic kinship" applies, in which people extend the expectations and patterns of familial relationships into other realms, such as business or politics (Joseph and Slyomovics 2001: 7).

As Abdellah Hammoudi has shown in *Master and Disciple*, patriarchal authority has infused social relations to the extent that almost all aspects of social life in the Middle East and North Africa are governed by it. Hammoudi traces the roots of authoritarian behavior, in which feminized subordinates are temporarily dominated by a superior, to the medieval Sufi diagram of master and disciple. The same model is operative in other relationships as well, such as that of husband and wife, father and children, supervisors and employees, even king and subjects. The effectiveness of the system rests in the possibility individuals have to seize power of some sort—be it familial, economic, or political. Within the master-disciple schema, temporary inversion, in which the power seeker is initially feminized and dominated, serves to "obliterate the reproductive role of women" (Hammoudi 1997: 6). After all, he asks, how else "could we expect this patriarchal society to accept the fact that women are responsible for the continuity of agnatic lines?" (6).[7]

The continued appeal of patriarchal social structures lies in the fact that patriarchy "provides the basis for a system of social security, and what is of undoubtedly even greater importance, the emotional comfort of personal identity" (Waltz 1995: 43). For many Fassis, membership in a renowned family line guarantees strong familial bonds that carry weight in the larger community as well. The ability of a male patriarch to protect female relatives supports his prestige as a leader not only of the family but also within the community (Rassam 1980: 172). In business transactions and even in interactions with local government, the prestige of family connections can result in favorable consideration or, at the very least, more attentive service. This security stands in marked contrast to the inadequate guarantee of services provided by the government (Joseph and Slyomovics 2001: 4). Individuals derive social and economic benefits from personal connections to others within the hierarchy, so that even at the highest levels of Moroccan society, patronage networks contribute to the formation of public policy (Waltz 1995: 46).[8]

Designed to protect the power of the patrilineage, the *mudawana* personal status code was the only area of Islamic jurisprudence maintained when Morocco became independent in 1956—criminal and business laws were modeled on European legal codes.[9] King Mohammed V favored a conservative *mudawana*, based on the Maliki school of Islamic jurisprudence that Morocco followed, which would appease kin groups on whom the monarchy depended for its legitimacy after independence. "The family law of newly independent Morocco," writes Mounira Charrad, "was a signal to notables in rural areas that the monarchy chose a law that conformed to the vision of the world held by the population of those areas. It also showed the determination of the monarchy to safeguard kin-based solidarities" (2001: 168). By favoring rural notables, King Mohammed V not only enhanced the stability of his regime but also weakened the popular urban-based Istiqlal party (Leveau 1976: 26). The Istiqlal party had hoped to abandon the system of power transferred through kinship in favor of alliances based on economic or social interests, but this was not to be the case. Rather, the alliance between the monarchy and the rural notables transferred to the level of government the "system of relationships which govern interaction between the local and rural elites, in which personal and family ties tend to reduce the importance of other ideals in motivating action" (Hammoudi 1997: 34).

At the time of Moroccan independence, the vision of a more liberal personal status code was not without its supporters. Istiqlal leader Allal al-Fasi advocated reforming family law to promote equality between men and women as well as stable conjugal units (Borrmans 1977: 128). Some of the reforms he argued for are the same ones that were considered controversial during my fieldwork, including the abolition of both polygamy and the marital guardian (*wali*), and raising the minimum age of marriage. Al-Fasi hoped that by altering the laws, kinship structures would gradually change, thus promoting not only national solidarity but also rights for women (Charrad 2001: 161).

In 1957, King Mohammed V resolved the issue of women's status by formalizing Maliki law into an organized code and eliminating local customary marriage practices.[10] The *mudawana* centralized kinship as a foundational organizing principle of Moroccan society. A strong family code thus allowed rural notables to maintain patrilineal control over women and resources, emphasizing the fragility of matrimonial bonds and giving significant advantage to agnates over spouses in matters of inheritance (Charrad 2001: 32). Although a few minor changes had been made to the *mudawana* in 1993, at the time of my fieldwork, the code had remained relatively unchanged since 1957.[11]

The *mudawana* covers all family matters related to marriage, divorce, parentage, custody, and inheritance. Over time, laws strengthened local customs and practices to increase paternal control over daughters (Borrmans 1977: 17). Marriage is defined as a relationship contracted to set up a family under the leadership of the husband. The husband is obligated to provide food, clothing, and furnishings for his wife, while she is expected to defer and submit to him (*mudawana* articles 1–31). While daughters have the right to refuse a marriage they have not chosen and to petition a judge to intervene if the father refuses to support a marriage, in practice a young woman would be unlikely to go to such lengths to defy the will of her family. At the time of marriage, control over the woman is transferred from the father to the husband. While a son is no longer under parental guardianship once he reaches the age of eighteen, the daughter continues to be until her marriage. Legally, her status is then subordinated to her husband.

In the national debates, proponents of the suggested reforms based their arguments primarily on sociological evidence and international human rights discourses. Arguing that Moroccan women had come to occupy many of the same positions in public life as Moroccan men, they asserted that their legal status must be elevated to keep pace with their accomplishments. Furthermore, they pointed out that the laws were inadequate, unjust, and unfairly applied. Opponents of the reforms insisted that the *mudawana* was Islamic and thus applicable for all times. Blaming a lack of enforcement for the inadequacies of the current laws, they also felt that Morocco's uneven reliance on Islamic and European legal codes demonstrated an overall societal weakness that could be remedied by turning toward Islam as a regulator of all areas of social life. Islam itself, they argued, contains the original principles of human rights. If women and men returned to their "authentic," traditional roles designated by Islam and practiced the proper division of the sexes, the *shari'a*-based family laws would adequately protect the rights and obligations of all.

In local debates, however, there was less of an emphasis on Islam or human rights arguments. Fassis who supported the existing *mudawana* held that law serves as a substitute where a male authority figure is unavailable to defend his interests. The code protects the ideals of patriarchal social organization even where such figures are absent and the mode of social organization has collapsed.

Khadija

An ardent defender of the *mudawana*, Khadija was a lawyer who specialized in family law. Attractive and poised, Khadija and her family had moved to Fes around the time she began her university degree. Although she was born in Meknes, her parents were "original Fassis" (*min asl Fassi*) and most of her extended family also lived in Fes. She did not cover her head and was not particularly observant, but her views about women were nonetheless conservative. When we met, she offered to spend time with me reading the laws in both Arabic and French to explain their social implications. During our first few meetings, she covered the structure of the personal status code, going over the rules for marriage and divorce and defending each one.

"The *mudawana* is a perfect document," she said. We sat in my apartment on Moroccan sofas, drinking steaming glasses of mint tea. At her side were several imposing legal tomes that she referred to from time to time. "There is no need to revise the *mudawana* because the Qur'an and the *hadiths* (sayings of the Prophet Muhammed) were intended to be eternal guides to human relationships. All the answers are here, perfectly suited to deal with the Moroccan family in the millennium."

Since the laws themselves were based on interpretations of the Qur'an and the *hadiths*, I asked her why she believed it was impossible to interpret them anew.

"Nobody is qualified to interpret the laws today," she said. "Society needs a guide to keep us from straying too far from the ideals of the religion."

I interviewed her extensively about the content and meaning of the laws. There were some aspects of current law that were different from the laws of the past, such as the fact that the original Maliki rites allowed child marriage, which was now illegal. Khadija had never heard this but said that there were valid reasons for keeping the minimum age of marriage at fifteen.

"I'm against raising the age of marriage," she said. "Here in the cities, girls don't get married until they are in their twenties, and they study and have careers beforehand. With girls like me, this law is meaningless, because we will wait until we're older to marry. But in the country, the women are not educated, so it's better they marry as early as possible so they won't get into trouble. If they are not allowed to marry, and if they do not marry by the age of twenty or so, something is wrong. They will have to go outside the home to work as maids, and then they will inevitably be raped by their employers. Then they would have a child out of marriage, and possibly this child would become an orphan. In Moroccan culture, people don't want to adopt orphans because of their illegitimacy, so the children won't have parents and they could grow up to be a problem for the state. Even if the mother does keep the child, she'll be stigmatized."

Although a new law allows Moroccan women married to non-Moroccan men to pass citizenship on to their children, illegitimate children are still not considered full citizens.[12] Khadija's logic emphasized the problematic sexuality of uneducated country women, who, if not married, would be raped by their urban employers. She did not present this as a disturbing fact, nor did she place the blame for a possible sexual assault of a vulnerable young woman on the employer. Rather, she felt that this outcome was merely the unfortunate reality of domestic work in Morocco.

"And all of this would happen if the age of marriage were raised to eighteen?" I asked. "Isn't it already happening? There are many women who come to the cities with illegitimate children."

"That's a result of uneven modernization," she explained. "That's what happens when you try to change people's traditions, which a new *mudawana* would make worse. The people in the countryside have a certain mentality, and to change their mentality would be to try to make everyone in Morocco the same. We must accept that traditions in the country are different from those of the city. Raising the age of marriage would only hurt their traditions and create chaos *(fitna)*. It would have no effect on *us* [emphasis mine] but it would be detrimental to them."

The prospect of change and the loss of tradition threatened social chaos. The urban-rural dichotomy visible in Khadija's argument mirrored the othering tendencies of rumors, discussed in the last chapter. Khadija highlighted a collapse in traditional values, rather than economic factors (such as the decrease in available work due to government-directed structural adjustment programs), as the reason for rural-urban migration. A different set of rules was needed for people from the countryside, particularly for poor, uneducated women. Khadija was well-off; her father, originally from Fes, owned several successful businesses and could afford to maintain two residences. She would follow through on her education and employment, marrying when she was ready, although she did occasionally express the fear that if she did not act soon, she might be considered too old to attract a husband.

"It is thanks to my father that I have accomplished so much," she said. "He facilitated my studies here; he made everything possible. Whomever I choose to marry, he will accept. I am very lucky." The migrants from the countryside, she said, could not count on the same support of their fathers, and thus they needed the *mudawana*, although the *mudawana* appeared to me to supplement patriarchal power, not stand in as a substitute for it. Migrants were "traditional," and thus in need of guidance. Here, the adjective "traditional" takes on a derisive meaning, implying a lack of education, an inability to control desires, and a subsequent need for legal ways to protect the honor of girls and women. The *mudawana* rationalizes social inequality by insisting that those who hold power and influence not only respect the traditions of the poor but also have their best interests in mind.

Father Knows Best

Khadija imagined that "traditional" people from the countryside needed the freedom of early marriages, but as Malika's story reveals, there is more of a potential for young women to be coerced. An early marriage had not saved her from social dissolution, forcing her to resort to extreme measures to escape, resulting in the same type of social chaos Khadija described as a consequence of women being refused the "right" to an early marriage. Obviously this "right" is of little use if the legal limits are ignored, and, as Malika's lawyer learned in the course of petitioning for a divorce, if young women "from the country" are used as pawns in a land deal. With the exchange of property as *sdaq* for Malika's marriage, the two parties who stood to benefit the most from her first marriage were her father and her husband.

The father's power to approve or refuse his daughter's marital choices was another area of proposed reform. The disproportionate power of the legal guardian (*wali*) over his daughter's marital rights could also disadvantage young men, as the example of Faris in the previous chapter indicates. Among all social classes, a malevolent *wali* can use his daughter's marriage to further his own wealth or social position. Although many middle-class Fassis told me they had married for love, most acknowledge that families still have the power to interfere with a marriage or forbid its taking place. Both men and women admitted having modified their marital choices to please family members, and there were some cases where a father's mercenary impulses were so strong that they resulted in a great deal of social embarrassment.

A case in point was the situation of Mouhsine, whose parents, the Ben Slimanes, lived in my apartment building. A dashing man in his early forties with twinkling eyes and thick black hair streaked with gray, Mouhsine lived in Spain, where he ran a successful café with his brother. He asked his parents to find out if there were any marriageable girls in the Lux neighborhood where he had grown up, and after making inquiries, they suggested a young woman in her twenties whose family also lived in the neighborhood. Mouhsine and Latifa began corresponding, and he returned for the engagement party, where he discussed the *sdaq*, or bride price, with Latifa's father. They agreed on an amount of fifty thousand dirhams, about five thousand dollars, which would be noted in the marriage contract.

By all accounts Latifa and Mouhsine were both excited about the marriage. They exchanged letters, and once a week Latifa would go to the cyber café to chat with Mouhsine over a webcam on the Internet. He began to process the visa paperwork to bring her back to Spain with him, and several months later the wedding was held in a spacious apartment belonging to Latifa's cousin. The bride entered in a beaded white caftan, and a small group of hired musicians played wedding music. Mouhsine and Latifa sat atop a mountain of pillows holding hands, while guests came forward to offer their congratulations.

The guests had already been celebrating for a few hours when the couple retired to a private room with both sets of parents and two religious notaries (*aduls*) who would execute the contract. But when Mouhsine stated the agreed-on bride price, Latifa's father shook his head.

"No," he said to Mouhsine, "that's not enough for my daughter." He demanded thirty-five thousand dollars more than the five thousand they had originally agreed on.

Mouhsine was stunned. The amount was far more than he could afford. The *adul* shrugged. What could he do, if the father refused to give away his daughter? Humiliated, Latifa begged for her mother to intercede. But her father called off the proceedings. The word went out immediately to the guests filling the salons: a disagreement at the last minute over the amount of the *sdaq*. The guests speculated: perhaps the father had learned something about Mouhsine's reputation that prevented him from giving away his daughter. Or maybe there was another contender for his daughter's hand? Rather tasteless, people agreed, to change the couple's fortunes at the last minute. Latifa's mother pleaded halfheartedly with her husband to allow the ceremony to continue. But the father refused, the wedding was called off, and later that week Mouhsine returned to Spain alone.

Before their son traveled, Mouhsine's family tried to negotiate with Latifa's father. But the father continued to refuse, claiming that Mouhsine did not value his daughter highly enough to give her a larger bride price.

"Do they think she's a piece of merchandise?" Mouhsine's mother cried. "Does he want to sell his daughter to the highest bidder?"

Mouhsine gave up and left the country. There were various rumors about why the father had refused, and the strongest among them seemed to be that he had heard Mouhsine had a fair amount of money tucked away in Spain. Latifa herself did not participate in the negotiations. Her father insisted that he knew what was best for her, and that these were matters beyond her understanding. Latifa had wanted to marry Mouhsine, and in fact, for months had been looking forward to moving to Spain. But she had no choice—under Maliki law, if her father refused, she would have to go to a judge, who would determine whether or not her father was being reasonable. How could she dispute his authority and risk alienating her family, who might then refuse to help her in the event of a divorce? It was better not to disrupt family harmony, especially when another candidate for Latifa's hand soon came forward: a man originally from the neighborhood who now owned a factory and could pay the full bride price that Latifa's father demanded.

I reported this incident to Khadija, who was patient with my neverending questions about the *mudawana*.

"It's sad, but the girl will get over it," she said. "She's young. She'll have other chances at happiness."

"But don't you think," I argued, "that it should have been her choice whether or not to marry him? Should the father have the absolute right here?"

Khadija sighed.

"In America, doesn't your father give you away when he walks you down the aisle?"

"Not technically," I said. "It's just a custom. We don't need our fathers' legal consent to get married."

"It's the same here," she insisted. "The *wali* is a custom. It's a safe-guard to protect the daughter from marrying someone who would be bad for her, especially in the cases where the girl is young, and she's marrying an older man. The daughter does not have the age and experience of her parents. They know what is best for her and could possibly keep her from marrying someone who would hurt her. We can still choose our husbands. In most cases, the parents won't interfere. They respect us. The law gives them the option of stepping in, if we're making a mistake. And if they eliminated the custom of the *wali*, and a girl married someone her parents didn't approve of, what if she had problems with him later? The parents would say, 'Well, we were not consulted to begin with, so we're not going to help you now.'"

Khadija did not know the Ben Slimanes but offered her own opinion on the situation.

"You said the husband was about forty, and she was no more than twenty or twenty-one; that age difference is a perfect reason why parents should be involved. How can a twenty-year-old know anything of the world? Does she know the man she is marrying, or what it means to be married? A father's consent is absolutely necessary. Probably he saved her from something she would have regretted."

The young bride, like the people from the countryside, needed protection. At issue was not only whether the bride lacked the common sense to contract her own marriage without a guardian's approval but also whether marriage is an affair of families or of individuals. The tension between the traditional view of marriage as a means of forming alliances, and the "modern" stance that marriage is based on love and the desire of the couple to establish a nuclear family, has still not been fully resolved.[13] After all, did Mouhsine not approach his marriage traditionally, seeking intermediaries to find him a wife?

Patriarchal authority is challenged by the suggestion that women should have the right to contract their own marriages without the approval of the *wali* or the marriage tutor (*mudawana* chapter III, articles 11–15). Under Maliki law, the bride's father, or another close male relative should the father be unavailable, must sign his consent to a woman's marriage. If the guardian disagrees with her choice or is unavailable, a judge may step in to act as *wali* on her behalf, should she take the matter higher. The 1993 modifications to the *mudawana* list the *wali* as the "right of the woman," stating that the *wali* may not give her away in marriage unless she consents (article 12). Additionally, the 1993 revisions of the *mudawana* give an orphan the right to contract her own marriage, while suggesting that she should designate a *wali* anyway.

Reformists have argued that if an orphan may contract her own marriage, why not extend this right to all women? Ali Boutaleb, the head of the commission that revised the laws in 1993, stated that the reforms had been moderate in the interest of protecting the family. "The role of the matrimonial tutor is mostly a moral role, with the goal of perpetuating family cohesion and solidarity in its dimension as a social institution" (*Le Matin*, November 15, 1993, 6). Boutaleb emphasizes again the kinship ties that the presence of a *wali* enforces. The laws are clear: marriage under the *mudawana* is a matter for families and not for individuals. Even the 2004 revisions, which allow the bride to appoint a male *wali* of her choice, while not doing away with the concept entirely, continue to support this principle.

Mouhsine's failed marriage was a hot topic of gossip in the neighborhood for weeks. Many agreed that Latifa's father was only being cautious. Immigrant marriages often failed, and then the bride was far from her parents. How could anyone know for certain that Mouhsine would treat her well? He had lived away from the neighborhood for over fifteen years. A large *sdaq*, which would serve as "insurance" and go to the wife in the event of a divorce, would demonstrate that Mouhsine was serious enough about Latifa that he was willing to take a financial risk to marry her. Taoufik, a neighbor in his thirties, put it bluntly, stating, "He has to pay a lot for her virginity, because if he is not serious about the marriage and he abandons her soon after, it will be harder for her to get married a second time. The *sdaq* is proof that he has the right intentions."[14]

In section 4 of the *mudawana*, *sdaq* is defined as "everything that is given by the husband that demonstrates on his part the strong desire to contract a marriage in order to set up a household and live in a state of mutual affection" (article 16). Traditionally the husband gives the money to the father of the bride, who then invests it in furnishings for the new house (*attat l-bit*), and thereafter, the furniture belongs to the wife. Today, the prospective husband often furnishes an apartment for his wife, and no money is actually exchanged between the husband and the *wali*, although the value of the furnishings is listed on the marriage contract and the husband may still give his wife a valuable ring or other jewelry. Occasionally, a bride price is deferred, with half paid at the time of the wedding and the remainder saved for a future moment in time. This custom serves as further insurance to protect the bride against a divorce (Rosen 1970: 35). In fact, studies have shown that in situations where considerable amounts of money and property are at stake, particularly in marriages among the elite where both bride and groom bring substantial resources to a marriage, marriages tend to be more stable.[15] A high bride price yet to be paid can induce a husband not to divorce his wife, although men, particularly if they are living abroad, can often get out of the marriage without paying.

Others took a more romantic view of Mouhsine's situation, lamenting the father's betrayal and the sad obstruction of true love. These were personal and not familial issues, they said. Those who spoke out against Latifa's father's intervention tended to view a large *sdaq* with suspicion, associating it with the family's intention to "sell" the daughter. They dismissed the notion that Latifa's father wanted to protect her, suspecting that he intended to take the *sdaq* for himself, which is forbidden by article 19 of the *mudawana*, but which nonetheless sometimes happens. A daughter was not a commodity! Where was progress, if girls could not even choose their own husbands, and if families continued to choose for them? Some young men, perhaps imagining themselves in Mouhsine's place, told me that people like Latifa's father were responsible for the imbalance in marriages that disadvantaged both unmarried young men and older women. Young men have no hope of marrying someone from their own age group as long as fathers demand large sums of money for their daughters.

In formal settings, such as in the press or in the media, Islam defined the terms of the general debate about the marital guardian. Those who argued for abandoning the custom of the *wali* were accused of being "against" Islam. The opposition would point out that the *wali* was only customary in the Maliki school of Islamic jurisprudence and not in the other three schools of *shari'a* law. Why not abandon this one restriction whose "Islamic" essence is questionable at best?

In Fassi discussions over what had happened to Mouhsine, the connections with *shari'a* and Islamic law were seldom mentioned. More significant were the social ramifications of the laws, and what the laws revealed about the ideal construction of the Fassi family. People's opinions varied depending on a number of factors, including the person's social status, educational level, and personal experience. My middle-class Fassi friends who were not proponents of *mudawana* reform and did not consider themselves particularly invested in politics tended to support the idea of Father Knows Best. Young men facing an uncertain future, like Faris in the preceding chapter, were upset that senior men continued to exert so much control over their daughters' marriages. Yet they seemed to accept this idea with resignation, perhaps since some of them (due to their own family status) might someday find themselves in the role of family patriarch. Locally, Islam almost never became part of the debate. Rather, the arguments boiled down to whether marriage is a contract in which a father gives his daughter to another lineage, or the establishment of a nuclear household based on mutual affection.

Polygamy

In the 1990s, a popular Moroccan movie was released that explored the deleterious effects of polygamy on the life of a Fassi jeweler living in the *medina*.[16] In director Abderrahmane Tazi's film, *À la recherche du mari de ma femme* (Looking for the Husband of My Wife), a polygamous jeweler performs the "triple divorce" formula in a moment of anger against his youngest, most beloved wife. In Islamic law, men have the right to pronounce, and revoke, the words of divorce three times in the course of a marriage, but saying the formula three times at one moment severs the relationship almost completely. The husband immediately regrets his decision, yet in order to take his wife back again, Islamic law requires that she must be first married to someone else, then divorced. The movie, which ends with the husband unable to find his ex-wife and her new husband, casts a critical eye on the institution of polygamy. Many Fassis I knew had seen the movie, either in the theater or when it was rebroadcast later on national television, and nearly all felt it had a strong moral message: that polygamy is nearly impossible to practice in the way Islam requires it. The movie elicited strong reactions among my Fassi friends, who could cite numerous examples of polygamous marriages gone wrong to support the film's criticism of polygamy. Yet almost no one, aside from a few activists and academics I knew from the NGO or from the local university, believed in banning polygamy entirely.

Polygamy is another social practice *mudawana* reformers proposed to eliminate, ultimately without success, though the 2004 revisions require both the wife's and a judge's consent.[17] In Turkey and Tunisia, polygamy is illegal on the grounds that most men cannot treat their wives with equality. The Qur'an states: "But if you fear that you cannot maintain equality among them, marry one only" (Qur'an 4:3). Another verse in the same *sura* offers further evidence of the difficulties of treating spouses equally: "You are never able to be fair and just as between women even if it is your ardent desire" (4:129). The idea of equality is essential to the just maintenance of a polygamous union, and men are expected to provide equivalent accommodations and spend equal time with both wives. While the rate of polygamous marriages in Morocco is fairly low, around 3 percent, it was nonetheless a topic that occupied a number of my conversations with middle-class Fassis about marriage and the *mudawana*.[18] Nearly all the Fassis I knew agreed that polygamy could not be eliminated because it was part of the *shari'a*, but most said that the practice was not recommended. Whenever I brought up the laws of

Turkey and Tunisia, the general response was that "taking the right away is still against Islam," and several argued that "the Turkish are not real Muslims." Asked to give reasons for polygamy, my Fassi friends cited the importance of polygamy in the early days of Islam, when men died in wars, leaving many women without husbands.[19]

Although I did not know of any polygamous situations among my network of Fassis under the age of fifty, when I asked what modern-day benefits polygamy might afford, a few people suggested that polygamy could offer unmarried women the chance to marry by becoming a second wife. High levels of unemployment meant that some men might never be able to support a wife, resulting in an imbalance of unmarried women. Making polygamy illegal, some said, would actually anger women who felt they were being deprived of their last chance to marry. Polygamy might also be necessary in cases where a first wife was barren and could not produce heirs, although in the six polygamous marriages I knew of in Fes, only one marriage had taken place as a result of this. Several women cynically speculated that men could get tired of their older wives and seek younger ones, but men never mentioned this reason.

Most of my Fassi acquaintances felt there was no longer any true need for polygamy in Moroccan society, and many stated their firm belief that a "modern" marriage was exclusively between one man and one woman. Although they could offer reasons for other people's polygamous unions, many women said they would prefer divorce to having to share a husband. Very few were willing to argue, however, that polygamy should be outlawed.

Khadija had strong opinions about the legality of polygamy. "The 1993 revisions to the *mudawana* accomplished all the reforms we need," she said. "Now, the man has a legal obligation to tell his first wife of his intentions to take a second. Before, this was not the case, so a man could be secretly married without either wife knowing. This new law respects the first wife's rights, within the framework of *shari'a.*" She added that if a woman does not want to be in a polygamous household, she can insert in her marriage contract the stipulation that she be granted the right to a divorce, should her husband take another wife.

"But why," I asked, "would a polygamous marriage be desirable?"

"It's simple. Even when they are older, men have *needs.*" She looked at me significantly. "You know, they can still have children when they are old. Women can't. If a legal, religiously permitted (*halal*) way for men to fulfill these needs does not exist, they might go with prostitutes and bring diseases back to their wives. Women, when they get older, can't keep up with their husbands' demands. They reach menopause (*sin al-yas*),[20] and they are unable to have sex anymore. The husband takes another wife so as not to inconvenience his first wife."

She said this with utter conviction, but then confessed that she had strong opinions on the matter for other reasons. Her father had two wives. She insisted that her mother had gotten along fine with her co-wife, and that she herself was as close to her half siblings as she was to her full siblings. Of course they had disputes, but those would happen in any family. Overall, Khadija said, they lived together amicably.

Accepting the idea of a co-wife had been difficult for her mother, but she was "older" and her father was apparently one of those men who had "needs." Also, her mother was very patient. Such a marriage would not work, Khadija said, if one of the wives was inclined to rebellion.

"So, would you be in a polygamous marriage yourself?" I asked her.

"No," she said with certainty. "I couldn't share a husband. But I don't have my mother's patience."

Talking with other members of polygamous families shed further light on the dynamics of these marriages. Khaled and Mounia, for example, were the son and daughter of a man who had two wives. Said's first wife was barren, but rather than divorcing her, he remarried, had four children with his second wife, and kept the entire family together for over twenty-five years. Khaled believed the relationship was harmonious, and said that he loved his stepmother as much as his own mother.

"She was like a mother to us," he said. "My father spent equal time with both his wives, and never stopped supporting his first. He took care of her. He did not throw her out on the street like some men do when their wives are unable to have children. He fulfilled his duty and continued supporting her. If he had decided to divorce her, she would have been out on the street. In this situation, polygamy is a benefit to the woman."

His sister had a slightly different perspective. While both wives had lived together amicably, Mounia told me that only the second wife derived status from being the mother of Said's children.

"Also, our mother was the second wife," she explained. "It was easy because in some ways our father preferred our mother. She was young and beautiful and always had a lot of energy. He was fifteen years older than her, whereas Fatima [his first wife] was his age. Sometimes he would take our mother on vacations and leave Fatima with us. But he never took Fatima on vacations. In general, of course, we were happier than most. But all things were not completely equal."

Economic concerns might also have been a reason the father stayed married to Fatima. The only daughter of a family more esteemed than Said's, Fatima possessed her own wealth and had even inherited the house they lived in.

"Do you think he could afford to live where he does on a waiter's salary?" Mehdi, the small business owner in his thirties who had once lived in Sweden, asked skeptically. "Fatima inherited the house when her father, who was very rich, died. Everything in Said's house is from his first wife. Of course he would not divorce her. If she had no money, I doubt he would still be with her."

Some Fassis mentioned the negative effects polygamy could have on children, whose experiences observing their father's actions might lead them to view women as expendable. Many felt that the husbands were using religious justifications as an excuse to have multiple sexual partners or to show off their wealth.[21] Mehdi, in the same conversation about Khaled and Mounia's father, told me this story:

Some of them do treat their wives equally, but just in terms of money. I know a man whose villa is divided down the middle, with separate entrances for both families. I went to school with one of his sons. I remember going over there to play. There was a cold war going on between the two wives. It was like Russia and America in the 1980s. They kept accounts of whether he spent more time with one of them. My friend said they didn't even share supplies between them. So if his mother ran out of eggs, she had to go to the *hanut* (grocery) to get more; she couldn't ask her co-wife. The father also owned a company, and he was sleeping with his secretary. You see, he liked a lot of women, and even two wives wasn't enough. But he made a big show out of his piety and how he treated them fairly. He liked it that he had a villa the size of two houses. And then you'd see him driving around in his Mercedes, stopping to pick up girls.[22] He kept an apartment somewhere, too, where he took his girlfriends. The funny thing is that the son had an affair with the secretary, too, and the father found out about it and fired her. Now the son is becoming like his father. He's very successful with girls, and he has several girlfriends. He knows how to make them jealous of one another, too, so that they're competing for his favors. Where do you think he learned that?

Fassis were less concerned with questioning the man's right to multiple wives and were more interested in how women coped with the situation. People drew attention not only to the unjust treatment of wives in actual examples of polygamy but also the continued importance of social networks and resources for women. Men I interviewed were more inclined to refer to polygamy as an aberration or an oversight, as a man's "failure" to get around to divorcing a wife who no longer interested him. Others speculated on the enormous cost of maintaining multiple wives, and wondered how men could do it. However, most surmised that remaining in polygamous unions was still desirable for some women.

Amina was a gentle, soft-voiced woman in her early fifties, thin to the point of emaciation from a lifetime of hard work. I came to know her through a friend, in whose house Amina worked one day each week as a maid. Deeply religious, she never went outside her house in the Fes *medina* without a headscarf and traditional face veil (*litham*). Amina supported two sons on approximately 120 dirhams a week (about $12). She rented a one-room apartment in a large *medina* house in which several families lived. Her husband had abandoned her twenty years earlier for a second wife, but he neither granted her a divorce nor supported his first family. The husband still lived in the *medina* and sometimes passed her in the street without acknowledging her.[23]

I mentioned the Najia Belghazi Center to Amina, thinking that perhaps she didn't know she had a legal right to maintenance (*nafaqa*) for the twenty years since her desertion. But she wasn't interested.

"God will give me my *nafaqa*," she said resignedly. "I know my rights. But to follow them through a court? I couldn't afford a lawyer. And he [her husband] would make trouble; he would find a way to show he did not have any money, and it would be bad for me. No, God will give me my justice in the next life."

My friend Naima, a lawyer who was one of the main volunteers at the Najia Belghazi Center, speculated that Amina's attitude reflected a passive sense of fatalism, and at first I agreed. After a while I realized that Amina did not want to be divorced, and that being alone but still married was, in many ways, preferable to being divorced. Amina explained, "I work for people sometimes [as a maid], but only for people I trust, and only if a woman will be in the house with me. If I were divorced, it would not be easy. People take advantage of divorced women. A wife is protected." Although she could not count on her husband for financial support, the fact that she was still married protected her. A divorced woman raising two children was more vulnerable than a woman who was known to be married. For Amina, living in a society where the ideologies of patriarchy remain strong, there were advantages in being nominally attached to a polygamous husband.

Loubna, a middle-class woman in her early fifties, was in a similar situation. In her twenties she became a third wife to a wealthy older man, and they had three children. But as the children grew up, Loubna became jealous of her husband's frequent absences, and she began to hear rumors that he was considering taking a fourth wife. Their frequent fights turned into a bitter separation, and her children inherited their mother's resentment of the situation and hid from their father when he visited. Eventually he stopped contacting them and ceased his monthly support payments. Unlike Amina, however, Loubna had a decent job as a civil servant and had inherited a family apartment in the Lux neighborhood where I lived. Over the years she achieved status in her work and could support her family comfortably.

Although Amina came from a lower-class background, was illiterate, and had few opportunities for employment, her situation and Loubna's were similar in one important respect. Neither wanted to be divorced, even though their husbands, for all practical purposes, had abandoned them.[24]

"Being married is preferable to being divorced," Loubna said, citing that people left her alone. She did not need her husband's support, and it was a matter of pride that she had never asked him for anything.

"It's between him and God," she shrugged, echoing Amina's comment. "For many years, I was angry, but everything passes. He will have to answer in the next life for what he has done in this one."

The similarities between Loubna and Amina perhaps end there, in the desire of both to remain in polygamous marriages. Their ages are also significant, as it remains unclear whether the same types of polygamy-related issues will affect younger generations. But in cases of abandonment, family resources cannot be underestimated. In Loubna's case, both her maternal and paternal kin were well established in Fes, and she relied on them for aid and employment connections. By contrast, Amina did not have relatives to whom she could turn for assistance. Her parents were now dead, and she was no longer in contact with her siblings. Her work as a maid allowed Amina a small measure of dignity, but she was illiterate and had few other options.

In the event of marital conflicts, kin-based solidarities are still the primary resource middle-class Fassi women turn to for support. Women with powerful families can use their kinship connections as a lever against wayward husbands, and, in the event of a divorce, can return to their parents' home and draw on familial networks for employment possibilities. As Joseph and Slyomovics have noted more generally in discussing the Middle East, since patriarchy infuses every sphere of social relations, women must be in familial relationships to make effective use of social institutions (Joseph and Slyomovics 2001: 5).

Fassis from influential families were thus unlikely to criticize the *mudawana*, instead insisting that the laws provide the same security for the poor, especially in the absence of familial support. Most of my middle-class Fassi colleagues, however, had little knowledge of how the *mudawana* affected the poor. The focus on the *mudawana* as a device for protecting those who have no other resources distracts attention from the customs these laws protect. These customs continue to favor an ideological system of patriarchy, in which men maintain legal control over marriage, divorce, resources, and family alliances. On a local stage, the ideology of patriarchy is visible in Fassi responses to individual cases that related to the *mudawana*. Most favored paternal control over a daughter's marriage choices to foster extended family solidarity, an early age of marriage for women, and the continuance of polygamy, which keeps families nominally united and offers a perceived societal protection for women from the threat of total abandonment.

On October 13, 2003, the king announced that he would revise the *mudawana*, easing women's abilities to obtain a divorce, raising the age of marriage to eighteen, and placing restrictions on polygamy, including the approval of a judge and the first wife. The revised *mudawana* further asserts that men and women are equal in marriage, and that the wife is no longer considered a minor under the guardianship of her husband. Divorce will require mutual consent, and in the event of a divorce, the revisions encourage a fair division of property, which makes spousal abandonment more difficult.

Despite the enthusiasm that greeted the revisions, many women's and human rights groups asserted that the revisions did not accomplish as much as they had hoped, especially since polygamy was not banned and the question of equality in inheritance had not been addressed. Criticism was muted on both sides, undoubtedly because the king had announced that the reforms agreed with principles for interpreting the Qur'an, stating in his address to Parliament, "I cannot authorize that which God has prohibited, nor prohibit that which the Almighty has authorized." As for the two most prominent Islamist political organizations in the country, the legal PJD (Party of Justice and Development) and the banned al 'Adl wa'l-Ihsan (Association for Justice and Charity), both were said to have backed away considerably from criticism of the reforms because the terrorist attacks in Casablanca of May 16, 2003, had led to a backlash against Islamist groups. Finally, enforcing the new laws was expected to be difficult, especially among conservative judges or in far-flung locations.[25] While my primary fieldwork research had already been conducted prior to the revision of the laws, the king's decision does not alter any of the arguments contained herein. Rather, observing how the laws both reflect and interact with the still-strong vestiges of patriarchal society remains an important strategy for understanding discourses that compete and coincide with one another to define the Moroccan social body. In resolving the dispute, the king continued to fulfill his role as arbitrator, offering solutions that appeased both sides while not overtly offending either.

It did not surprise me that Khadija was a proponent of the institution of polygamy, since it allowed her to benefit from familial resources and kept the family unit intact even after her father had taken a younger wife. Her perspective on the *mudawana* revealed that for her, the existing family structure that it promoted still functioned, while Malika had not benefited from the laws at all. Interestingly, as the resources provided by kinship were usually unavailable to poor women, some of the women who came to the NGO spoke of volunteers in a familial idiom.

Malika referred to the women who worked there as "my sisters," and on more than one occasion she said that they were like a family to her. Idioms of kinship spread into the world of the nongovernmental organization, which provided the support and advice that Malika had never received from her own family, facilitating her access to resources, and enabling her to obtain a divorce. The following chapter explores the work of the NGO that helped Malika in a slightly different light: in terms of the resistance Fassi society offered to the NGO's other possible successes.

Chapter 4

Solidarity with Distinctions: The Limits of Intervention at a Fassi Nongovernmental Organization

The judge told me I needed evidence [to obtain a divorce], evidence that my husband mistreated me. But how can I find witnesses; do you think he will do it in the street? The judge asked when my husband last beat me. I didn't know the month. I told him it was when the last of the cold came. But this is not evidence. The judge had no patience with this answer.

—Touria, on her failure to obtain a divorce in Fes

To be honest, I don't think I would benefit from helping them. The women who go there do not actually want help. They want money, and as soon as they understand that you are not going to give it to them, they will stop coming. If you have time, it is better to help someone you know, especially if they are in the family. You will see the results [of your assistance], and you can be sure they will be grateful.

—Khadija, a Fassi lawyer

The sky outside the windows of the Najia Belghazi Center was beginning to darken, and soon it would be time to go home, where tonight my mother-in-law was going to teach me to prepare her *sopa*, the vegetable soup she often cooked on cold winter evenings to serve with bread and a Spanish omelet. All afternoon Naima and I had been at the Center listening to women talk about their legal problems. Naima, a lawyer in her early thirties, was one of my closest friends in Fes, and she was kind enough to let me spend Friday afternoons with her as she dispensed free legal advice at the NGO where she volunteered. So far the day had been filled with the usual issues: cases of divorce, abuse, and abandonment. Naima was pleased when she could be helpful, when the questions had straightforward answers. The law was clear on most matters, and at the very least it was satisfying for her to be able to respond, whether a woman had a valid case to pursue or not. But for our final client of the day, there were no easy answers, and long after the woman left, I would be puzzling over her story, helpless in the face of the hopelessness of her demands.

A thin, disheveled woman in a stained purple *djellaba* came into the small consultation room, her hennaed hair falling out of the sides of a hair clip. Halima could have been in her forties, or else she could have been younger, aged prematurely by a difficult life, but it was impossible to tell. She started with what seemed like a simple request: how to get child support from her ex-husband, who worked illegally but claimed to the government that he had no income or employment. She was desperate to feed her two children, she told us, and her work as a maid did not always pay the bills. Pulling her *djellaba* off her shoulders, she showed us the discolored bruises where the male head of a household where she had been working as a maid had beaten her.

"How did that happen?" Naima asked, her eyes widening. The head of the household had picked her up as usual for work, but instead of going directly to his family's house, he had taken her to an unfamiliar apartment.

"I knew something was wrong, so I tried to leave," Halima said. "I ran into the street, but he came after me. He chased me with his car and tried to hit me. Then he sent someone else after me, and I fought him there in the street. That other man hit me with a bottle, but I escaped."

"Did you go to the police?" Naima asked.

"No," Halima replied. "I came here because I heard you helped people."

Halima's story suggested the often blurry line between domestic work and prostitution. Remarriage would give the husband the right to take custody of the children, so many poor, divorced Moroccan women try to find work as domestics, the one job they are qualified for. When this fails, prostitution is often the only remaining option.

"Can you go back to your family?" Naima asked.

"They wouldn't take me," she insisted. "And they're too far away. We moved here years ago from the countryside. I don't know what to do."

"What is it you are hoping to accomplish?" Naima replied, asking the type of neutral, open-ended question volunteers had been told would encourage women to think about what they could do, and not solely what the Center could do for them. Halima offered a response I had heard from a number of women who came to the center.

"I want my rights. I want justice (*haqq*). Can you help me to see justice?"

Justice, I was realizing, was a slippery word. Perhaps Halima wanted economic justice, the opportunity to earn a living without having to resort to prostitution in a market that was glutted with too many illiterate maids.[1] The Center could direct her to its plumbing and gardening training programs. Was she looking for a way to press charges against the person who had given her the bruises? Did she truly want to know the steps to take in order to pursue the child support issue with her husband, or was it a hopeless cause, since he did not declare his income? Or was she simply seeking a sympathetic ear, someone who would take her seriously and not dismiss her as a discarded person on the margins of Moroccan society? The kind of justice Halima sought was broader than anything the law could address. Social justice seemed to best approximate the sum of this woman's complaints: the possibility of living in a fair and equitable society, the protection of her basic human rights and physical security, and the ability to seek viable economic opportunities.

Encounters between clients like Halima and the volunteers who staffed the Najia Belghazi Center indicate both the possibilities and the limits for NGO-led interventions in the Moroccan context. Many women, like Malika, whose story I tell in Chapter 3, did obtain clarity over legal issues, leaving the center with new information or strategies to help them pursue their cases through the labyrinthine Moroccan legal system. Clients also participated in some of the center's other offerings, such as literacy or job training classes. But cases like Halima's were numerous and had no clear answers. I had heard other women relate similar stories, women who started out by recounting narratives whose multiple legal and social issues were buried deep within, becoming murkier and more hopeless with every word. After several minutes went by, it became clear that their problems were greater than the need for clarification of the intricacies of the law. In addition to *mudawana*-related issues such as divorce and abandonment, substance abuse, poverty, rural-to-urban migration, and illiteracy were frequently part of the story. Proving a deadbeat husband had sufficient resources to send child support was difficult at best, but in entering the legal system to pursue a case, many women had too much to lose.

Halima's demand for justice, which was echoed by many who came to the Center, hints at some of the complex problems for which there is no quick legal fix. Her story speaks not only of individual suffering but also of the failures of a legal system based on cultural and religious prescriptions that are frequently contradicted by the structural conditions of inequality in contemporary Moroccan society. Although religion lies at the core of Moroccan family law and is used in defense of its immutability, a society organized around patriarchal family structures provided the social context for the *mudawana*'s initial codification in the 1950s. As I have shown in the previous chapter, arguments for maintaining the laws in their supposedly original, authentic form were not merely about religion, but concerned vestiges of male familial authority that some were eager to maintain, although many in Moroccan society had long since lost the benefits and protections these laws might once have afforded.

In Halima's case, other factors in addition to the patriarchal character of the law were working against her: her lack of education, resources, or family connections, and the absence of labor opportunities for unskilled women. Indirectly, her presence in the city of Fes was also the result of larger political and economic forces, which can be traced back to Morocco's adoption of structural adjustment programs in the 1980s as well as its entry into the global market. The declining need for rural agricultural labor has led to mass urban migrations and high levels of unemployment, and therefore resulted in the disintegration of local networks and familial resources that are a woman's first recourse in the event of a divorce.

Because of these changing socioeconomic circumstances, NGOs such as the Najia Belghazi Center were altering their own aims in order to create new forms of support and solidarity for women. While Naima might not have been able to offer any legal consolation to Halima, she could direct her toward other programs the Center was experimenting with. Often the volunteers' networks and access to resources could provide the bridge that women needed in order to advance beyond the limits of their situations, when both the nation-state and family had failed to offer any support.

Despite some of the Center's success stories, such as that of Malika, there were also many interactions that clients or volunteers deemed failures. Sometimes clients arrived at the Center assuming that volunteers would give them money, intervene in a family dispute, or offer shelter from an abusive husband. From the other side, volunteers were frustrated by clients' assumptions that the Center had unlimited resources, and by the fact that clients seemed determined to enact patron-client relationships with the volunteers. This directly contradicted the Center's desire to produce forms of solidarity among women, in which the hierarchical relations that structured Moroccan society would magically vanish. In effect, it was solidarity with distinctions, whereby volunteers tried to assert that all Moroccan women were victims of violence, albeit a different type of violence depending on one's social position. Solidarity was ephemeral and momentary, usually achieved during brief transactions rather than sustained within long-term social relations. For all those women who seemed to gain something from their interactions with the volunteers, there were just as many who left frustrated and never appeared again. Were these failures mere products of entrenched class relations, or did they reveal something more?

New Forms of Space

The Najia Belghazi Center was a new space for women in urban Fes. On rare occasions a man would come in, a father accompanying his daughter to ask about a divorce claim, or a doctor giving a lecture to the women about health issues. But the Center was staffed by women and visited by women, who usually came first for legal advice, bearing documents as evidence. The documents attested to their mistreatment at the hands of men. They came with divorce certificates they could not read, wanting to know the terms under which they had been abandoned. Brandishing their documents, they asked if they had a case, usually financial, to demand money from the former husband, to return to the house they had lived in for thirty years, or to get support for their children.

Some women learned they needed other kinds of evidence. Divorce on the part of a woman required substantial proof of the husband's cruelty or abandonment. Photographs were good. The volunteers at the Center encouraged women to document their abuse, to go directly to a photo lab on Boulevard Hassan II, to sit before the neutral passport backdrop, and to wait for the blinding flash to illuminate the bluish shadows of a black eye, the red seam of a knife wound. The camera would serve as a witness, would assist women in their claims for a divorce. Some women learned this from the police, some of whom had been "sensitized" by the Center. Still, the rumor was that there were police who answered complaints of mistreatment with "Call us when he kills her." But the "sensitized" policemen encouraged the women to file reports, visit the photo lab, and then to go directly to the Najia Belghazi Center. At the Center they kept a folder of these photos, an album of unsmiling women displaying the souvenirs of their husbands' rages.

However, there was much that could not be documented, cases that were therefore harder to "prove" in the eyes of the law: the philandering husband who smoked too much hashish and brought prostitutes home in the wife's presence, the husband with the alcohol problem who sometimes crawled into bed with his own daughters, the husband who assaulted his wife in ways forbidden by the Qur'an but too shameful to discuss in a court of law.

Sometimes, as I noticed with Halima, pieces of the story were missing. In other cases, it was unclear who sought the help of the Center, the victim or another family member. I remember listening to the story of one girl, no more than fifteen, who had been raped by a neighbor who was now in prison. He could be released instantly if the girl agreed to marry him. The girl's mother spoke for her, trying to convince both the lawyer and the daughter of the correctness of marriage between the rapist and his victim. The mother talked of honor, and the family's reputation in the old *medina*. The girl never spoke. The case itself revealed the clash of two sets of laws: the French criminal codes that dealt with rape sitting uneasily with the possibilities of marriage under the *shari'a*-inspired *mudawana* laws.[2]

Talaq, talaq, talaq, the easily pronounceable divorce formula, was the sole provenance of men, requiring only that they register the divorce officially, despite a 1993 addition to the *mudawana* that encouraged a judge to counsel the couple before "they" took this extreme step.[3] For the women who came to the Center, divorce was not so easy, and many wanted desperately to be divorced but could not get their husbands to agree. All expressed their frustration at this unilateral right of men to divorce, dismiss, and abandon. A woman must go to a judge, must prove beyond the shadow of a doubt that her husband is impotent, has abandoned her, or has physically damaged her beyond the everyday "disciplining" that is a husband's right. A man does not even have to give a reason.

I first learned about the Najia Belghazi Center from a colleague, who gave me a business card for one of the volunteers. Most of the volunteers had day jobs—they were professors, doctors, lawyers, or psychiatrists. A few volunteers had university degrees but no work, and so they spent most of their time as administrative personnel, most of them unsalaried, but with a deep commitment to advancing the cause of women's rights in Morocco.

For several weeks I tried to get in touch with the woman whose name was on the business card. We spoke, made vague plans to meet, the woman announcing she would call me back in a few days once she had a better idea of her schedule. After a while, she stopped returning my calls, and I began to wonder if I had been too pushy. I waited a few weeks, then decided I would simply go out to the Center myself.

In one of the lower-middle-class suburbs of the Ville Nouvelle of Fes, set back from a busy street filled with taxi stands, drygoods stores, and discount clothing shops, the Najia Belghazi Center was located in a building identical to the other buildings surrounding it.[4] A locked gate kept out unwanted visitors, which I learned later included enraged husbands who heard their wives had been there. I rang the bell, peering through the iron gate at the sidewalk and the bare, unlandscaped garden on either side.

Finally a thin, dark-haired woman in slacks and a heavy red sweater came to the door. Samira was one of the volunteers who did not have a day job, and she usually answered the phone and staffed the front desk. I explained who I was, and why I was interested in the Center. She was friendly but reserved, explaining that while none of the other volunteers were there at the moment, I could browse the library, or come back in the afternoon when someone could tell me more about the Center. She gave me a tour of the building: a basic two-story apartment duplex that had been transformed into offices. It was January and the building was freezing. On the first floor was a conference room with a long table, and a space for prayer in the corner with a small, folded-up prayer rug. The second floor consisted of the offices and library, and a room with a sofa and a few chairs where the "*écoutes*" took place—where women would meet to discuss their problems with a trained counselor. We ended up in the library, which contained half-filled bookshelves, a table, and two spindly metal chairs. Samira brought me Nescafé and a plate of cookies, leaving me to my own devices.

For an hour I browsed through the reading material: copies of the *mudawana* in French and Arabic, books about sexual harassment and violence against women, pamphlets from NGOs in France. Then another volunteer, Saida, arrived. A cheerful woman in her early twenties, Saida was more effusive, kissing me on both cheeks and announcing with confidence, "Now I will tell you everything there is to know about what we do."

Since the agitation for *mudawana* reform had begun in March of 2000, centers like this one had begun to spring up all over Morocco. Initially opened to provide legal advice for women in matters of marriage and divorce, the Najia Belghazi Center gradually came to deal with issues ranging from domestic abuse to job training. Saida listed cases the Center had been involved in, and she opened a photo album to show me photos of women they had tried to help. Domestic violence was widespread, she said. But there was so much to do. There were many women like Halima—abandoned by their husbands and forced to turn to prostitution to support their children. The Center was training them to become plumbers and gardeners, a radical new program, since these were not traditional women's professions in Morocco. Volunteers held literacy classes, health education sessions. They explained the intricacies of the *mudawana* family laws to women who could not read.

Saida herself was thrilled to be a part of the whole endeavor. She had wanted to become a lawyer, she explained, but her entrance exam scores were not high enough to receive admission to law school. A professor at her university had encouraged her to get involved with the Center, and it was something to do while she considered the next step in her career.

"Most of the serious work happens in the afternoon," she said. "That's when the volunteers with law degrees and medical degrees come, so we usually ask women with questions to come back then." Women trickled in throughout the day, some stopping by just to chat, others to update the volunteers on the status of a case they were involved in. But the formal sessions—classes, legal consultations, and so on—happened in the afternoon, when the professional volunteers would take off from work. Saida told me to come back when Naima would be there: Naima would explain everything.

Although I got to know almost all the volunteers at the Center, I became closest with Naima. A lawyer in her early thirties with long, brown hair and intense dark eyes, Naima herself was no stranger to hardship, which made her a strong advocate for the disenfranchised women who came to the Center. As a child she had received a tainted vaccine that damaged her health and partially paralyzed her. She preferred crutches to a wheelchair, although she walked with difficulty. At every turn Fassi society had tried to marginalize her, equating physical with mental handicaps and assuming she lacked the intelligence to succeed on the same terms as everyone else. But her family was supportive, and her father was her greatest advocate. A school administrator, he pushed her to excel in her studies, and when she was older, he encouraged her to strive for the best possible career she could have. Against great odds, she passed the bar exam and became a lawyer, despite efforts from a few Fassi lawyers to keep her from taking the exam. She had her own office in the middle of the Ville Nouvelle, where she practiced with her brother-in-law. She lived at home with her parents and two other sisters, whose pride in her was apparent. Naima constantly challenged herself to test the limits of society, and her latest venture had been to buy her own car (specially designed with hand controls, imported from Spain) and to receive her driver's license.

Over the months Naima was to offer profound insight into gender issues in Fassi society. Her own situation had made her deeply reflective on Moroccan social life. Early in our acquaintance, she gave me an unprecedented opportunity: to sit in on her Friday afternoon legal consultations at the Center. For several hours each Friday, women would come for fifteen to twenty minutes of legal advice, alone or in pairs. Naima would explain to them that I was writing a study about women's rights (*huquq al-mar'a*), and asked if the women minded if I listened. I wondered if it would be strange for the women to have a foreign observer present, but for the most part they seemed uninhibited by my presence. One woman even asked me if I was an international human rights observer, there to help Moroccan women finally receive justice. The comment intrigued me, but it was also vaguely unsettling, as it hinted at the almost colonial dynamic in which the Westerners are the ones with "human rights," to which non-Western "others" must measure up. But in the six months that I watched and listened, only one woman asked to speak to Naima alone. Naima later explained that the woman had been one of the few middle-class clients who came to the center, and that she was worried about her social position and did not want others to know her problems.

I recorded my observations between sessions, since sometimes the sign of pen in hand, Naima explained, reminded clients of the bureaucratic nightmares they had already endured in trying to get the officialdom of Fes to hear their concerns. Writing represented authority, the literacy many of them lacked, and the power to scribble a judgment that would forever alter women's lives.

A Typical Day

On the day Halima arrived, the type of cases we had heard were typical for what I usually witnessed on Friday afternoons. Naima's first client was an older woman whom I had seen earlier, praying in a corner of the Center. At two o'clock she entered the office, sinking down into the chair with a sigh. She was probably in her sixties, and she was coming, she said, on behalf of a neighbor, who had just been divorced by her husband of forty years.

"He put her out on the street. She has nowhere to go. Doesn't she have any right to the house? She lived there forty years. They live in the *medina*." Naima shook her head and told her no, that she only had a right to what she legally owned, and what had been declared in her marriage contract as the *sdaq* she had brought to her marriage.

"You see, he installed a new wife in the house already," the woman continued, as if more evidence of the husband's misdeeds might make the case stronger. "This new wife made my friend leave, and now she's staying with her son, but she doesn't think that's right. To make her leave the house she lived in for almost all her life? The house she raised her four children in? The son begged his father to change his mind but he said there was nothing he could do, that the new wife doesn't get along with her."

"Did he divorce his first wife?" Naima asked.

"Yes, without giving her a warning. She was not expecting it. That was a few months ago, and immediately he took another wife. For awhile she stayed in the house, and then they made her leave. The children are grown, and she can go to them, but she wants her house back."

"I'm sorry, but unfortunately the house is not hers if her name is not on the contract of ownership," Naima said.[5] "This is the law. The husband only has to support her if there are children who are not grown, or unmarried daughters. Does she have any daughters who are not married?"

"No."

"Then she will have to go live with the family. There is nothing else that can be done, the law is clear on this. It is up to the mercy of her husband."

"After so many years. . . ." The woman shook her head. "And her son's house is full. It's not easy for her to stay there."

"It's sad," Naima said, "but if the husband has no compassion, what can be done?"

"Thank you," the woman said, shaking her head. "I'll tell my friend there's no reason for her to come here."

"I wish there were something we could do, but the law is very clear," said Naima. The woman sighed and left the office.

Samira brought an older woman and her daughter up the stairs to meet us. Mothers and daughters often came together, and usually one outlined the problems of the other. The mother was dressed in a *djellaba* and a headscarf, which was tied around her head in an old-fashioned style that I had noticed on older women. Her daughter wore the long, gray housecoat and tight headscarf that had become the symbol of young Islamists in Fes. She was young, probably in her early twenties, and had a smooth, round face marred only by a faded yellow bruise under her eye.

"Tell me what's going on," Naima prodded gently. The mother drew a deep breath.

"Her husband is a bad man," she began. "Do you see her face? He did that when he came home drunk last week. It was not the first time. They live in the *medina* in a house with other families, and there is a neighbor who is divorced, and he spends time with her too. He only works part of the time and spends his money on alcohol and women. He's also addicted to hashish. She wants a divorce. What can we do?"

"Do you want a divorce?" Naima asked the young woman. At first she did not respond. "Has he hit you before?"

She nodded.

"Show her," the mother ordered. The daughter lifted her hand to show a large purple mark on her palm.

"How did that happen?"

"I was at the stove and he pushed me."

"Do you want to be in this marriage?" Naima asked again.

"I'm afraid," the woman said.

"Maybe one day he will kill her," her mother said.

"Do you mean you're afraid of your husband or afraid of a divorce?" Naima said.

"She's afraid he'll tell lies about her in the court," the mother said. "She's a good girl. She does all her prayers. She cooks for him, she cleans; she's a good wife. But you never know what the men will say, and the judge will believe him."

Naima explained that they would need evidence: neighbors who were willing to testify that they had witnessed the abuse, photographs of the damage he had done, or police reports. Then the daughter would have to file for divorce, making sure that she had these forms of evidence with her to show the judge.

"The police came last week," her mother said. "A neighbor called the police and they filed a report."

"A police report is good," Naima said. "You need evidence. You said he doesn't work much. We can also argue that he does not provide for her, and if this is true it can also be used to get a divorce. Does he bring home enough for the house?"

"He's in construction, but he doesn't always go to his job," the mother said. "There is a neighbor who will testify that the man comes home drunk, so he is spending his salary on alcohol. There are others in the house; they hear him. And they hear what he does to her."

"Those are all good reasons. But you have to want to do this," she said directly to the daughter. "Is it you who wants the divorce or your mother?" The daughter lowered her eyes and did not answer. "We've found that men like this never stop," Naima continued. "I must explain to you that this is not going to end. He is not going to stop hitting you. If you want a divorce, I can tell you the steps you need to take, where you need to go, which papers you have to have. If you are not ready, you have to be ready. The next time he hits you, you need to take a picture of the bruises. Go to the big photo lab on Hassan II Street, tell them to take your picture. Ask for Amina. Don't be embarrassed; she has an agreement with us. She will help you. And talk to your neighbors to see if they will testify in court."

The mother looked at her daughter. "What about a lawyer? Will you be our lawyer?"

Naima smiled. "I am only here on Friday afternoons to answer questions. There are lawyers who cost money and there are also free lawyers provided by the state. When you go back downstairs, ask Samira for a list of the lawyers who can help you. And if you can't afford a lawyer, here is the address of the office where the city can refer you to a lawyer free of charge." She scrawled something on a sheet of paper. "But you know you can come back here any time and someone will be here to talk to you and answer your questions."

"But you seem good, can't you be our lawyer?" the mother continued.

"Yes, of course, but in my practice, it will cost you money. If you decide you want to pay for a lawyer, you can come to my office during normal business hours. Samira can give you the address downstairs."

"Thank you so much," the mother said, getting up. "I told her that he wasn't going to stop, but she refuses to believe me. I told her she

needs to get a divorce, that she is still young, and she could marry somebody who treats her well and doesn't drink. She's a good girl; she should
not be with a man like this. But she believes him when he tells her he
won't do it again. Tell her she ought to get a divorce."

"I can't tell her what to do," Naima sighed. "That's between the two
of you to decide. It is true that men who beat their wives do not usually
stop. You have to decide if you can live with that," she said to the daughter. "You have to want to be divorced. Then we can help you, then a
lawyer can. . . . But you have to want it yourself."

"But, the last time, when he beat her, it was the worst time yet, and
you haven't even seen the marks on her back from where he used his
belt. He doesn't do it when he's sober, but he's got a bad temper, and
he's not well raised at all, and I tell her, you have to leave him before
there's children, before he gets you with a child."

Naima gently cut her off.

"I'm sorry, I have other clients waiting for me. I can't tell you what to
do here. She has to decide. We are not here to tell you what to do. We
do have meetings where women can come to talk about these kinds of
problems. There are other women with husbands like yours, and Samira
downstairs can tell you more about these meetings, if you want to talk
about it. Sometimes it is nice to know you are not alone."

"I didn't want her to marry him," the mother said. "And you see, this
is what happens when the children don't listen to their parents. I tell
her that now, but it's not too late for her, is it?

"No, of course not. But I can't resolve this for you. She has to want
the divorce. You'll have to decide this yourselves."

The women got up reluctantly, the mother talking half to Naima, half
to her daughter, as they slowly made their way out the door. Naima
called after them, "Don't forget to get the addresses from Samira. Please
come back for one of our groups if you want to talk more about this; the
groups are very good." She shut the door.

"You see, the daughter isn't ready for a divorce," Naima told me
before the next client arrived. "The mother dragged her here, because
she wants someone else to tell her daughter to get a divorce. I can't do
that. I can only say that statistics show that the men are unlikely to stop
abusing their wives. But they want someone in a position of authority to
tell them what to do. All I can do is tell them how to proceed. Even so,
what is dangerous is that the mother probably tries to fight with the husband, and if she or the daughter tells him that a lawyer told the girl she
should get a divorce, there is a chance he could find me and take it out
on me. It has happened before, at other centers in Morocco. Not yet
here, fortunately, but we're still new to this."

Another mother and daughter entered, both in *djellabas* and headscarves. Their clothes were slightly nicer and they seemed more articulate than the previous women. This time, the younger woman talked more, although her mother began the story for her.

"Her husband is an immigrant in France," the mother said. "They were married and she went to live with him. He stole her jewelry and her passport! She just wants them returned."

"We lived in Lyon," the daughter added, taking over the story. "I was there for six months after we married. We came back to Morocco for vacation and he left early. He took my passport and said he needed it for some paperwork at the consulate. I came here to Fes to stay with my family. I waited two months for him to send the money for the bus so I could join him, and he said he would send my passport back to me. Then three months passed. One day his family called from Casablanca and said my husband wanted a divorce." She paused for a second. "I had just spoken to him and he hadn't said anything to me about it."

"His family is terrible!" the mother exclaimed. "Casa people![6] Not a good family. Our neighbors are related to them. They suggested the marriage, but our neighbors . . . well, we did not know their family was like this. They said he was from a good family. Of course you never can tell with the ones in France. Who knows what their intentions are? We suspect the family wants him to marry someone else."

"So what can I help you with?" Naima asked.

"He only paid half of his bride price (*sdaq*)," the mother explained.[7] "He left her here for three months, he refuses to send her passport, and she left her jewelry and some other things of value with him in France. What can we do?"

"We see cases like this a lot," Naima said.[8] "When the husbands are abroad, it is often difficult to get the authorities in France to help us, although it has been done. They may not enforce the three months of support (*nafaqa*), but they can try to make him give back your passport and jewelry. Sometimes there is more cooperation than usual, but it depends on the town, how close the Moroccan consulate is, and whether the local authorities are helpful. But there are a couple issues here. The divorce has to go through a judge in Morocco, and it sounds as if he has not paid his *sdaq* as well as the three months of support he owes you. You will have to provide proof of his employment, and often the husbands pretend to be unemployed so they can pay less support. The judge can order the husband to return your jewelry, but there is always a chance he will lie about it. Was it part of your *sdaq*?

"Some of it was," the daughter said. "There was a gold belt and a ring, as well as some things my mother gave me. But I want my passport back. I have the visa now, and what if I want to travel? He refused to give it back. Once he said that he was my husband and he has the right to forbid me to travel. Then another time he said he did not have it."

"Once he is not your husband, he cannot forbid you to travel. You may want to get a lawyer," Naima advised. "These cases are a little more complicated. Can you afford a lawyer?"

"Of course," said the mother.

"I can recommend a few who deal with issues like this across borders," Naima said. "Ask Samira downstairs for the list. Tell her you want the ones who help with marriages to immigrants."

"Will the lawyers help us to see justice?" the mother asked. The daughter looked slightly embarrassed.

"*In sha'llah*, God willing, but you will have to follow the case as closely as you can. What often happens in these cases is that if he refuses to pay, the judge issues a court order to arrest him when he enters Morocco. Once they are threatened with this, they usually find the money. Unless they have no intentions of ever coming back."

The mother and daughter left the office looking hopeful. So far, the cases were typical examples of what I usually saw. Women often came with questions about the divorce petition, and whether a woman had a right to more than what she had received. Abandonment was common, as was expulsion from the marital home.[9] The second case just described involved allegations of abuse, recounted not by the woman who was abused but by her mother. This was also a common strategy, for one woman to talk for another one when they came for consultations, sometimes out of shame but other times in search of a mediator. Transnational marital disputes were prominent, as the third case demonstrated. Many Moroccans felt that Moroccan immigrants abroad often married women for sex but had no intention of fulfilling their contractual responsibilities to them. Abuse, finally, was a common thread, as Halima's case had demonstrated.

But Halima left without Naima being able to offer her any sense of resolution. Like many women, she never came back. Had the Center failed her in some crucial way? What had Halima hoped to gain by coming to the Center, and what were they capable of giving?

Failures of Solidarity, Failures of the Nation-State

The first of its kind in Fes, the Najia Belghazi Center was not directly associated with a political party or religious organization. The volunteers perceived their center as existing "outside civil society," asserting that the term "civil society" had been coopted by male elites, both secular and religious. They expressed their desire to transcend divisions of social class and forge links among all Moroccan women, hoping that the women who visited the center would also be able to envision this possibility of solidarity. However, clients and volunteers often found themselves at cross-purposes, and efforts to establish links across social classes that might lead to larger structural changes improving the status of women were not always successful. Despite the valuable new role NGOs play in Moroccan society by creating new spaces for discussions of women's rights, much of the local resistance in Fes reveals impasses of class, ideologies of patriarchy, and beyond that, the need for government intervention in larger structural problems.

The failures of one NGO to help women "solve" all their problems cannot solely be attributed to insurmountable class differences but must be considered in the light of the problematic role of the nation-state in an era of globalization. As in other regions of the Global South, globalization in Morocco has been accompanied by increasing market liberalization, which has involved deregulation, privatization, and an increase in consumption. IMF-led structural adjustment programs (SAPs) of the 1990s have led to declines in government spending and high rates of unemployment, with no safety nets to assist those who fall deeper into poverty (Pfeifer 1999: 25). In response, the Moroccan government has encouraged the formation of NGOs to ameliorate resulting social problems.

In an era when globalization has supposedly undermined the nation-state's hegemony, NGOs represent one among many possibilities for community and solidarity. However, NGOs are often overstretched and understaffed, in addition to facing resistance from both within and outside the larger communities in which they are based. These resistances and failures of solidarity should not be taken as evidence that NGOs are not useful or necessary but suggest that they are only capable of doing so much. The struggles of the Najia Belghazi Center indicate not that the nation-state is disappearing or powerless but that it is simply evading its responsibilities to its citizens.

In the case of the Najia Belghazi Center of Fes, the NGO's attempt to assert a vision of community encompassing all women met with both local and class-based resistance. Much of this resistance stemmed from core structural issues that demand the intervention of the nation-state. While NGOs can certainly serve as agents of change, the assumption that NGOs can solve major social problems allows the state to evade its responsibilities for suffering brought on by cuts in government spending as a result of SAPs or by government laws and policies that legitimate discrimination against women.

At the time of my fieldwork, many of the difficulties reported by clients at the Center related specifically to laws that favored male authority above all other interests. However, many of the original safety nets that were designed to balance out the uneven effects of the law were missing, particularly for lower-class women. For example, in the past, a woman entering a marriage contract could count on a strong extended family structure to support her should the marriage fail. A sufficient dowry negotiated by a woman's family acted as insurance against a bad marriage, and the necessity of maintaining harmonious group relations among families led to greater pressure for the husband to treat his wife with dignity. If a couple divorced, the woman could usually return to her family, counting on male family members to wield sufficient influence to ensure that she left the marriage with all her dowry.

However, women in Morocco today, particularly from lower socioeconomic groups, are less likely to have this community support. From the 1960s onward, tribal models of production gradually came to be displaced by the impersonal demands of a capitalist economy, which frequently necessitated women's participation in a cash economy. Family structures deteriorated, particularly among the urban poor, though laws and local attitudes about women's rights and women's place in the public sphere remained conservative. For urban women, Ennaji and Sadiqi have explained this crisis as "a clash between an essential tribal superstructure and a production system whose economic logic was alien to the traditional communal mode" (2006: 94). Structural adjustment programs have further contributed to rapid modernization and a deterioration of extended family structures, and the laws have made women the most vulnerable. Women who came to the Center for help often lived far from their families, in addition to lacking the literacy to negotiate the law and the job skills to enable them to support themselves and their children once divorced. NGOs such as the Najia Belghazi Center quickly moved to serve as a resource for all these problems, but as nonprofits they were unable to tackle some of the basic structural causes that have led to a rise in marital problems as well as to the community fragmentation that resulted in women's loss of support.

The Moroccan government has nonetheless placed its support behind the creation of NGOs designed to tackle a range of problems, from orphans to women's rights. Movements of association have a long history in Morocco, although in recent decades, they have taken new forms and begun to deal with issues such as human rights. The origins of the Moroccan feminist movement can be traced back to 1946, when the women's branch of the nationalist Istiqlal party demanded greater representation in the public sphere and an end to polygamy (Ennaji and Sadiqi 2006: 96). Unveiling and nation building became part of the nationalist project when King Mohammed V unveiled his daughters in public. As in other parts of the Middle East and North Africa, progress in the nationalist movement was measured by the attainment of European

Figure 3. Cigarette and candy saleswoman, Fes.

standards concerning the treatment of women. Middle- and upper-class women entered the public sphere through education and high-status professions, and female journalists and writers in the 1960s and 1970s promoted ideas of equality through what Ennaji and Sadiqi call "feminist hagiography," that is, journalistic biographies of famous world feminists as a way to introduce feminism without directly implicating the writer (98). During this period, women's progressive political parties (such as the Union Progressiste des Femmes Marocaines in 1962 and the Union Nationale des Femmes Marocaines in 1969) and women's professional organizations began to appear as well.

It was not until the 1980s that national women's associations, such as the Association Démocratique des Femmes du Maroc, began to appear outside the political parties, and not surprisingly, many of these associations were founded by women who felt their concerns had not been addressed in the political arena. *Mudawana* reform has been a primary goal of many of these groups, along with ending discrimination and violence against women. As of 1990, there were twenty-nine formal women's associations in Morocco, sixteen created in the past decade (Belarbi 1992: 187). Government statistics list thirty-four associations in 1997, but since then, many more have appeared (*Population et développement au Maroc* 1997: 153). The creation of so many organizations since the 1980s has been attributed to a number of factors, including new political openness on the part of the monarchy and a growing awareness among citizens that existing societal structures are insufficient to address social problems among the poor and disenfranchised (Belarbi 1992: 187).

Many Moroccan women's associations are concerned with ameliorating social hardships as well as helping women to obtain a better standard of living. Others are overtly activist-oriented, promoting legal reform or the insertion of more women into the political process (Ennaji and Sadiqi 2006: 106). In addition to humanitarian, political, and feminist organizations, there are also professional associations for women in different high-status careers, including administration, law, and business. Some areas of activity among the organizations overlap; for example, both political parties and feminist groups offer activities such as literacy training, prenatal care, and legal awareness seminars. Other organizations focus both on reforming the *mudawana* as well as on sensitizing Moroccans to a variety of social issues. "Their objective," writes Aïcha Belarbi, "is not to integrate women into a system of production which rarely benefits them, but to increase awareness, to arm them to become active and effective agents in the dynamic of social transformations" (1992: 192).

Often funded by governments and organizations throughout Europe and the United States, many Moroccan NGOs have a degree of independence from the state that allows them to operate without excessive recourse to bureaucratic procedures. The anthropological literature on NGOs reveals two general trends in the perception of their effectiveness: either NGOs are contributing to the workings of the nation-state in an era of neoliberal capitalism, or they work outside the state in processes that will hopefully transform society (Fisher 1997: 445). To proponents of the first viewpoint, NGOs provide evidence of a strong civil society, one in which citizens are actively engaged in renegotiating the relationship between individuals and the state, and in the process, reimagining forms of community and creating new arenas to support those whom the system has failed. Some analysts have pointed to the importance of the role of NGOs in an era of neoliberal capitalism, whereby NGOs are expected to contribute more rapidly and efficiently to processes of "development" than governments (Fisher 1997: 444). Their presence is believed to offer evidence of democracy, and in the case of women's associations, to indicate the participation of women in Moroccan society. Proponents of the second viewpoint argue that NGOs offer what Michel Foucault has called an "insurrection of subjugated knowledges," politicizing previously taboo subjects and demanding radical societal change (Foucault 1980: 81). NGOs like the Najia Belghazi Center fit into neither of these paradigms perfectly. The presence of NGOs offers a positive international image for the Moroccan government, giving the appearance of a strong civil society in the absence of real democracy. However, while the Center promoted many initiatives related to the government's plan to integrate women in development, the Center was unable to efficiently solve the overwhelming number of problems brought by clients.

Violence and the Limits of Solidarity

In Fes, volunteers at the Najia Belghazi Center felt compelled to officially tone down any elements in their discourse that might have been perceived as radical in order to try to gain acceptance by a locally conservative society. Refusing to take a public stance on *mudawana* reform, the volunteers insisted that their goals were strictly apolitical.[10] They wanted to stay outside the domain of politics while quietly working to inform women of the legal rights they did have. Violence was the larger umbrella that was supposed to envelope everyone. On numerous occasions the volunteers echoed the assertion that all Moroccan women were victims of violence: juridical, physical, or structural violence. This broad stance allowed them to assert solidarity across social classes with their clients, most of whom were lower class, economically disenfranchised, or illiterate. Rather than interacting in typical patron-client patterns, at the Center, volunteers hoped that they could meet with clients on more neutral grounds, united by the shared theme of "violence" inflicted by patriarchal social interests.

"When we started out," the Center's founder and president, Alia, told me, "we had no idea the violence problem was as extensive as it is." Alia was a serious woman in her early fifties who taught at the university and was deeply dedicated to women's rights. "At first we were more informal in our '*écoutes*,' and we were not trained to handle violence-related issues. We made many mistakes. But after our first year of operation, when we looked back at the data from the women who had come to us, we realized violence was prevalent, especially among maids and women in lower socioeconomic groups, both married and unmarried. We looked at government statistics on violence and found them to be greatly underreported. In determining how we could best serve the population in Fes, we realized we needed to offer more support in these areas, and also that we needed to sensitize the police to such issues."

The Moroccan government confirms Alia's statements. Between 1995 and 1997, over 20,000 cases of violence against women were officially reported (*Arabic News.com* 1998). According to the former Moroccan secretary of Family and Child Protection, Mohamed Said Saadi, the actual numbers are probably much higher, as ideals of shame and honor lead many women to keep silent about matters of abuse (*Arabic News.com* 1998). Additionally, these figures do not include prostitution, rape, or sexual harassment.

"We were also looking for ways we could get a better idea about the level of violence, outside of institutional strategies such as statistical measurement," Alia added. "But more than that, we knew we needed to come up with strategies, not just for how we handled violence issues here at the center, but for how we could help these women to take control over their lives. They need to be able to get along in society, and to earn a living, without intermediaries. They need to have work in a viable profession."

As Margaret Keck and Kathryn Sikkink have shown in an important work about transnational advocacy networks, the supposedly universal character of "violence against women" became a means of unifying feminist groups across transnational lines in the 1980s (1998). As a way of encouraging "first-world" and "third-world" feminists to see their concerns as related, the definition of "violence against women" as universal was also intended to facilitate transnational conversations and promote global solidarity among feminist groups. Efforts to fight violence against women became a central concern of international development programs, achieving full prominence in the United Nations Fourth World Conference on the Status of Women in Beijing in 1995. However, anthropologists have criticized the supposed universality of these discourses, which promote a Western individualistic concept of rights and ignore global inequalities as well as local contexts and cultural variables.[11]

The volunteers of the Najia Belghazi Center did participate in transnational conversations about women's rights, maintaining networks and exchanging visits with women's NGOs in Europe and North America. Sometimes I helped Alia, who was fluent in French and Arabic but not English, to write letters to NGOs she had visited in the United States. These networks served as a valuable source of information concerning grant possibilities, training initiatives, and the latest research on forms of violence. At times, volunteers were even able to call on NGOs in cities in Europe for assistance in marital disputes involving Moroccan migrants. Through the intervention of a French partner NGO, for example, the woman who sought the return of her passport and jewelry might have been able to obtain a search warrant of her husband's house from French police. But despite these transnational links, volunteers were quite conscious of the culturally specific forms and causes of inequality and violence against women in Moroccan society. They were further aware of the potential didacticism involved in identifying common concerns among women of different social classes, but they nonetheless attempted to bridge these differences in their efforts to promote women's full participation in society. As Alia told me, "We are united more generally by juridical violence, which all of us face. Here, our motives are different: to create a space for activism, and to achieve women's full participation in society. Legally, women in Morocco are given the same rights as children. This has become insupportable."

For the Najia Belghazi Center's volunteers, legal, physical, and economic concerns were perceived as intertwined. With grant money received from foreign funding agencies, NGOs, and even governments, they created various programs aimed at training women who had no resources to work for themselves, frequently in nontraditional positions. With control of an income, female dependence on the quixotic whims of husbands would decline, women would become savvier about their rights, and some of the social structures that continued to replicate this dependence on men would themselves dissolve, whether or not the laws themselves followed suit.

Despite volunteers' insistence that these concerns were not political, to many Fassi Moroccans they appeared to be explicitly so. Some of the Center's failures were rooted in Fassi rejections of the Center's claims that challenged entrenched notions of patriarchy, class, and social structure. While it sought to create a distinctive space for women outside the confines of civil society and the nation state, the forms of solidarity the Najia Belghazi Center attempted to forge were often fleeting, dissolving in the face of other cultural and class-based pressures, with all their accompanying ideologies.

While public debates over changing the *mudawana* focused on law, Islam, and the permissibility of new interpretations of the religion, within the NGO activists were working to effect change by encouraging women to see themselves as sharing common concerns with all Moroccan women. Rather than publicly criticizing the *mudawana*, the volunteers at the Najia Belghazi Center avoided taking sides by arguing that within the existing laws, there was room to maneuver. Additionally, the Center's official position—that all women were united by gendered experiences of legal, physical, or psychological violence—led them to consider women's legal rights as related to larger issues of inequality in Moroccan society. This shared experience of what the Center's president called "juridical violence," and the attempt to make client-volunteer interactions as equitable as possible, were two examples of strategies employed to promote solidarity among women. Volunteers insisted that visitors to the Center understand that volunteers were not interested in perpetuating the patron-client relationship, in which people seek a benefactor in exchange for services.

However, there were limits to these attempts to create solidarity. Activists at the Center distanced themselves from personal experiences of physical violence, identifying with the more abstract notion of "juridical" violence and with the sexual violence that comprised basic street harassment. Although volunteers often cited the statistic that domestic violence crosses class lines, the volunteers were quick to point out that they themselves had never been physically victimized. Physical violence was perceived as a problem specific to lower socioeconomic groups, a problem that could be ameliorated with access to education and employment. Bringing poor women to the centers to discuss physical and sexual abuse was touted as progress, as "lifting the veil of shame on this taboo subject," as one of the volunteers once said to me. Yet the subject of physical violence among the middle and upper classes remained a taboo among the educated volunteers, as if it were presumed not to exist at all. Ironically, "lifting the veil of shame" for lower-class women but refusing to discuss the possibility of physical violence among the middle and upper classes perpetuated the same class divisions that volunteers sought to overcome.

Class divisions and a general suspicion of the NGO's altruism were also reflected in outsiders' perceptions of the Center. The majority of middle- and upper-class Fassis I asked about this topic still felt that marital problems should be resolved within families. Many of the Fassis I knew considered it shameful that the women who visited the Center aired intimate details of their domestic life before an audience of strangers. They doubted the honest intentions of the Center's volunteers and asserted that the volunteers must be pocketing their grant money.

The Center also met with resistance among some academics I spoke with, who offered a more sophisticated critique of the NGO along the lines of its supposed subversive intentions. A few academics perceived the creation of the NGO as a blatant ploy to influence the *mudawana* debates. Driss, a university professor, described the work of local NGOs as "cultural imperialism," equating it to missionary work.

"They want to accomplish legal reform to give Moroccan women the same rights as European women," he told me. "But they're ignoring our traditions, and our heritage." This was also a common argument against altering the *mudawana*—that any changes to the existing laws somehow threatened to destroy Moroccan culture. Issues of violence and poverty, or more significantly, the structures of patriarchal social relations and patron-client ties, are effaced in favor of a view that sees Moroccan women as repositories of traditional culture. The territories of ideology, when described as an eternal and unchanging "culture" or "religion," were very difficult to overcome.

Because of these public perceptions, the Center faced difficulties recruiting professionals interested in volunteering their time, which made the task of solving such a wide range of problems even more overwhelming. The woman whose business card served as my initial connection to the Center was no longer a volunteer and had not, according to Naima, been truly committed to their purpose. Volunteering in the Western sense of donating one's time to help strangers in an impersonal location with no expectation of personal gain did not fit in with standard notions of aid, many of which revolved around the idea of mutually beneficial patron-client relations. Many middle-class Fassis are accustomed to dispensing aid through preexisting social or kin-based networks, a practice unavailable to rural-urban migrants who typically arrive in the cities with no such networks in place.

"The idea of 'volunteering' [*se porter volontaire*] does not really exist in Moroccan culture," Naima explained to me, slipping the French term into our conversation, which was in Moroccan Arabic.[12] "In Casa and Rabat, there have been associations like ours for years, so people are accustomed to them. In Fes, we are the first, so we have a hard time getting professionals who are willing to work without pay." I asked if volunteering would be considered positively as an Islamic duty, a required form of charity. "People don't think of it that way. It's alien to them; they are used to giving money to beggars or helping out unfortunate family members, but volunteering to give time to strangers is something new. I have tried to convince other lawyers to work with me here. Many of them say they already help their families and that they don't have time."

In this respect, the comments of Khadija, who had refused an invitation to volunteer at the Center, were telling. As Khadija's quote at the beginning of this chapter demonstrates, some professionals believed that the women who come to the Center only want money, and the relative anonymity of volunteer-client interactions meant that it was impossible to measure the effects of intervention. Khadija herself was willing to help only if she could be certain her assistance would truly be appreciated, and the best way to assure this was to work with family members.

In fact, many of the interactions I witnessed between clients and volunteers did attempt to draw on this patron/client model. In the eyes of the volunteers, patron-client relations were part of a larger societal problem, yet ironically, producing these types of relations was, for many clients, the only culturally familiar way to gain access to resources. Women often recounted long and painful sagas of abuse, divorce, and expulsion from the marital home, which ended with a plea for the Center to provide them with a free lawyer or money. Occasionally clients tried to offer their services as domestics in exchange for a lawyer. And although the volunteers tried to maintain their neutral and egalitarian position, it was difficult to elide the perception that their legal knowledge represented the formal domain of law and state authority. The earlier example of the young woman who was ambivalent about a divorce from her abusive husband despite her mother's insistence was a common type of interaction—the mother clearly sought the mediation of an educated authority figure when all Naima could do was to "inform" her that abusers were statistically unlikely to stop. Ideally women would come to the Center to gain a better sense of the path they needed to take in the judicial system; they might also take advantage of literacy or job training classes and then promote themselves as entrepreneurs. However, upon hearing that the Center was not offering money, free lawyers, or dispute resolution, many women left and never came back.

Class differences—here exemplified by the promotion of solidarity with distinctions, the sense among Fassis that only the poor and uneducated would air their marital grievances at an impersonal NGO, and the difficulties of convincing educated professionals to volunteer—mask a larger problem. This is that the Moroccan government itself has in some sense contributed to the creation of these problems, and by encouraging NGOs to solve them, is ignoring the larger structural causes. The structure of social relations has broken down due to rapid modernization brought on by economic policies, and the government, rather than developing social services to aid in the resulting societal transformations, has actually taken them away. Expecting one non-profit to bear the burden for an entire city's problems with domestic violence, illiteracy, divorce, and abandonment; and blaming these problems on a lack of education, poverty, or social class—this tends to abstract these issues from their true causes. The illusion of a flourishing civil society, in which impartial, uncoerced NGOs stand between the government and the population, allows the government to receive accolades from human rights groups for its openness, while obscuring the true causes of human suffering. For Halima, her suffering visible not only in the bruises that colored her shoulders but also in her distraught monologue and vague demands for justice, monumental structural obstacles were also at work.

The Death of the Nation-State?

As labor and global capital cross borders with increasing ease, unimpeded by traditional regulations such as tariffs or labor laws, the provocative idea of the "death of the nation-state" has often been asserted as a byproduct of globalization.[13] According to this formulation, nations have lost their ability to legislate and are made irrelevant by powerful flows of global capital. Economic deregulation leads to higher corporate profits, as companies relocate to areas in the Global South with weak unions, low wages, and the fewest restrictions on labor practices. Within Global South economies, IMF-led programs of structural adjustment promote globalization by offering loans on the condition that recipients privatize public assets and cut government spending. However, structural adjustment programs, rather than leading to economic growth and improvement, often result in economic recessions, greater unemployment, and poverty, particularly for women. The loss of public-sector jobs and an accompanying shift from formal to informal employment have increased women's work while failing to improve their decision-making power in the household. With less education and lower status than men, women find themselves in lower-paid, riskier, more labor-intensive jobs. Employment instability and job loss contribute to marital tensions and an increase in domestic violence. As the weakened nation-state is no longer able to offer services to combat issues related to the feminization of poverty, we see a rise in the number of NGOs devoted to addressing women's concerns.

Yet globalization does not simply happen to passive, helpless actors, whether nations or individuals, and assertions about the death of the nation-state are perhaps premature. Saskia Sassen has noted that globalization requires active implementation on the part of nation-states to facilitate the movement of capital and labor, and that globalization is, in fact, embedded in the national (Sassen 2000: 217). In Morocco, structural adjustment programs have led to an improved standard of living for some, but in other respects have hurt many citizens. An IMF study of the effect of SAPs from 1980 to 1996 shows that Morocco did not improve in the rate of exports of goods and services or in its trade balance (Pfeifer 1999: 24). Debt rose in the 1990s, the rate of investment continued to be low, and—most significantly—unemployment increased.

The efforts of the Najia Belghazi Center to attack a wide range of social problems met with resistance from well-meaning volunteers, clients, and citizens. Effacing class differences was difficult when volunteers distanced themselves from forms of violence particular to the lower classes, or when clients affirmed these class differences by attempting to seek a patron-client relationship with the volunteers. Middle- and upper-class Fassi observers who benefited from the patriarchal social structures in place to resolve marital differences within the family disapproved of the NGO's perceived intervention in marital disputes. The Moroccan government, it would seem, offers the least resistance, as it allows the NGO to operate with considerably leeway, pursuing whatever agenda the NGO deems as important.

Yet blaming the failures of solidarity on the NGO's founders, volunteers, clients, or local citizens obscures the fact that many of these problems might not be so pronounced had underlying economic problems not contributed to them. In 1983 the monarchy signed on to structural adjustment programs without consulting the people, and to this day economic reforms are a result of top-down, hierarchical state policy. The flourishing of NGOs conceals the absence of a strong democracy. Rather than disappearing, the nation-state still plays a very pronounced role in the lives of citizens. On a local level, NGO solidarity has failed for two reasons: first, divisions of social class created obstacles to solidarity; and second, these class-based divisions often existed as a direct result of state policies that undermined the core issues the NGOs attempt to address. These policies included legalized inequality between men and women, structural adjustment programs leading to "official" unemployment rates as high as 25 percent, and finally, the failure of government to offer creative solutions to the feminization of poverty. NGOs in the Global South, while making a valiant attempt to address these issues on a small scale, are insufficient as the sole recourse for marginalized citizens. But the state, it appears, has left them to address the crucial issues that contribute to poverty, marginality, and disenfranchisement.

Nonetheless, organizations such as the Najia Belghazi Center must be lauded for their creativity and their initiative in tackling these monumental issues. Other women's associations promoted "women's work" such as embroidery or weaving as a means of income for poor women who had been divorced, but the Najia Belghazi Center had begun to pursue a different strategy.

"So many women know how to embroider that it is not profitable; they have to struggle to make money at it," Naima told me. "Artisanal work is nothing new; it has always been considered women's work." In Fes, "cooperatives" often meant nothing more than collecting a group of women together in one place, offering them materials to work with, and then giving them a daily wage that was far below the end value of the product. Associations that promote "traditional" work initiatives for women do little to expand the stereotypical images of Moroccan women as keepers of the domestic flame, or to alleviate their status as legal minors (Belarbi 1992: 189).

The Najia Belghazi Center's employment initiatives, however, attempted to create new categories for female labor participation. A training program that instructed women in plumbing and gardening had just commenced as I was finishing my fieldwork in June of 2002. Plumbing and gardening were not traditional women's professions in Morocco. Yet if women were the only ones at home, Moroccans considered it inappropriate for an unrelated male to enter the house. The Center proposed that women should be trained as plumbers, reasoning that there was a need for this service that women could ideally fulfill.[14] The first training session was comprised of twenty-six women who had been abandoned by their husbands and were currently having difficulties supporting themselves and their children.

While the training aspects of the program had been worked out, the

Center did not have a clearly defined strategy for promoting the plumbers and gardeners once they were ready. There was some talk of drawing on connections with owners or managers of local hotels, who might employ the women to tend to their large gardens. Alia suggested that the women could promote themselves, and gain self-esteem through doing so, by forming a "committee of entrepreneurs." To Alia, the question of how to publicize the workers would be solved when the time came; the larger problem in her eyes was whether or not male relatives or husbands would try to take away the women's earnings.

"It is important," she said, echoing a sentiment that I heard from numerous Moroccans, "that women have their own incomes in order to take control over their lives."

Yet I wondered whether the promotional aspects of this program would succeed, and what sort of "committee of entrepreneurs" might result. Would women need to rely on traditional forms of networking in order to gain clients for their services? The following chapter offers one such example of how "traditional" kinship networks involving women have expanded to involve non-kin and to deal with contemporary situations. While the woman at the center of this network was a middle-class Fassi, membership included Moroccans of other social classes. NGOs are a new resource, but it is possible that their success may depend on the degree to which they involve culturally accepted networks and forms of communication.

Chapter 5

Kinship: Seeking Sanctuary in the City

The sun had just set as I walked from my apartment in the Lux neighborhood over to Huriya's place just a block away. I dodged the cars that were pulling out of the daytime parking lot next to my building, bank employees and civil servants leaving their offices in the city center to head to apartments in the suburbs. In a few months the parking lot would become another high-rise apartment building, so rapid was construction at that time, in the early part of the millennium. But that night the parking attendants in their blue coats were still hard at work, waiting for the last of the cars to leave so they too could go home. Although evening, it was still warm, a sign that summer was almost here, since in spring the nights could be chilly. People had thrown open their windows, and Fes felt open to the world, the boundary between home and outside blurred, as women called out to their neighbors in other apartments, their voices carrying as they exchanged bits of news. Sons lingered to play soccer in the street just a few minutes longer, and in the boulevard below, café tables spilled out across the sidewalk and men lingered there, enjoying the weather. Soon everyone would begin pouring out into the gardens beneath the palm trees in the middle of Hassan II Boulevard to escape the nighttime heat hemming them into their apartments. It would happen suddenly, as if all at once, everyone was in agreement that summer had arrived at last.

I stepped through the small courtyard on the ground floor of the Tazi building, greeting Huriya's neighbors, some of whom were her family, others renters who were "like family," unless there was a dispute, whereupon the ties of fictive kinship no longer applied. Still dressed in an embroidered lavender *djellaba* for work, Huriya kissed me on both cheeks, and we went inside, where a pot of mint tea was coming to a second boil on the stove. I kissed Huriya's daughter Yasmin, my sister-in-law, who was visiting from northern Morocco, and lifted up her four-year-old son. We moved into one of the salons, where the television was tuned to a cooking show we all enjoyed watching.

It was not uncommon for Huriya to receive visitors from outside the family, and when the bell rang she jumped up to see who it was. A woman none of us recognized stood in the courtyard beyond the iron bars of Huriya's doorway, and she announced her connection to Huriya, along with her reason for being there.

"I'm sorry to be disturbing you like this. My name is Fatima. My neighbor is Asma Majid, who rents the apartment you own in the *medina*. She told me you would hear what I had to say, and that you would be so kind as to advise me on my problem."

Huriya turned the key in the lock, and the door swung open. The woman wore a plain beige polyester *djellaba* and headscarf. She carried a plastic shopping bag, and her shoes were scuffed and worn. After a year in Morocco, I could tell from Fatima's clothes that she was not well off. I had begun to understand the subtle cues of social class from clothes that, at the beginning, all looked unfamiliar and exotic to me.

We moved into the nicer of the two salons, the one Huriya reserved for guests, and Yasmin disappeared into the kitchen to make more tea.

"My daughter-in-law. She's American," Huriya said, introducing me. The woman nodded and then turned back to Huriya, stating her problem in a voice that was at once both desperate and imploring.

"My husband," she began, "drives a *grand taxi*." Grand taxis were cars that traveled between Moroccan cities, leaving for their destinations as soon as they were packed with at least six passengers. "Brahim is a very honest man. Never any trouble, a good husband, a provider to his children. But last night the police came for him." Huriya's eyes registered no surprise. Working in the courthouse, she was used to these stories, and had seen all sorts of human vice in the city of Fes. She waited to hear the crime of which Brahim was accused.

A month before, Fatima continued, Brahim received an opportunity to take a British tourist to the airport in Casablanca some four hours away. It was not Brahim's normal route, since he was licensed to drive between Meknes and Fes, but the tourist had been willing to pay a fair amount, and Brahim did not want to turn down the opportunity to make some extra money. Unfortunately, one hour away from the airport, his taxi had broken down on the highway. The British tourist was growing desperate about missing his flight, and Brahim flagged down an empty *grand taxi*, whose driver agreed to help them out. Not understanding what had just happened, the British tourist recorded Brahim's license number, just in case something went wrong. Brahim gave the driver the remainder of the fare to take his passenger the rest of the way.

At the airport, the second taxi driver demanded more money, insisting that Brahim had given him nothing. The incensed tourist argued with the driver but finally ended up giving him the extra money. From England, however, he wrote several letters to various officials in Fes, reporting Brahim's license number and accusing Brahim of ripping him off. Now Brahim was in jail, unable to support his wife and four children. Because they had no money, Fatima feared they would have to rely on state-appointed lawyers, who were notorious for their neglect of nonpaying customers. Neither Brahim nor his wife Fatima had relatives in Fes who could help, so in desperation, she had come to Huriya.

I listened as Fatima told her story, noticing how she casually mentioned other details about her life that might evoke sympathy and suggest possible ways she could give something back if Huriya helped her.

"I clean houses sometimes, but I haven't managed to find steady work. I have nobody to turn to. We have almost no family here in Fes, although there is one brother-in-law who sells sofa wool in the medina. The finest wool—the best quality. If you ever are interested, I will make sure that he gives you a good price." Huriya promised to do what she could for Fatima.

"What can you do for her?" I asked, after Fatima had left. "Is she telling the truth?"

"I believe so," Huriya said. "Sometimes people don't know what they need to do to get themselves out of these problems. If her story is true, then the tourist would have written down the other driver's information as well. I will help the husband to find this information."

The next day, Huriya spoke to a connection in the police department, who agreed to release Brahim. She then recommended his case to a lawyer she knew who would accept a lower than normal fee. Huriya advised Brahim how to find the other driver, and he subsequently managed to save himself from prison.

Huriya did not hire Fatima as a maid, but she recommended her to a friend who was seeking one. Finally, when a newly married family member was setting up his household and needed some wool to make traditional Moroccan sofas for his salon, Huriya herself called on Brahim's brother, who gave her the wool at a good price.

I was impressed by the smoothness of these transactions, which unfolded over the next few months. When Huriya was invited to a wedding in the *medina* of someone associated with the family who rented the apartment she owned there, we saw Fatima, who kissed us on both cheeks and greeted Huriya warmly. Although Huriya and Fatima were of different social classes and clearly had access to different sets of resources, both women gained something from the encounter.[1] Huriya had used her resources to assist Fatima, who was now obligated to return the favor, which she did by connecting Huriya to her brother-in-law, offering another service from which Huriya indirectly benefited. Americans would have called this networking, a neutral term that gives no indication of who operates from a comparative position of power, but in the anthropological literature, the term often used to describe it is the more cynical sounding "patron-client relations." The centrality of kinship to these networks, and the ways women navigate ties of kinship as well as the more impersonal ties forged as a result of their own public positioning, is the subject of this chapter.

Kinship as a Middle-Class Resource

For the middle class of Fes, the traditional resources provided by family and kinship practices have continued to remain an important form of economic and social support, even as public attention has turned to newer forms of assistance provided by nongovernmental organizations (NGOs) in an era of decreasing state intervention. Structural Adjustment Programs (SAPs) introduced by the International Monetary Fund (IMF) in the 1990s have led to declines in government spending and high rates of unemployment, with no safety nets to assist those who fall deeper into poverty (Pfeifer 1999: 25). The rise in the number of NGOs, many of which offer support to poor, working-class Moroccans, can be attributed in part to these processes.

While SAPs have directly and indirectly affected the forms of assistance available to lower-class Moroccans, government policies also shape changes to kinship structures. Mandatory education for girls, the almost equal rate of male and female students at the university level, and women's salaried or hourly wage employment are all processes originating at the level of the state that have brought great numbers of women into the public sphere. Yet the impersonal nature of wage or salaried labor has not led people to be completely independent of the need for the resources provided by kinship. In Fes, a city characterized by declining economic conditions and insecure employment prospects, kinship networks offer a degree of certainty and security no longer promised by the nation-state. As Huriya's story indicates, women's significance in kinship networks not only highlights women's changing role in the Moroccan public sphere but also indicates the flexibility of kinship principles once thought to be the provenance of men only.

Literature on civil society in the Middle East and North Africa (MENA) has tended to focus not on kinship but on the appearance of newer forms of association not directly connected with the nation-state, such as NGOs. NGOs have been called on to offer a variety of social services that one might argue are the provenance of the nation-state. As I have shown in the last two chapters, NGOs offer some limited support, particularly for rural-urban migrants with weak or absent support networks. For the middle class, however, kinship networks can be quite robust, essential resources in the face of demographic changes, modernization, and an unreliable economy. Significantly, women are often at the center of these networks, which are no longer exclusively restricted to family or gender.

In the rush to define and critique the role of NGOs in the MENA region, kinship has been understudied as a form of civil society (Antoun 2000). The importance of strong family ties in maintaining elite economic hegemony has been described for other regions of the global South (Creed 2000: 329–55). Other works focusing on the MENA region have usefully addressed the role of the household in local, national, and global economies, particularly the creation of women's economic survival networks.[2] Kinship networks, once thought to be fragmenting due to modernization, remain significant in the MENA region, as a number of recent studies have indicated.[3] Viewing social, economic, and demographic changes through the lens of kinship enables us to consider how middle-class families update and make use of kinship principles in an uncertain world. While membership in kinship structures is not voluntary in the sense that civil society organizations are often defined, what people make of kinship structures is less predetermined.

Revisiting Hildred Geertz

In this chapter, I explore the strength of kin relations for middle-class Fassis, examining how these kinship networks function while also drawing attention to women's prominent roles. An ideology of kinship, closely associated with patriarchal social organization, remains strong in Fes, reflecting a taken-for-granted belief in the essential importance of family ties in negotiating social, economic, and political worlds. As I have shown, the belief shared by many middle-class Moroccans that family interests remain paramount in marriage considerations, and that patron-client ties are a natural way to forge relationships between those seeking and distributing aid, demonstrates a significant territory of ideology that must be negotiated not only by women, but also by the Moroccan government as it encourages *mudawana* reforms and NGO-led social initiatives. For middle-class Fassis in the Ville Nouvelle, kinship retains certain characteristics even as the content of its forms changes, and revisiting earlier studies gives a sense of how basic Moroccan principles of kinship have been modified in response to large-scale societal transformations.[4]

Conducting research in a multigenerational household in Sefrou, Morocco, during the period 1965–71, anthropologist Hildred Geertz found that rather than approaching kinship in an ordered sense, families viewed kinship as fluid, guided by a "person-centered ethic" in which choice of residence and familial alliances were determined not by rules, but by the flexible dynamics of particular situations (H. Geertz

1979: 316).[5] Following this "person-centered ethic," individuals developed various relationships: marital, patron-client, personal, social, and economic. Frequently, the kinship networks Geertz examines center around a senior male or family patriarch, and she describes women's networks as "unseen" and therefore harder to study.

As the number of female-headed households has increased, and as more women have entered the visible public sphere for reasons of employment, middle-class Moroccan women have come to take on kinship roles similar to those described in the past for men. The Fassi networks of patronage described in this chapter often contain a woman at their center—not a prominent man, as was the case for families like the Adluns of Sefrou that Geertz described in the 1970s.[6] Property ownership and employment status give women an advantage in many situations, especially over unemployed male relatives. Among the Adluns thirty years ago, men owned the property, held wage-earning jobs, and were responsible for the economic well-being of their families; among the Tazis of the Lux neighborhood in Fes, many of the women are both property owners and wage earners.

While "person-centered ethics" still guide the formation of Moroccan kinship networks today, demographic changes have radically altered household structure. According to official statistics, 69.7 percent of households in Fes are now nuclear, with 30.3 percent containing extended families, a shift that reveals an increase in nuclear households over the past few decades (Guerraoui 1996: 166). Censuses reveal that women play a significant economic role in their families. Among families who work in civil service and commercial occupations, the wife's income serves as the primary means of familial support in one out of three households.[7] In addition to economic practices, social practices related to gender have also changed radically since Geertz's fieldwork. The creation of visible patronage networks notable for the presence of a woman at their center is not uncommon, nor does this centrality necessarily confer a lack of prestige to those involved. Examining the circumstances of one middle-class family is a useful means of understanding both change and continuity in the prevalence of kin-based networks.

My ties with the Tazi family are extensive, and I grew to know the family well during the course of my fieldwork.[8] My husband is a member of the third generation of this family, and the Tazis have been unanimously generous in welcoming me.[9] Through the Tazis I met other middle-class Fassis, some of them connected by marriage to other "original" Fassi families now living in the Ville Nouvelle. Their stories proved useful in helping me to understand the changing position of women among the middle class in Moroccan society. The Tazi family was not exceptional in having prominent female members with their own public networks that

extended beyond the family. Other middle-class Fassi women I met possessed similar networks, founded not only on the basis of their connections in the public sphere but also on their own access to resources,
property, and other assets both inherited and acquired.

In some ways, my identity as both a daughter-in-law and a foreign
anthropologist placed me in a bind. My intimate knowledge of one family provided a wealth of useful anthropological information, but at the
same time, I was conscious of the need to protect stories the Tazis shared
with me. Some incidents, particularly related to marriages and divorces
within the family, would be considered too personal to share with outsiders, and I have often changed telling details that would enable other
Fassis to identify someone. If a certain distancing sometimes creeps into
this narrative, this is not due to any sense I have of myself as an objective
observer but more to my feeling of protectiveness over the personal
details of family life. Turning family into "informants" or characters in
an ethnography has significant ethical implications, so I have attempted
to avoid writing about sensitive family issues and to create composite
details wherever possible.[10]

"Tazi" is an illustrious, "original" Fassi family name, but the multiple
branches of this family that exist today throughout Morocco are only
distantly related, if that. This particular branch of the Tazis is one in
which nine out of eleven adult siblings occupied the same family-owned
apartment building together with their descendants. Six of these individuals were women, and all but one of them were widowed, divorced, or
never married.[11]

Like other "notable" families of Fes, the Tazis trace their origins back
hundreds of years and have a sense of identity that is deeply tied to the
city's history. After Moroccan independence from the French in 1956, a
number of affluent Moroccan families in cities across the country left
the *medina* to occupy buildings abandoned by the French and, more
recently, by Jewish families emigrating to Europe, Israel, or North
America. Many of the large, palatial homes of the ancient *medina* were
subsequently broken up into multiple apartments and rented to
migrants from the countryside. Upon emigration to Israel in the 1960s,
a Jewish family sold their apartment building to the patriarch of the Tazi
family, Si Mohammed, who died in 1972. During the period of my
fieldwork from 2000 to 2002, the majority of both Tazi occupants and
renters had lived there for twenty or more years. The inhabitants of the
building were solidly middle class by Moroccan standards, with at least
one person working full time in each family. In four of the nine families,
a woman's income was the principal form of financial support. Family
members' employment ranged from education to business, from civil
service to secretarial. The younger children of the third generation, the

grandchildren of the late patriarch, ranged in age from ten to forty-five and were educated to varying degrees, with most having stopped after the high school level.

Today, the three-story building, with its shutters and art deco balconies, is one of the few French structures remaining in the neighborhood, and the street is dominated by high-rises built during the last several years. The high-rises are characterized by the anonymity that one associates with urban dwellings in the West, where neighbors are unrelated and do not socialize with one another. However, the Tazi building preserves aspects of sociability common to Moroccan culture that are, in urban areas, dying out. The Tazi building is centered around a courtyard where families often talk to one another while shelling vegetables for lunch or hanging laundry. A spirit of mutual assistance pervades, and anyone who is doing spring cleaning or preparing a special feast can count on cousins, sisters, and aunts to come to her aid. The top two floors each have four apartments, and a staircase leads up to the roof, where the families hang their laundry and gather to enjoy a bit of sun and gossip during the cold winter months. The roof also serves as the site of sacrifices during the annual Feast of the Sacrifice, when each family's sheep, tethered at a corner of the roof, awaits the butcher. During the day, women are the primary occupants of the domestic space, though the men come home for lunch and gather around television sets at night. Outside on the main street, a few of the apartments are rented out as shops, for income that the entire family shares. Four of the building's apartments are rented by nonkin who have been living there almost as long as Mohammed Tazi's descendants. They are considered "like family," except when there are disputes or someone forgets to pay the rent.

Despite widespread public education and the ability of some unconnected individuals to advance based on factors other than family status, family names still carry weight in Moroccan society. The principle of *nisba*, indicating attachment to a particular kinship group, is still significant to Moroccan identities.[12] The Tazis are a large, well-known family in Fes, and other relatives, both near and distant, have moved to Casablanca to Rabat, where they have become very successful. "Original" Fassis in the financial and political capitals maintain the widely held Moroccan stereotype that people of Fassi origin constitute the majority of those at the center of power, money, and influence. Among the particular branch of the family described in this chapter, money and influence had dissipated, yet kinship was an important resource that allowed many of them to maintain middle-class status even though Fes was no longer the dynamic economic and political capital it once had been.

Many practices that Hildred Geertz associates with men's kinship networks in the 1960s are now practiced by women. Patron-client networks are still a significant means of allowing individuals to navigate a not-impartial bureaucracy for which social connections and influence are still essential, but with increased migration to the cities, it is not always as easy for individuals to develop these face-to-face relationships as it once might have been. Women's access to education and employment in the public sphere has allowed them to be at the center of kinship networks. What interested me as I came to know the Tazis was how family ties often brought together families of women—families in which the most senior member was a woman who owned her own property, gathered her descendants about her, and had a network of people who depended on her for support or patronage.

Among middle-class Moroccans, residential patterns have changed to accommodate a new emphasis on the conjugal unit, with couples less likely to live with the husband's family. The Tazi family was no exception, as the married children of the third generation lived mostly in separate apartments in other parts of the city. In addition, marriages are less likely to be arranged among members of the same social grouping, and although choice was a factor applauded by many, when marriages failed, family position was often the first factor people suspected. Within the Tazi family, kinship served as a kind of insurance, and when a relative fell on hard times, he or she could count on other family members to pool together resources of support. What amounted to mini patron-client relationships seemed to develop within the Tazi family, as those who received the generosity of other family members went out of their way to help with domestic tasks and other nonmonetary exchanges. Kinship ties prevented some family members from falling into abject poverty, and better-off family members were sympathetic to their own kin, blaming their circumstances on bad luck rather than laziness and constantly providing them with assistance.

Women at the Center of Patron-Client Networks

The significance of patronage networks in maintaining the Moroccan political system has elsewhere been described, particularly how patron-client relations structure social relations from the level of the monarchy on down to interpersonal fields of exchange.[13] In these theoretical models, patron-client ties are modeled on that between the king and his subjects, with the client always feminized by his dependence on the dominant party. Clients become "indentured" out of economic or social necessity and may improve their status to create their own patronage ties with subordinates, yet there will always be more powerful patrons who require placating (Smith 2002: 115). Examining patronage relations on a micro level demonstrates how individuals benefit from connections with a prominent individual. An example of how women's patron-client relationships are constructed illustrates the expansion of women's networks beyond the household. Huriya Tazi, who worked in a local government administrative office, was perhaps the most prominent woman among the children of the late Mohammed Tazi.

In a number of ways, Huriya had been a principal inspiration for my research. I first met my future mother-in-law a year before I began my fieldwork, and she seemed a powerful role model. Huriya's empathy, strength, and good judgment led Fassis both related and unrelated to the Tazi family to turn to her for assistance in economic, legal, and personal matters. The incident I witnessed with the wife of the taxi driver brings together a number of themes associated with the study of kinship in the Moroccan context, most notably the development of patron-client relationships where powerful individuals are able to intercede on the behalf of the less powerful. Because of her years working in local administration, and because she came from an influential family, Huriya was known by many important people in the community. Her stature and reputation were sufficient to open doors for her, and she did not have to offer bribes. In such situations, people like Huriya were indispensable in providing a link between the disenfranchised and the influential.

An attractive and charismatic woman, Huriya had raised five children who, at the time of my fieldwork, ranged in age from twenty-five to thirty-three. Since her husband's death in 1978, she and her children had lived in their own apartment in the Tazi building. Her daughters were now both married and living outside Fes, while her three sons owned and operated a small business in the family property facing the street and still lived at home at the time I met them. Huriya, who had recently begun to wear the headscarf (*hijab*) and had made the pilgrimage to Mecca, worked full time while also keeping up with household cooking, washing, and cleaning. Her energy seemed tireless, but her children also helped out with whatever they could, and the household impressed me with its intensely cooperative spirit.

All five of Huriya's children were under ten years old when she was widowed. At that time, her father's brother, a well-connected religious scholar, helped her find a civil service job. Since then, Huriya had relied on her salary to support her family, supplemented by rent from an apartment she had inherited in the *medina*, and by her share of the proceeds of the rent from the unrelated neighbors in the building. As the children got older and began to earn money of their own, they also contributed to the household income. Her choice to live with her own family resulted from a sense that she would have more control over her own children, with no interference from in-laws. Relations with her late husband's family were cordial, although Huriya's family played a much more prominent role in the everyday lives of her children, who saw their father's family infrequently, usually on special occasions.

Within the family, Huriya also provided advice, financial support, and access to her connections in city administration. She gave small sums of money to a female relative who was divorced and in poor health but still had adult children living at home with her, only one of whom worked. In exchange, this relative and her daughters often did housework for Huriya. Tazi family members, however, resisted my attempts to attach the label of "patron-client" relationship to Huriya's actions, preferring instead to couch her generosity in terms of familial love and altruism. This was not because of Huriya's gender, as the Tazis also disliked the description for an uncle who served a similar role. Patron-client relationships, one Tazi family member of the third generation told me, were about "big men [who] are always trying to obligate you, to have you in their debt. [Our uncle] is not like that. He does everything because he likes to help people, not because he cares about having influence." Although some Tazi family members were indebted to others and tried to repay them in small ways, they did not like to see this as an obligation. Generosity was just a part of being "family," they asserted. Patron-client ties, another Tazi man told me, were for people outside the family.

Conflict within kinship networks can arise when someone refuses to participate in acts of reciprocity, leading to feelings of bad will. As Marcel Mauss might remind us, rejecting an offer of aid is tantamount to refusing a gift, which can damage the complex web of reciprocity that sustains social relations among Fassis (2002). Tazis maintained patron-client relationships as long as they remained in balance, and as long as both parties felt they were benefiting from the arrangement. However, these relationships were delicate. People were suspicious of gifts given for no reason, particularly if it seemed the giver harbored intentions for the other person to become indebted. A perception that the other person was seeking an advantage could immediately damage relations not only between the two individuals involved but also among entire branches of the family.

Marriage Practices

Women in the Tazi family also played a prominent role in forging links with other families through their children's marriages. In the past, Moroccan women exercised indirect influence in terms of selecting partners for their children, while male relatives handled the technical and legal aspects of the union. Today, sons and daughters frequently control their own incomes and choose marriage partners for themselves. Families are involved to a lesser degree than they used to be, although approving a potential spouse and determining the degree of freedom allowed in premarital interactions is still a parent's prerogative. Because women headed six of the nine Tazi households in the building, women were often the primary negotiators in marriage contracts for both their daughters and sons. Huriya, for example, went to the household of her prospective daughter-in-law, whom her son had met on his own, to negotiate the arrangements of the marriage on his behalf.

Within the Tazi family, choice of residence did not always follow the custom of living with the husband's family after marriage. Although the rise in the number of nuclear families reflects the increased importance of the conjugal unit in Moroccan society, among many Fassis, economic concerns were cited first and foremost in determining where a couple should live. "If a good job takes someone away from their family, they should follow the work," one of Huriya's sisters once told me. We were discussing a Tazi cousin who had just gotten married, and her husband was planning to leave his work in Fes and move with her to Rabat, where she was employed. Was this normal, I asked. "Anything is possible," she said. "If it happens that the woman's job is in Rabat, and she is making more money, then they should go there."

There were numerous exceptions to the custom of going to live with the husband's family, often related to spatial issues or future projects couples had in mind. The Tazis considered it important for a husband and wife to have their own living area so that they would not be "living right on top of one another, like everyone in the *medina* does," as one man expressed it. One of the three adult children of Si Mohammed Tazi who did not live in the building, the widowed Najia lived in a traditional *riad*, a house in the old *medina*, with her son and daughter, both of whom were married and had families of their own. Souad, her daughter, could have lived elsewhere, with her husband's family or in an apartment of their own, since the husband had a good job. Souad, who was in her late twenties, told me that because her mother's house was so large, each couple had its own floor and thus a measure of privacy. Also, Souad and her husband saved money they might have spent on rent for traveling, and for a future home of their own. Convenience and practical necessity thus often dictated where people would live.

While marriage still remains a goal for most middle-class Fassi women, they now have other aspirations that bring them into the public sphere, once strictly the domain of men. Two adult daughters of Si Mohammed Tazi who kept apartments in the building, Bouchra and Aicha, lived active lives that revolved not around the domestic space but around social networks forged outside the home. In this building where many women lived without men, Bouchra and Aicha represented different possibilities for women who do not marry or have children, and both were intensely involved with other families.

Bouchra was a large presence, a robust woman in her early forties with a terrific sense of humor. She received income from a number of sources, including an aunt in another city who was fond of her. Without children or a husband to occupy her, Bouchra had turned to religion to occupy her time, and she wore a conservative headcovering and overcoat more reminiscent of Islamic fashions from the Middle East than those of Morocco. Bouchra divided her time between Fes and Casablanca, where her best friend Zakia lived. The deeply religious Zakia had been a lifelong friend and was described in fictive terms as a "cousin." Zakia's family served as a surrogate family for Bouchra, and she often brought Zakia's children to Fes and took them around with her as if they were her own.

For Bouchra, being unmarried was more of a reflection of the overall economic situation in Morocco than of personal inclination.

"It's not as if I didn't have offers, especially when I was younger," she assured me. "There was one man who asked, but he was unreliable and did not have a job. What would I do with a husband like that? There are so many without jobs, they can never afford to get married, and that means a lot of women who will never marry either, since men always want to marry somebody who is a lot younger than they are. But anyway, I like my independence. The older men who would marry me are just looking for someone to take care of them, to be their maid, and I don't want to do that." Bouchra was content with her life, with her extensive network of friends in Casablanca, and her freedom.

Where Bouchra emphasized religion as her primary activity, her unmarried sister Aicha, also in her forties, worked full time as an administrator in the school district and was intensely involved with her work. In addition to her apartment in the Tazi building, from her salary she had purchased an apartment in a new neighborhood on the outskirts of the Ville Nouvelle, which she rented out. Like Bouchra, she had close ties to other families. She spent much of her time living with her best friend's family, whose house was near the school where she worked. Aicha helped to tutor her friend's children, who called her their aunt. Aicha also had other significant ties that were as intense as family connections. During vacations, she traveled to Tangier to visit a family with whom she had forged a friendship in the 1970s. Aicha still maintained an apartment of her own in the Tazi building and ate her meals with family members whenever she was around.

Family size had declined steadily among the Tazis, following national trends. Although Si Mohammed Tazi had twelve children by the same wife, family size for the second generation was smaller, featuring on average four children per household. Among those of the third generation who had grown up and started families of their own, they had an average of two children each, and most stated a preference for having no more than three. The younger Tazis were great believers in family planning, and had absorbed government messages about the ease of providing for a small family. Family planning (*planification familiale* in French or *tandim al-usra* in Arabic) has become another indicator in Fassi eyes of class differences. People who consider themselves to be well raised (*mrabiyin*), one Tazi woman in the third generation told me, knew better than to have more children than they can reasonably care for. Large families are associated with generations past, and Fassis told me that "in this modern era there's no reason to [have a big family]; there are not enough jobs or money to go around anymore." Scarcity of resources is one reason offered for having a small family, not only because one might not be able to provide for offspring, but also because of the dearth of employment opportunities children will grow up to face. Many middle-class Fassis compared families with many children to "machines" or "animals" who gave no thought to how they would feed so many mouths. In contrast, families who practice *tandim al-usra* consider themselves to be rational, intelligent humans, capable of planning for the future.

A large family size is linked with poverty and a lack of education, and middle-class Fassis from the Ville Nouvelle associate large families with life in the *medina*, where people live "right on top of one another in quarters that used to be for horses," having "baby after baby." "This is not a farm; this is the city, and extra children are only going to make more problems for society," one Tazi male told me.[14] Others mentioned the fact there are "fewer people who can help" to raise a family, as more women now work, and finding reliable maids is said to be notoriously difficult.[15]

Nisba and the Significance of Family Origin

Although endogamous marriage was rarely practiced in the Tazi family, many Tazi family members stated a marriage preference for Fassis with similar social backgrounds, that is, those from larger networks of old families who trace their origins back to Andalusia.[16] Tazis did marry those whose names placed them outside the pantheon of "good Fassi families," and there were some marriages with Moroccans who did not come from Fes at all. If the marriage was a success, the spouse's origin was a non-issue. But in difficult marriages the offender's family background was often cited as the first sign of trouble. "Her husband doesn't come from a good family," one man, Kamal, said when I asked him to explain why a woman in the Tazi family was having marital problems.

When I pushed him to clarify what he meant, he explained, "The family isn't known. They're not of Fassi origin." Or, when another couple was on the verge of divorcing, the Tazis said the marriage was ill fated from the start. "His family is from Casablanca and nobody knows them. How are you going to know whether he will treat your daughter well if you don't know his people?" one woman asked rhetorically.

Family names are profound social identifiers in Moroccan society, as Geertz and Rosen have noted (C. Geertz 1979, Rosen 1984). The principle of *nisba* concerns a linguistic form that indicates not only the kin group to which a person belongs, but also other information such as hometown, profession, or religious brotherhood (Rosen 1984: 20). Derived from the Arabic root *n-s-b*, meaning "ascription," the various meanings of *nisba* include, according to Clifford Geertz, " 'ascription,' 'attribution,' 'imputation,' 'relationship,' 'affinity,' 'connection,' 'correlation,' and 'kinship' " (1974: 39). In particular, the *nisba* system is still used to indicate membership within a prominent family. The *nisba* system reflects a belief in Moroccan culture that "a very considerable part of an individual's character is constituted by the social milieu from which he draws his nurture. . . . To be attached to a place is, therefore, not only to have a point of origin—it is to have those social roots, those human attachments, that are distinctive to the kind of social person one is (Rosen 1984: 23).

Family name and place of origin are closely interlinked in conversations about others. In Fes, family names were deemphasized by those who did not come from families considered prestigious, who argued that *nisba* was a prejudiced strategy designed to maintain the power of particular families. Scheherezade, the self-made woman described in Chapter 2 whose family originated outside Fes, claimed that "the same people have been using their names for years to stay in power. They only help each other out." But to the Tazis, the *nisba* system was still significant in the way they understood others; for example, in explaining the reasons a marriage might have failed. In marriages, family origin is a pragmatic concern as well. Because of the relative imbalance in men's and women's legal power in marriage, a wife often needs her kinspeople to intervene with the husband's family to help resolve difficulties. When the family is unknown, and when they live far away, the traditional networks for persuasion are absent. To marry one's daughter to a non-Fassi is thus still considered a gamble, as the husband may reveal himself to be unreliable once the marriage takes place.

Name and place are significant to the point where, when the Tazis talked about a notoriously noisy and disruptive family who lived in the neighborhood, they attributed the family's difficulties to the grandmother's Algerian origins. These concepts are operative in business

Figure 4. Fassi weddings are festive, all-night affairs where female guests feel comfortable dancing in mixed company. Here, the author is preparing to make her entrance into her own wedding. Her husband is at the right.

deals as well, where a prominent family name can make someone more disposed to potential transactions. While non-Fassis downplay the prestige of certain names, many people still consider them to be significant. Names are a starting point for approaching strangers by understanding to whom they are connected. As Lawrence Rosen has written, Moroccans see "a contextualized individual . . . and it is through this individual's situated actions that place and attachment to one's own network of affiliations may be known and shaped" (Rosen 1984: 59).

In terms of naming conventions in the neighborhood, the building was referred to as the building of the Tazi family (*l'immeuble dyal-'a'ila Tazi*). Everyone owning an apartment in the building was a Tazi, as the female daughters of the late patriarch still keep Tazi as their surname, following Moroccan custom. Significantly, Tazi remained the primary familial attachment for most of the daughters' children as well. Habiba, another widow in the building, lived with her adult son, who had inherited significant property from his father yet now had little contact with his father's side of the family. In another example, Mounia and Ahmed, a Tazi brother and sister who were both living in the building with their families, had at one time both been married to siblings in a family from Meknes. When Ahmed divorced his wife, Mounia and her husband relocated to Fes from Meknes to live in the Tazi building with their children. Finally, although Huriya's children had a different patronym from their mother, when identifying themselves to other Moroccans who asked them what family they came from, they frequently responded, "My father was a Berrada, my mother is a Tazi," thus indicating their membership in two lineages.

In Sefrou in the late 1970s, when asked to describe genealogy, Sefrawis commonly mentioned first the older, influential men, with emphasis placed on individuals with whom they had patron-client ties. Women were never mentioned. Geertz calls this the "name cluster," whereby people see individuals as related to surrounding circles of people, obligated to them in various relationships of patronage. For the Tazis this principle is still operative, yet with the significant variation that people consider women as heads of households in their own right, and people often stated a woman's name when I asked about Tazi family structure. Granted, the last name itself still revealed its patrilineal origins. Yet Tazis did not automatically mention an older, influential male when asked to describe their kinship attachments. The daughters of Si Mohammed Tazi, who owned their apartments, were not simply skipped over in favor of an adult son or the long-dead patriarch. Rather, people who knew the Tazis, as well as the Tazis themselves, conceived of social arrangements emanating from particular households within the building. In this conceptualization, women are at the center of networks involving reciprocal relations and obligations that have been erected over the course of the adults' lifetimes.

Conclusion

A shift in women's remunerative employment to the public sphere since the 1970s has been accompanied by other changes in living arrangements, particularly in matters of marriage. Despite some of the changes, many couples still live in the Fes Ville Nouvelle surrounded by kinspeople, in networks of support and patronage that echo the arrangements of the past. The form of these relationships is still based on ties organized along patriarchal lines, yet women have often stepped in to fulfill male roles in their dealings with both kin and non-kin. Many Fassis have moved out of the old *medina*, where women were once sequestered within the domestic space, leaving only to visit family or go to the public baths. Women now have more opportunities in the work force, education, travel, and mobility. Furthermore, the available living spaces themselves dictate a change in patterns of living. In the Ville Nouvelle, familial living patterns have shifted to accommodate the types of structures available—French-built apartments rather than traditional houses centered around a courtyard, for example.

For the Tazis, consanguineal ties are the most significant ordering principle for life in their family-owned building. The renters, many of whom have been there just as long as the family, were sometimes spoken of as fictive kin, but this was not always the case. Family remains the most secure resource for financial support for the Tazis, and although not all family members are equally well off, the Tazis take care of those who have fallen on hard times. Family members rely on each other for connections leading to employment, and in an economy where very few have access to resources, for the middle class, family ties are often the most important source of stability, encouragement, and advancement. Women draw on kinship ties in matters of marriage and divorce, which is why Fassis emphasized the importance of marriage with other known families, who could be counted on to share the same values concerning arbitration or familial pressure in the event of marital problems.

Having done well by one's family, by supporting them both emotionally and financially, earned respect for Tazi family members both male and female. Huriya commanded esteem for her career, her wisdom, and the admirable work of having raised five children. Income was also a factor in how the siblings related to one another. Regardless of their gender, the Tazis who had more money than others were linked in ties of patronage with other, less fortunate siblings and with non-kin. They lent or gave money and hand-me-down clothes when needed, while in return, the person receiving the favor might send a child over to do a laborious task, such as cleaning sofa covers, or doing the family's laundry.

Life in the Ville Nouvelle has become more compartmentalized than in the *medina*, as each family occupies its own apartment, with individual facilities for bathing and cooking. Yet aspects of communal life still remain important to the Tazis, maintained by the constant visiting among family in their building. Although women are no longer secluded within the home, strong echoes of social mores discussed by Hildred Geertz for Sefrou in the late 1960s nonetheless remain. When not working, shopping, visiting friends, or going to school, women spend a great deal of time at home, sharing news with one another as they prepare food or help each other with housework. Friendships between cousins, sisters, aunts, and nieces are enduring. Men prefer to socialize outside of the home, in the streets or in cafés with their friends, although both male and female relatives often gather together at night to watch television.

Concerning the importance of kinship, David Schneider distinguishes between the normative system, consisting of "rules and regulations which an actor should follow if his behavior is to be accepted by his community or his society as proper" (Schneider 1972: 37), and the cultural system, which is more abstract. The cultural system consists of a shared sense of "how the world is structured," how men and women perceive their environments, and how they give meaning to existence. Although more static than the norms, the cultural system is amenable to change. In addition to understanding the connections among kin (by blood, marriage, and so on), it is important to grasp how people make use of these connections. In the case of the Tazis of Fes, and more generally in Moroccan kinship practices, the norms have expanded to allow a much greater variety of kinship networks, particularly those involving women. Environment, personal circumstances, and economics often contradict older "norms" such as seclusion and gender hierarchy. Kinship is one set of ordering relations in Moroccan society, at a different level from the state, and from other networks in which an individual might find him- or herself. Where possible, people draw on family ties for support, and family remains the most significant and dependable source of aid in times of crisis. Yet each situation is unique and complex, and "norms" cannot really tell us about the intricate relationships forged among individuals, based on a lifetime of knowledge of the debts and obligations incurred among them.

The ambivalence of Moroccan naming practices (noted elsewhere by Hammoudi 1993), which exclude women from the patriline while simultaneously depending on them for its maintenance, continues to exist, yet women's public significance to family kinship and social networks has increased. As property owners and salaried workers, they control resources that, if managed correctly, place them in high esteem among their neighbors and kinspeople. While thirty years ago, women's networks were "unnamed" and therefore harder to see, in the case of the Tazis, they are apparent in everyday interactions with people from the neighborhood and beyond. An increase in women's employment and the acceptance of women's presence in the public space has widened the range of potential contacts a woman can form during her lifetime. Social networks create a web of complex interrelationships that demonstrate the mutually beneficial possibilities for those who are included in such networks.

However, these social networks are not without conflict. Tensions are not uncommon over property or marriage, and as property values in the neighborhood rise, the Tazis have begun to disagree over whether or not to sell the property. Located in the center of Fes, the real estate itself carries a high premium, since apartments in newly constructed apartment buildings frequently fetch up to $80,000. In recent years, a popular tactic of developers has been to tear down the historic French buildings in favor of rapidly constructed modern high-rises. An old cinema and café, sources of many fond memories for the Tazis, have disappeared, and the buildings that remain are dwarfed by the new construction. Tazi family members sometimes talk of leaving, of selling their joint interests for a high price and moving to quieter neighborhoods on the outskirts of town. No one has yet made the move to do so, and turning out the renters, who are said to be "like family," and who pay around three hundred dirhams monthly rent, would inevitably be difficult.[17] Undoubtedly the sale of the property would also cause conflict among family members in terms of the division of proceeds.

Despite widespread accusations non-Fassis often made of the power and influence of Fassis, it was not clear that kinship networks would be sufficient to negotiate an increasingly globalized world. Among the third generation of Tazis, although some had managed to secure employment in small family businesses or local civil service positions, others had left the country seeking work elsewhere in Morocco or in Europe, the Gulf states, or the United States, and many were simply unemployed over the long term, with no immediate prospects. In this younger generation of Tazis, the hold of family ties remains strong, but migration and economic pressures dictated that many of them would move elsewhere.

Fassi social networks are often useless in other cities. Although distant relatives who have the Tazi last name can be found in the highest offices of government and commerce, the Tazis who remain in Fes have often lost contact with branches of the family who have moved elsewhere. Social networks facilitate everyday interactions, local business deals, and bureaucratic processes, but in an area where there are few jobs and many unemployed, these networks can only go so far. Emigration is becoming more and more common among Fassis, who, while they still maintain their old ties with family, are unable to actively participate in the day-to-day maintenance of these networks that determine status and social position among those who have stayed behind.

Kinship relations are not fixed but are flexible and fluid, constantly shifting as people age, change jobs or residence, marry, divorce, retire, migrate, or experience interpersonal conflict. Since the time of my fieldwork, the Tazi family has experienced many of these changes, which have altered the networks described herein while not eliminating them. With changes in demographic structures, and with more women likely to be employed in the public sphere, residential and financial patterns have been significantly transformed over the past thirty years. One out of every five households is female-headed, and in many cases, even when a husband is still present, residence can be matrilocal. Women incur prestige not only through their family names but also through their own social networks (extending beyond the family), management of property, and resourcefulness. While person-centered patron/client networks such as the ones Geertz describes for Sefrou are still significant, we are now more likely to see women at the center of these networks.

These patron-client ties have been described as features of patriarchal social organization, and they serve as a conduit between state, local authorities, and the neighborhood itself. The presence of the same family, living in the same building for thirty years, is not unusual in the Ville Nouvelle, and neighboring dwellings are also composed of families who have been in the area for just as long. Despite the transience of urban life and the passage of time, such families continue to anchor the neighborhood, although as children emigrate and the old buildings are torn down to make way for high-rises, the continuity of these social networks remains uncertain.

Chapter 6

Occupying the Public: New Forms of Gendered Urban Space

He who takes his wife out in public divorces her.

What a woman sees of the sky is only that which passes over the circle [the open roof over a household].

—*Moroccan proverbs*

Scene one: late spring 2002, a warm, sunny day near the central market of the Ville Nouvelle. On the sidewalk of a busy street, a woman sat with her baby, begging. People stepped over her, largely ignoring her chanted litany.

"Please, some of God's charity. Sadaqa min Allah. Please, money for bread."

Near the spot where the woman was sitting, I waited for photos to be developed at a one-hour lab. I stood close to the photo lab, which was full, knowing that to stand too far from my destination meant I could not duck inside if someone approached me. To be too stationary in a public place was to invite harassment—a woman not constantly in motion must want something. To make eye contact with anyone was also risky. I adopted my usual closed body posture, trying to look hostile, ignoring the occasional "hellos" from men as if I were deaf. As a point of reference I kept my eyes on the woman, watching her as she pleaded with passersby, her baby cradled in her arms. The woman's djellaba was dirty, her bare feet rough and callused. Across her face, under her eyes, she wore a litham, *a black face veil. The hood of her djellaba was pinned over her head. The way she wore the hood and the* litham *was an old Moroccan style, seen only on very old women in the medina. Now, young Fassi women who want to cover up favor silk scarves and neutral coats imported from Egypt.*

I had asked Fassis about the beggars who always stationed themselves outside the shops on Mohammed V Avenue. They were heavily concentrated in this area, the ones with extreme disabilities closest to the central market.

Fassis were dismissive, stating that begging was a profession like any other, and that these people were "bused in from the countryside" and that they went home every night laden with coins. Many claimed the women borrowed other women's babies to use as props.

But this woman looked particularly mskina (poor, to be pitied), and the baby, I soon realized, was definitely hers. Too young to walk or even sit up, the baby, who had been sleeping when I arrived, began to cry. The wails grew louder and louder, the mother attempting to quiet her small charge, but to no avail. Finally, she unbuttoned the front of her djellaba and pulled out her breast, which the baby quickly latched onto. Until the baby drank its fill, they sat there like this, the veiled woman with her breast in full view, the child sucking happily away. I looked at the faces of the people passing by for a reaction, but they barely seemed to notice.

Scene two: a posh exercise club in one of the wealthier new neighborhoods of the Ville Nouvelle, near the crumbling French army barracks and an old French-built racetrack once used for horses. American Steel Fitness was the first club in Fes to have separate floors for men and women, so people could exercise every day, rather than on a rotating schedule, as in the other clubs. Women could pass through the men's space on the ground floor, but men must never come upstairs. Yet the club was poorly constructed, and over the space women used for aerobics classes, slanted mirrors revealed everything to the men lifting weights below. When the club owners, an American and a Moroccan American who had come from the States to try out a new business venture, realized this oversight, they quickly installed curtains to appease their female customers.

It was late in the spring of 2002, and the days had grown quite hot. In the exercise club, all the heat rose up to the women's area, and while there were never more than two or three men downstairs during the day, the upstairs area was always crowded with women. About ten of us waited in the aerobics space for the teacher to begin her class. There were a few students, well-to-do housewives, cosmopolitan women wearing stylish exercise outfits. Already sweat trickled down our faces, even before we had begun exercising. The teacher came in and started the music without closing the curtains. I was grateful—the curtains were heavy, dark blue affairs, and once they were shut, all circulation of air ceased. But others were not so happy. A woman in her thirties, who always exercised in a headscarf even though she wore a tight leotard that left nothing to the imagination, angrily strode over to the curtains and resolutely closed them. Another woman, one of the perfectly made up beauties who often crossed over into the men's section for weightlifting demonstrations, argued with her.

"Come on, it's so hot," she said. "I'll stand there where they can see me if you care so much."

"Shame on you!" the other woman snapped. "They don't have the right *to look at you or at me. It's forbidden (haram) for the men to be able to leer at us while we exercise."*

"There's nobody down there!" the second woman said. "See for yourself. There are no men there right now!"

"She's right, if you stand over there, they won't see you with the curtains open," the instructor said. "That would be the easiest solution."

"Do you have no shame?" the first woman said. "The curtains stay closed, or else I'm leaving the club!" she threatened. Shrugging her shoulders, the instructor began to teach the class.

We sweated through an hour of aerobics, the woman with the headscarf taking her usual position close to the mirror where she watched herself the whole time, never paying much attention to the teacher, while the second woman visibly displayed her unhappiness about how unbearably hot it was. Afterward, in the dressing room, the drama continued.

"Who does she think she is?" said the woman who had argued for the curtains to be left open. The veiled woman was nowhere in sight, but could have still been within earshot, and the speaker spoke loudly, as if hoping her nemesis would hear. "She's no prize. Does she think the men want to look at her anyway?"

"It was soooo hot!" someone chimed in sympathetically.

"She acts like she's so pious, but it must come from the heart, it's not how you dress or whether or not the men can see you!" insisted the woman, still loud enough that anyone standing at the door could hear her. "Those fundamentalists (ikhwaniyin), we can't understand them. They wear tight clothes, they cover their heads. She's crazy, that one. This gym, it's not for the fundamentalists. If she doesn't like it, she needs to stay in her house." The woman grabbed her shampoo bottles and wrapped a towel around herself, storming off to the shower. Her friends shook their heads sympathetically and followed her.

Scene Three: a cyber café in my neighborhood of the Ville Nouvelle, one of the many Internet locations that had cropped up all over Fes in the past few years. The customers ranged in age from seven-year-olds playing games to men in their fifties, with men outnumbering women. Some used the computers to work on their résumés, others to search for jobs online. A few boys played video games, while older men scanned visa and consular information, hoping to learn something that would help them get out of the country. There were always religious people looking at Saudi websites with the latest sermons from mosques all over the Middle East, sometimes playing Qur'anic recitations loudly until the cyber café owner asked them to turn the volume down. The high, nasal warble of the recitations contrasted radically with the American hip-hop someone else blared from his computer station, and with the din from the café that was below us, which was full of people in late afternoon.

At this time, high school or university students occupied most of the twenty computers. As usual, most were doing Internet "chats," typing messages in transliterated Moroccan Arabic, French, or English (but usually French), with Moroccans or foreigners from all over the world. Next to me, three teenaged girls wrote messages to a boy in Tangier. It was clear that one in particular had her sights set on the boy, and their messages to one another grew more flirtatious as the other two girls giggled. She typed rapidly in French, responding to questions about how she looked, her age, and what she liked to do for fun. "Can we chat on the phone sometime?" he asked. "What's your cell phone number?" She typed that in for him, and they made plans for a rendezvous. "Now I'm going to send you my picture," she wrote, taking a diskette from her purse, and expertly pasting a file in an email attachment for him to see, and sending it off. They waited a few minutes for him to get the message. "Vous êtes très belle," he responded. "I want to meet you," which set the three girls off into paroxysms of giggles, the main one blushing and covering her face with her hands.

"Wait, wait, look, he asked you something else," one of them said, pointing at the screen. The girl read his question out loud. "'You are a virgin?' Eh, of course! What does he think I am? Shame (hshuma) *on him!" she scoffed indignantly, then typed in "Bien sûr!" She looked at both of her friends. "Hshuma!" she announced again.*

What is the anthropologist to make of these three episodes? I witnessed all of them as attempts to consider the broad question of "women in the public space." The thread of "shame" is an element running through all three episodes, although this did not become apparent to me until later. In the retelling, the three anecdotes seem disconnected, evocative of vast class disparities in Moroccan society. What are the connections among these incidents: a beggar breast-feeding on a street corner, two middle- or upper-class women arguing at an exercise club, and a lycée student challenged over the internet about her virginity?

This chapter explores the changing nature of public space, and the ways space in Fes is contested, appropriated, and defined by its users—here, with an eye toward the gendering of new urban spaces. In every place, whether at the beach, market, office, street, or café, the mixing of unrelated men and women is an endeavor fraught with tension. When women intrude on "male" spaces, they will be reminded of their transgression, whether by the catcalls and invitations that follow them down the street or by the male gazes that seem to sear the body with intimate, shameful knowledge.

What are the rules for women's presence in different public spaces?[1] These "rules" are constantly discussed, challenged, and negotiated. The male presence is never questioned; at issue is not the mixing of genders,

but the limits that women may not cross. The transgression of these limits could lead to chaos, but contradictorily, the limits themselves appear
to be constantly receding. No space is neutral, and context and timing
are everything. What may be perfectly fine at four in the afternoon is
wrong at midnight. What is acceptable when a woman is accompanied
by several friends is wrong when she goes alone. Frontiers and limits are
constantly under discussion, erased, and produced anew. In efforts to
define space, it sometimes seems that Fassis are arguing with themselves
as much as with others. Which vision of their city, of their nation, are
they arguing for?

By examining Fassi women's social performances in everyday situations, we can better understand how people navigate among competing
ideologies to test the limits of gender in a variety of social situations.
Through "everyday practices," practitioners of culture regain their
agency as they manipulate the basic rituals and rules of social organization and turn them to their own ends (de Certeau 1984: xiv). The
preceding examples of women's spatial practices highlight the incon-
gruities, possibilities, and conflicts inherent within Fassi social life.

Over the past fifteen years, the appearance of new spaces for social
interaction in urban Morocco suggests that a straightforward analytical
division of Muslim social spaces into "public/male" and "private/
female" is inadequate for comprehending the ways Muslims actively
construct gendered social space.[2] During my fieldwork, I noticed that
arguments over how women should occupy particular social spaces often
prompted discussions about the appropriate place of women in Moroccan society. In local disputes concerning how to regulate interactions
between unrelated men and women in spaces that often seem designed
to facilitate them, there was often more at stake than a single place.
Debates over the possibilities and limitations that delineate gendered
urban space speak to larger contestations over the position of women in
modern Muslim nation-states such as Morocco. As Diana Taylor has written, "battles for land and national identity have been staged on, over,
and through the female body—literally and metaphorically" (1997: 32).
Space becomes an extension for debates taking place elsewhere in society, such as over the proposed revisions to the *mudawana* personal status
code.

Divisions of space such as "public" and "private" are too often
mapped out onto gendered space, with the assumption that one gender's entry into another's space constitutes a social transgression. However, as women and men in the Middle East and North Africa
increasingly occupy the same public spaces for social and economic reasons, women's presence and movement through public space must be
reexamined. Urban spaces in particular offer an opportunity to examine

how discourses of modernity are accepted, contested, or transformed by their users. Here, my concern is with the gendering of social space in the city of Fes. I examine women's disputes over social space to show how people navigate among competing ideologies to test the limits of gender. In the Moroccan context, two particularly prominent ideologies are represented by gender-focused discourses of the nation-state and its Islamist critics. The nation-state characterizes the Moroccan female citizen as simultaneously modern, secular, and Islamic, while an oppositional religious discourse frames the nationalist vision as hopelessly enslaved to Western secularism, suggesting that the Moroccan woman needs to "return" to an authentic, "traditional" Muslim identity, modeled after the imagined example of the Prophet.[3] The spread of both discourses has been influenced by the increased flow of Moroccan migrant populations between Morocco and Europe, North America and the Middle East, as well as the proliferation of new technologies of communication such as satellite dishes, the Internet, and cell phones.

Responding to both positions, Fassi[4] Moroccans often draw on local meanings to create identities for themselves that both resist and transcend these ideologies. These include notions of what it means to be Fassi and female, shame as a positive attribute, and hospitality. I use Michel de Certeau's concept of "everyday practices," to show how middle-class Fassi women manipulate competing ideologies and turn them to their own ends (1984: xiv). Whether Moroccan women are arguing over the divisions of space in an exercise club or over how to respond to an invisible suitor met over the Internet, their everyday practices indicate how users appropriate social space, articulate conflicts, and respond to ideologies in locally meaningful ways.

The Ville Nouvelle of Fes offers a unique opportunity to observe these processes in urban areas of the Muslim world that are not considered central to political and economic operations of power.[5] An examination of provincial cities complements existing anthropological studies of urban areas of the Middle East and North Africa that have focused on cities that are loci of government and political power, such as Cairo or Casablanca.[6] The provincial character of a city like Fes, with a population of over a million residents, makes it an interesting area for inquiry. Competing discourses concerning the identity of the nation-state are received and transformed in innovative ways that may be lost in studies that focus on capital cities, despite the attention paid to individuals who are themselves marginal to operations of power.

Recent studies that focus on the lived experience of individuals in Moroccan urban environments have focused on the hegemonic effects of media, modernity and globalization, and on the hybridity of women's expressive discourses in the marketplace.[7] In *Picturing Casablanca*, for example, Susan Ossman characterizes Casablanca as a postcolonial space predicated on representation and colonial planning, governed by abstract media images that lead to a fragmented existence. In part this reflects a trend in anthropological studies of urban space since the 1980s to focus on representation and on the city as text (Jacobs 1993: 827). While indirectly concerned with similar issues, I am seeking to revive the specificity of a lived city, examining how discourses from outside are received and interpreted by individuals.

In the case of Fes, academic research has further ignored the Ville Nouvelle in favor of studies of the ancient *medina* as a site for religious learning and a place where "traditional" trades and professions are still practiced. Yet Fes, like many other Moroccan cities affected by French colonization, is divided. The Ville Nouvelle possesses its own substantial population of modern city dwellers, virtually ignored in the literature. How do individuals in Fes, particularly women, consider their relationship to the built environment? How do local and global discourses interact in the gendering of modern Muslim cities? More important, which discourses are most salient to women as they determine the "rules" for occupying new urban spaces? Attention to these questions sheds light on the ways in which national and global processes play themselves out in specific local settings.

A focus on "everyday practices," or on individual efforts to contest or manipulate discourses of power, enables a shift away from framing this inquiry as a study of the ways "traditional" people deal with "modern" spaces and ideologies. The reified nature of this construction is limiting, as it continues to associate tradition with all that is "native," while modernity implies something imposed from above, usually from the West. Moving away from considering colonial and postcolonial space solely in terms of issues of representation and reception, De Certeau's emphasis on individual tactics that insinuate, manipulate, and finally reappropriate social space is more useful for highlighting human agency in response to powerful ideologies. Everyday practices consist of those small, sometimes fragmentary tactics that represent "the ingenious ways in which the weak make use of the strong" (de Certeau 1984: xvii). In Fes, women give meaning to urban social spaces by using their own cultural categories to shape space in a way that reflects the construction of a female, Moroccan, Fassi identity. This is not a neutral process, however. Through the ways in which people contest urban social space, more is at stake than just the creation of an individual identity. In defining the meanings and uses of new spaces, Moroccans are also making a claim for a collective vision of gendered identity and relations between men and women. Everyday practices, rather than being mere individual tactics, are profoundly social. In this case, gendered everyday practices assert an individual's idea of the proper place for women while simultaneously responding to and transforming various discourses about women's position in Moroccan society.

Moving beyond a focus on the *medina*, on Fes as an "Islamic city," or on representations of the city's colonial past, this chapter seeks to examine individuals in the Ville Nouvelle and their concrete ways of transforming urban space according to distinctive local conceptualizations.

The Public/Private Dichotomy: North African Meanings and Contexts

Attempts to view culture in terms of oppositions have been significant since at least the days of Claude Lévi-Strauss. Different conceptualizations of "public/private" or "domestic/political," have captured the attention of anthropologists for decades, and are often part of efforts to understand why gender inequalities exist in Euro-American contexts. The domestic realm comes to represent "lower-level, socially fragmenting, particularistic sort of concerns," while the public realm is the space of politics, religion, and other inherently "cultural" activities (Ortner 1974: 79). The tendency to perceive women as devalued by all cultures was later explained to be a function of "muting," whereby anthropologists themselves were guilty of privileging men and their worldviews. In actuality, the nature/culture dichotomy was an "ideological discourse" that had come to appear natural (Bloch and Bloch 1980: 26). This discourse, rooted in the Enlightenment tradition, had the added effect of dichotomizing and potentially oversimplifying what was once a more complex system of thought.

In the 1970s, anthropologists tried to complicate these oppositions. How were domestic/public dichotomies blinding anthropologists to other realities of the society under question? Mediterranean societies proved particularly useful in exploring this dichotomy, since men's and women's social worlds were largely separate. In Rayna Reiter's eyes, the rise of state societies was to blame for a decreased emphasis on the social worlds of women, which may have been more important in the past. Michael Herzfeld argues that while gendered oppositions did exist, they had become reified and told anthropologists nothing about lived social experience or meaning. In Greece, for example, people manipulated gendered oppositions, which were largely symbolic, and could be used to articulate a national identity vis-à-vis outsiders and foreigners. While social worlds were fairly segregated, this was due more to common interest than to any explicit devaluing of women's status. Public/private dichotomies have thus arguably been overemphasized at the expense of a nuanced understanding of other factors at play. Herzfeld wrote of a woman entering a café to publicly berate the proprietor; although she had entered a male space, her presence in the café would not have been questioned had it not been for her actions.

Similarly, in the Moroccan city of Fes, the gendering of spaces depends on the time a woman enters a space and what she intends to do there. At night, for example, Fassis do not consider it appropriate for women to wander the streets, but this is not, my friends insisted, because the street has suddenly become a "man's world" from which women are restricted. Rather, nighttime in Fes is when drunks tumble out of the bars looking for fights, when the glue sniffers (*shemker*) roam the streets in packs, and when prostitutes troll for customers. Women who are in public at this time risk association with this world, and even the men I knew preferred not to wander too far from home, but rather to "hang out" on familiar street corners within their neighborhoods, within safe reach of their homes. At night in the Ville Nouvelle of Fes, the street becomes a lawless place. Yet during Ramadan, the opposite is true, as everyone pours into the streets, fortified after the breaking of the fast, to shop for pastries, visit family members, or amble around with friends.[8]

Social scientists working in the Middle East and North Africa have long noted the culturally idealized orientation of women toward the home and men toward the street. "The most important rule in the code of movement," writes Willie Jansen about Algeria, "is that one should remain within the space reserved for one's own gender. . . . The feminine space is directed inwards, toward the courtyard; the masculine space is directed toward the outside, the streets. The difference in available space reflects the social hierarchy between the genders" (Jansen 1987: 183). Other analytical representations of the public/private dichotomy locate this divide within Islam and the idea that mixing between the sexes will lead to social chaos.[9] The street has been described as a place of reason, as opposed to the irrational, emotional world of women and the home.[10] However, more recent work has challenged the public/private dichotomy, arguing that much like Orientalist writings about the "Islamic city," the public/private dichotomy reflects Western secular biases and a tendency toward binarisms.[11] Some examples of recent anthropological scholarship that demonstrate a more nuanced view of the meanings of public and private include ethnographies that document women's roles in the marketplace (Kapchan 1996), as political and religious activists (Deeb 2006), and as transformers of social networks (Holmes-Eber 2003).

Spatial seclusion of women was a feature of urban Moroccan society until the 1940s.[12] In 1943, King Mohammed V presented his daughter in public without a veil, and around the same time, Moroccan nationalists instituted programs promoting education for girls (Mernissi 1987: 155).

After Independence, particularly in the 1970s with the government's creation of civil service positions, numerous women entered school and the workforce. In the 1960s, female employment increased 75 percent. The large majority of female workers during this period held jobs either as low status domestics or higher status government civil servants, while jobs in agriculture and textiles came next.

Despite the fact that spatial seclusion of women, particularly among the urban elite, was a more prominent feature of Moroccan life prior to the 1940s, it should not be assumed that women had no place in public life until the postcolonial era. Describing the seclusion of urban elite women, colonial officials and historians of the region imposed Eurocentric interpretations of public and domestic space onto North African contexts, which meant that women's activities often went undocumented and unnoticed. In North Africa, women always played a significant role in regional economies, although they were underrepresented in French colonial statistics because work was only counted in terms of observable markets and not domestic economic production (Clancy-Smith 1999: 28). In actuality, the spaces in which women moved always depended on environment, economics, and social class, and were not easily reducible to a set of rules or prescriptions.

Moroccan sociologist Fatima Mernissi has written of how women compensated for spatial restrictions by transgressing other boundaries. Mernissi recalls fondly how the women of her family employed tactics such as stealing a key to a forbidden radio that, once the men were out of the house, would link them with visions of the outside world, with romance and fantasy and freedom. The forbidden radio transmitted ideas that came to affect Mernissi's conceptions of the world, and through it she was exposed to news about feminists in Egypt, subversive nationalist discourses, and music from France and the Middle East.

Even within a single household, women were not of one mind about their seclusion. Many longed for the day when their activities would be less constrained, while others argued fiercely for maintaining the traditional divisions. Yet Mernissi argues that "roaming freely in the streets was every woman's dream" (1994: 22). When she went to visit her grandmother in the countryside, she noted that women's freedom of movement was much less restricted than in the city. Her grandmother Yasmina's harem "was an open farm with no visible high walls. Ours in Fez was like a fortress. Yasmina and her co-wives rode horses, swam in the river, caught fish, and cooked them over open fires" (41). Thus, even between city and countryside there were distinctions.

During much of her childhood, Mernissi sought to understand the boundaries of her existence. She even came to view the city of Fes as cordoned off into restricted areas, with the French imprisoned by fear, afraid to exit their safe zone and trespass into the territory of the Moroccans in the old *medina*. A cousin pointed out that "the frontier is in the minds of the powerful." Yet, as Mona Fayad has written, "It is up to those *inside* the frontier, however, to determine whether or not to recognize the frontier, whether it is established by colonialism or by patriarchal control" (2000: 89). The harem in which Mernissi grew up was contested, trespassed, and transgressed; it was "no more easily defined than the notion of boundaries which, the narrator remarks, continue to be elusive" (Fayad 2000: 91). In fact, Mernissi's experiences with her grandmother's living situation, and with the differing viewpoints of the residents of her own household, led her to conclude that the harem was a microcosm for the Moroccan nation itself, uncertain of its own boundaries, limits, and self-definition.

These communities of the past were not rigid and static, but were, in fact, "engaged in a process of redefinition that is in constant flux" (Fayad 2000: 93). From city to countryside, from wealthy to poor, spatial organization and restrictions on women varied widely. What is certain is that women contested, challenged, supported, and transgressed society's physical boundaries, even if this resistance was not always visible in the "public" sphere. Women in Mernissi's household were at the center of the stories they told, and they actively engaged with the nationalist movement, which aimed to resist French occupation and create new spaces for women in society. Mernissi's autobiography, then, reveals the dangers associated with perceiving the changing dynamics of physical space as evidence of some sort of cultural stagnation that existed prior to the "modern" era.

Because the visible range of movement for women has expanded in the past forty years in response to changing political and socioeconomic conditions, examining specific ethnographic performances can provide a useful view of how women themselves conceive of their presence in different spaces, especially as literal boundaries between domains are fluid and seem often to have disappeared. As urban women increasingly come to occupy previously "male" spaces, a breach in territorial distribution and domination opens up, limits are crossed, and the separation between "male" and "female" space is called into question.[13] Navez-Bouchanine has suggested that while traditional spaces in urban Morocco often sharply demarcate public and private space, the structure of the Villes Nouvelles lends itself to space that is neither public nor private but often both at the same time (Navez-Bouchanine 1990: 135).

Especially today, strict dichotomies such as "public" and "private," are insufficient for understanding Moroccan women's "ways of operating" (de Certeau 1984: xiv). While the range of movement for women has expanded radically in the past forty years, we must still interrogate specific instances to understand the meaning of women's presence in public spaces. Thus, "private" and "public" serve as loose, often metaphorical concepts that Moroccans consider "good to think with" (to quote Levi-Strauss), often juxtaposed as "inside" (*dakhl*) or "home" (*dar*) versus "outside" (*ala brra*). Context-specific, contested, and constantly shifting, these terms contain a range of meanings that may or may not be opposed. Metaphorically, *ala brra* can mean anything beyond the home's threshold, extending from the local market to the transnational contexts of migration outside Morocco. Fassis speak of "inside," or *dakhl*, to indicate a space currently inhabited, or to refer to one's own social milieu, class, or gender. *Dakhl* also means the careful balance (for women) of being seen yet maintaining concealment by refusing to acknowledge that one has been seen at all. Here, the term conveys a space of interiority. In the street, Fassi women project a desired image by remaining silent, and by never responding to the verbal overtures of men.

The idea of "home" (*dar*) is polysemic, having connotations not only of a place to dwell but of a familial space, symbolized by wives and children (Bourquia 1996: 23). The word contains significations beyond that of the individual dwelling, as even in the earliest days of Islam, *dar as-salam*, "house of peace," signified those lands in which Islam reigned, contrasted with *dar al-harb*, "house of war," meaning those lands which lay beyond the reach of Islam. Fassis move comfortably between "home" and "outside," yet the larger sense is always that "home" represents stability against the unknown, even as household compositions shift, and even as the nation-state fails to provide opportunities for its citizens.

Through discussions *about* place, Fassi Moroccans attempt to negotiate and sometimes delineate space and the rules for inhabiting it. Whoever defines a space assumes that he or she refers to a set of rules all can agree on; however, often individuals contest both the space and the rules for its occupation, particularly in the case of new spaces. At times, women extend principles for conduct in the home to a public space. The code of conduct for women requires that women "*t-hasham*," which literally means "to be ashamed," though Fassis explained that "*t-has-ham*" means being polite, obedient, pleasant, and demure, particularly in front of elders, men, and non-kin. All my colleagues from the Ville Nouvelle agreed that *t-hashaming* was a positive attribute best demonstrated by Fassi middle-class women, in contrast to the conduct of *medina* women, whose country origins led them to be loud, ill-mannered, and uncouth.

Other principles of conduct are more nebulous. Some Fassis stated their belief that women should not be seen by unrelated men without being fully covered. This belief extends to the idea that unrelated men and women should not share the same space, which was disputed by women who frequented cafés, claiming that ignoring the men who shared the same space was sufficient. Being associated with a particular family is also thought to guarantee a good reputation, particularly in cafés. Public spaces contain conflicting resonances, encouraging women to be both visible and invisible, simultaneously acting in the public realm yet out of reach. The threat of incurring social judgment, circulated by "gossip," *klam dyal nas*, is always present. As a bewildering array of "new" social spaces open up, whether to label them as "public" or "private" becomes less important than comprehending why Fassi Moroccans contest those spaces, and in which instances a particular viewpoint will prevail.

Moroccan society is still highly gendered, with many social activities limited to interactions with persons of the same sex. Examining the complex tactics of women's everyday practices sheds light on the logic of gendered social space in urban contexts. Through these tactics, women not only define their presence in physical and metaphorical spaces (such as the cyberworld) but also assert divisions according to social class, age, employment status, education, and religion. Many still associate women with domestic space, so that women's occupation of public space is often inflected with attempts to redefine such spaces as partly domestic or private, hence suitable for female presence.

Frequently, men and women are present in the same places but are associating solely with their own gender. In cases where the inevitable mixing of unrelated men and women takes place, Fassi women borrow from available rules for interaction, such as attempting to remain unseen or ignoring the presence of men entirely. When conflicts result, the concept of "shame" (*hshuma*) may be invoked to trump an opponent, suggesting that the other has strayed too far and is in danger of losing all morals. In new spaces people quarrel fiercely over how men and women should relate to one another and how women are to occupy the space. It is notable that I never witnessed similar debates concerning the presence of men, and also that most of the debates I heard were between women. When prompted, men made statements about women and space, but the actual disputes seemed to take place among women.

Common Domains: Street and Café

An example of the way women have integrated two historically "male" spaces in the Ville Nouvelle should offer context for the examination of new spaces. The complex "rules" for occupying the mixed spaces of cafés and streets involve successfully balancing appearances with actions,

with the threat of being perceived as sexually promiscuous as the punish-
ment for transgressions.[14]

Women were more likely to be present in the Ville Nouvelle cafés than
they were in the cafés of the *medina*, where I almost never saw women.
Among my middle-class Ville Nouvelle colleagues, younger professional
women and students (ages 20–45) went to cafés, whereas older women
and those who did not work or attend university never visited them.[15]
Rarely do the professional women who visit cafés sit with men, although
they often greet fellow coworkers at other tables before sitting at their
own. Female university students, however, told me that they go to cafés
to study but also to talk and flirt with the male students.

Although men claimed to have no problem with women's presence in
cafés, they sometimes qualified that there are certain cafés where
women might not feel comfortable. "Some of the cafés just aren't clean
(*naqi*)," Karim, an unemployed man in his thirties, said. "A place should
be clean if it is for women. Women would not like the popular (*sha'bi*)
cafés because they are so dirty (*musikh*)." In the Ville Nouvelle, *sha'bi*
cafés are often places that were built by the French, with décor that
seems not to have changed since. However, describing a café as "dirty"
(*musikh*) also conveys class differences. Middle-class residents of Ville
Nouvelle frequently refer to cafés in poorer neighborhoods or the
medina as *musikh*. A café that is *musikh* might also, I was told, be filled
with smoke and men who are *zufriya*, types who are inclined to bother
women, drink alcohol, and start fights. There are also upscale cafés that,
while physically very clean, are known meeting spots for prostitutes.
These have attracted the label of *musikh*, further illustrating the fact that
in this context, cleanliness is a social category that has more to do with
morality than dirt.

The level of comfort professional women expressed about particular
cafés often related to whether proprietors were cognizant of a woman's
place within familial, professional, and social networks. Association with
a particular family guarantees that café owners will be hospitable and
that women will not be harassed. The guarantee of hospitality in this
context transfers principles from the private domain into the public, as
a householder would never allow guests to feel uncomfortable. "Everybody here knows me," my lawyer friend Naima said of the café near the
courthouse where she worked. "I work with all these people, and the
waiters will not let anyone bother me." This tactic loosely applies rules
of hospitality and respect for guests to a world that was once solely the
domain of men.

For women, streets, unlike cafés, do not encourage lingering. The
street is a pathway between destinations: market, school, work, or home.
While women are always in motion, men lounge on corners or outside

Figure 5. Women outside a newsstand in the center of the Ville Nouvelle.

cafés. For men, the street outside one's building is an extension of the home, and a place to hang out with friends or relatives. However, men also tend to remain in the street closest to their own homes unless they are visiting friends elsewhere, and streets in unfamiliar neighborhoods possess a quality of unwelcomeness that encourages men to keep moving as well. During the daytime hours, women run errands or take walks with their girlfriends, but at night (except during the month of Ramadan), Fassi women do not go out.

My friends told me that Fassi women distinguish themselves by their demeanor, and that they should not be too aggressive, loud, or forward. Girls must conduct themselves unobtrusively, and those who do not fall in line are scolded that they "have no shame." Young, unmarried women are at a dangerous, vulnerable age, and they should do everything possible to avoid gossip (*klam dyal nas*). Yet at the same time, they need to dress stylishly, wear makeup, and be visible to attract potential husbands, who might see them in public and then ask around the neighborhood about the girl's family and marriageability.[16] Street harassment is still a problem, and the severity of harassment depends on factors such as tightness of clothes, facial expression, and the time of day, all potential indicators of sexual availability. In fact, the most common explanation Fassis of all ages gave for harassment was that it was a way of determining who might be a prostitute.

"Men just talk to see who might go with them," a middle-aged woman, Bouchra, explained, "and if the woman answers, it means she is fair game. A good girl (*bint an-nas*)[17] is ashamed and will never answer them."

Women's presence in the streets is fraught with more tension than within the domain of cafés. Young Fassi women in their twenties spoke to me of the social pressure they felt to be seen in public wearing the latest clothes, yet they walk a fine line in trying not to accrue negative judgment. This constant balancing act often results in a split in women's self-image. Fassi Moroccan culture insists on an acceptance of some parts of a modern, Western-oriented image and a rejection of others— yet just which parts are to be accepted and rejected is uncertain.

Media images contribute in no small part to this confusion, and satellite televisions, now accessible to all middle-class Fassis, send up provocative images from MTV, European and American movies, and soap operas. Simultaneously, satellite programs from the Middle East convey the contradictory message that the acceptance of Western fashions represents the Muslim world's dependency on and enslavement by the Christians. Some Fassi women have adopted a more Islamic style of dress in response. The practice of veiling (here meant to describe the wearing of a headscarf or *hijab*) is one tactic that many younger women have begun to employ within the public space. Whether they do this to avoid harassment or demonstrate their piety (as a few women who wore *hijab* told me), this concealment has variously been interpreted as extending the private space into the public, or as signaling the wearer's intentions not to engage the public at all.[18]

Tactics in New Spaces: Exercise Clubs and Cyber Clubs

As the preceding section demonstrates, in public spaces women must maintain a careful balance between visibility and propriety, advertising their beauty while creating a sense of separation between themselves and the words and gazes of unrelated men. But what are the rules for spaces that are neither exclusively public nor private, such as a mixed exercise club or a cyber café?

When American Steel Fitness opened up in the winter of 2001–02, it was all the rage among affluent Fassis. I joined ASF shortly after it opened, when a friend of mine who was an aerobics instructor left another club to work there, and over the next several months I became acquainted with some of the other members. Founded by a Moroccan American and his American business partner, ASF advertised itself as an American club. Equipment was imported at great cost from the United

States, classes were to start on time and with a high level of professionalism, and in the future, the male and female floors would be mixed.

At first, middle- and upper-class Fassis responded enthusiastically, and the club was always packed with women. In locker room conversations, women bragged about their travels overseas—summers on the Costa del Sol in Spain, and the "mixed" exercise clubs they had experienced in France, where men and women exercised together with no problems. A few women even trickled down into the men's section to observe "weightlifting demonstrations." For a while, the club was a symbol of a new cosmopolitanism that well-to-do Fassis previously had to go outside the city to find.

Yet gradually the novelty began to wear off. The aerobics instructors complained about their low, "un-American" wages. The showers were often broken. These were American prices for Moroccan quality, people grumbled. But the most contentious issue became the fact that men and women were sharing the same space, albeit on different floors, and that men could gaze up into the women's space from the mirrors. Amina was the most vocal in pointing this out, and before every aerobics class, I heard women wonder whether one of the "fundamentalists" would show up and insist on the curtains being closed.[19] Amina complained that the men might one day try to sneak up to the women's section, although I never witnessed anyone trying. Initially most of the customers had accepted the premise of the owners that Fes was "ready" for a Western-style club in which men and women would eventually exercise together. But with the increasingly strident voices of the "fundamentalists," the other women became more hesitant. Many ceased asserting their opinions that the club should be mixed. Soon the only women speaking were the ones who insisted on the closing of the curtains.

In the scene I described earlier, tensions that had been simmering finally came to the surface. Miriam, who wanted the curtains open because of the heat, described her opponent as being attentive only to the surface appearances of piety. Those who desired a strict separation of men and women ought to stay at home where no one could see them. But Amina, whom I interviewed about her views on the club, did want the convenience of belonging to an exercise club that was open to both sexes every day.

"I know in America this is how you do things," she told me. "But this is Fes. We're Muslims. It's *haram* (forbidden) the way some of the women act here." Amina, who was in her early forties, had recently started wearing the *hijab* and seemed interested in pointing out to other women that they were, as she said, "not acting like Muslims." She stated that it was important to remind people of the proper distance that should exist between men and women. Creating this distance was the issue, particularly due to the problematic placement of the mirror, which revealed what the separation of floors should have concealed.

Miriam, who argued with Amina but did not criticize her to her face, did not seem cowed until Amina had accused her of having no shame. Her religion was her business, she said, and Amina had no right to judge her. Shortly after this argument, she stopped coming to the club, and membership as a whole dropped off. Eventually the two owners returned to the United States, leaving the management of the club in the hands of the Moroccan American owner's family. The owners expressed their disappointment that Fassis "were not ready" for such a club. Miriam agreed, distancing herself from the women who wanted the curtain and calling them "typical Fassis." Although she was born and raised in Fes, she was not interested in claiming to be a Fassi, and she instead called attention to her Meknes roots. When I spoke to her about the fact that she had stopped coming to ASF, she told me in French, "I can't stand to be around hypocrites. It's because of people like them that this city does not progress." She distinguished between her own open-mindedness and the Fassi obsession with decorum, which she felt was entirely on the surface. Again, appearance and not reality was what Miriam felt the "fundamentalists" were focusing on, but she also emphasized that her differences with Amina related to categories of identity and not religion. Although most of the middle-class Fassis I knew were decidedly nonjudgmental about religious matters, they did distinguish subtly between their own moral behavior and that of Moroccans from elsewhere, a distinction that Miriam had turned on its head to emphasize not morality but hypocrisy.

The exercise club was not easily classifiable as "public" or "private," male or female, and thus, women argued over the physical separation of male and female space within the club, even when no men were present. Arguments in favor of the curtain posited the culturally valued attribute of "shame" over the cosmopolitanism and class-bound distinctions that the club originally carried. Assumptions that middle upper-class Fassis would accept "American" ideas about the appropriateness of mixed exercise clubs proved not to be true, and in this case, neither social class nor age were significant predictors of how women would respond to the issue of the curtains. While women who shared Amina's point of view about the curtains did not manage to convince the others of the correctness of their position; once the concept of "shame" was invoked, many simply left the club.

Cyber cafés are another new setting where men and women occupy a mixed space, both literally and metaphorically, as they browse the Internet. Diverse groups of people share the cyber café for multiple purposes, ranging from job hunting and game playing to looking for a

Figure 6. Upper-class teenagers at a mixed dance party.

spouse online or listening to Qur'anic recitations. Over time, the fees have gradually decreased to around 50 to 70 cents per hour, which has made Internet use more widely available to educated middle-class Fassis. Most of the customers at the cyber cafés are under the age of fifty, with the majority under thirty.

Young people have colonized the cyber cafés in Fes, both in the *medina* and the Ville Nouvelle. "Chat" programs, conducted in French or English, are popular with unmarried men and women, especially high school and university students. For women in particular, having a boyfriend in cyberspace can mean escaping the watchful eyes of parents and community. I knew unmarried professional women in their twenties and thirties who forged relationships with Moroccans in other cities that occasionally resulted in clandestine meetings, and of others who conducted "forbidden" relationships with foreign men.[20] Fassi men use the Internet to meet foreign women, and many marriages (and emigrations) are facilitated as a result. There is even a marriage service for the very religious, where devout Muslims all over the world post personals.

The Internet has undoubtedly assisted in the widening of social boundaries, offering increased opportunities for interaction between men and women.[21] The Internet also provides safety for those who wish to hide behind its anonymity. Yet certain Fassi values, such as the honor of maintaining female virginity prior to marriage, are still emphasized, as revealed by the conversation between the young women and their faceless male interlocutor. In the episode described earlier, Zahra was quick to send her photo to her chat partner. When he inquired about her virginity, she accused him of "having no shame," not because this was an embarrassing question, but because she was offended that he did not automatically assume her purity and good intentions.

The cybercafés themselves, as well as the metaphoric "space" of the Internet, are new sites in which interactions between men and women are not strictly regulated. As with the regular cafés, in the cyber cafés men and women sit at neighboring computers but most of the time do not interact with one another. In cyberspace, however, mixed-gender conversations are the order of the day. Women control to whom they will speak and what they will reveal, and whether to arrange physical meetings or limit their encounters to the printed word.

The narrator in Algerian novelist Assia Djebar's *Fantasia* writes, "When I write and read the foreign language, my body travels far in subversive space, in spite of the neighbours and suspicious matrons; it would not need much for it to take wing and fly away!" (Djebar 1993: 184). Writing in French in the Internet "chat" programs, the Moroccan women were like the three Algerian sisters in Djebar's novel *Fantasia*, who created a "secret spirit of subversion" by conducting pen-pal relationships with men all over the world (12). That French was the language of colonialism was not an issue for the young women I described in this incident. They came from the neighborhood where I conducted fieldwork, and they normally spoke Moroccan Arabic but conducted their chats entirely in French.

"It's just easier," Zahra claimed. "I don't know how to type on the Arabic keyboard." She admitted that her parents would not have approved that she was chatting with boys, but she said, "The people you meet [on the Internet] are not in the same room with you. There's no danger. I haven't done anything wrong." As for the people who shared the physical space of the cyber café with Zahra, she never talked to them, and she almost always came with her girlfriends. The presence of her friends as witnesses to her online relationships may have served as proof that Zahra was not doing anything wrong, but Zahra simply said she liked to go to the cyber café with her girlfriends because it was "fun." Other young women, however, did use the Internet alone.

The world of the Internet allows Fassi women to create new relationships that might transgress community standards of morality while simultaneously upholding personal moral codes. Using programs designed in other countries for use in languages that are not their native tongue, young Fassi women nonetheless make the space of the Internet their own. Demonstrating agency in manipulating the technologies and languages of others for their own purposes, they simultaneously exhibit a strong sense of adherence to local value systems. Such instances demonstrate that while "rules" for women's behavior in new spaces are not always clear, women themselves navigate among competing ideologies to occupy those spaces according to their own standards.

Imagining Poverty

The idea of "shame" had no bearing on how middle-class Fassis interpreted my description of the veiled beggar breast-feeding her baby on the street corner. I initially assumed that people must be shocked by the contrast between concealment (her face veil) and display. Was she crazy? Why did nobody seem to notice her? Was this not considered shameful? But when I described this scene, I received a surprising variety of responses that again revealed the anxieties of class and the projections Fassis placed on "others" they knew nothing about: here poor, possibly rural-urban migrants.

Most stated that the woman's actions, both the breast-feeding in public and the begging, indicated that she was "beyond shame" to begin with. People hypothesized that the woman probably came from a small village and now lived in one of the outlying neighborhoods in Fes. She was a rural-to-urban migrant, they imagined, who had gotten pregnant without a husband. Maybe she had tried to find work as a maid and ended up as a prostitute. Regardless, she did not "belong" in the city and lacked the skills and networks to make ends meet. She had no network of kin who could support her and was probably alone and destitute. Pregnant and unable to return to her family, she might have gotten mixed up with a network of beggars, whose leader gave them bus fare into the city center and positioned them at "stations" throughout the city. She would beg all day and then take the bus back to her neighborhood at night, where she slept in a rented room with other women. The leader would take the majority of her earnings and leave her with enough to buy food.

"But what else can she do?" Naima, who worked with many destitute cases at the Najia Belghazi Center, said. "Those people come to the city and have nothing—no family, skills, or education."

The display-and-concealment I had found so striking in the beggar's exposure of her breast was not an issue people found significant.[22] Rather, this anecdote elicited broader observations from a few women, who viewed this scene as a comment on social issues such as poverty and economic development.

"People like that have no shame," said Amina, who had little money herself. Amina was the woman I described in Chapter 3 who worked as a domestic and had never been divorced by her husband. "But they have no shame because they can't afford to. I might live a modest existence, but at least I have shame. If times are tough, there is always something you can do to avoid having to beg, even if you have no family to help you out, even if you have to work as a maid for a little while."

Middle-class Fassis made similar comments. Even if she had chosen to emigrate to the city, circumstance forced the beggar into her position, and there was something wrong with a system that produced so many people like this. Although Fassis suspect many beggars to be frauds, the sign of the child at the woman's breast indicated that she was genuinely without resources. The act of begging alone was considered worse than breast-feeding in public, a last-ditch tactic, the most visible proof that a person was absolutely desperate, forced to abandon "shame." "Having shame" is almost a commodity, something that gives women social capital. Moreover, "shame" is an attribute that women are proud of because it represents a civilizing force.[23]

"The veil doesn't mean what you think," Huriya explained. "It doesn't mean anything except that she doesn't want people to know who she is."

"You never know, the city is small, she might see someone from her village, and then it would be embarrassing for her to be seen begging," Rachid asserted.

"She can't help it," Amina said, in another conversation. "When the baby cries, you have to feed it. When you have to sit in one spot all day, you can't get up to look for a place to feed the baby. The streets aren't for feeding babies, the streets aren't a place to live, yet some of those people have no choice; this is where they live." She shrugged. "This thing is sad (*had shay hzin*), but it's God's will. There are poor and there are rich. Such is life."

Ultimately, in Fassi interpretations of the situation, the display and concealment I had thought was so dramatic meant very little. This was a mother feeding her child, and her status as a beggar and an outsider pushed her beyond the framework of Fassi judgment. What she did in the streets had no bearing on "normal" women's behavior, because already her actions placed her in a different category, as someone whose total loss of shame was not a symbol of defiance but of circumstance. At this point the beggar was concerned with mere survival, and not with trying to obey Fassi moral dictates related to shame. In imagining her life, Fassis were sympathetic. The story stimulated recognition that something was wrong with Moroccan society, in fact with any society in which such poverty exists and where people are allowed to fall through the cracks, abandoned by families, governments, and economies. The beggar was beyond judgment, and her incongruous actions said less about her and about the rules for gendering a space than about the failures of humanity.

Conclusion

These debates resonate well beyond the individual cases that I provide, as they speak to a larger vision of the role of women in the Moroccan nation-state. Images of how Moroccan women should occupy public space are abundant in magazines, newspapers, television, and government discourse. On the one hand, the Moroccan government promotes a unitary vision of the "Moroccan woman" as "the guardian of Moroccan cultural values at home and the proponent of modernity outside her house" (Moroccan Government website 2006). Meanwhile, the Islamist position, represented by nationally known figures such as Nadia Yassine and Abdelilah Benkirane, leader of the religiously oriented Party of Justice and Development, argues that the Moroccan woman's entry into the public sphere and demands for equality threaten the integrity of the Moroccan family and, in fact, the strength of the entire Moroccan nation.

These representations of the ideal Moroccan woman respond to other issues in Moroccan society, most notably the 2000–2003 conflict over legal reform of the Moroccan personal status code (*mudawana*) governing a woman's rights in marriage and divorce. As I have shown in previous chapters, the media tend to dichotomize these debates, representing positions over women's status as falling either into the more secular government camp (which nonetheless claims a religious basis for its formulations) or the more explicitly religious one. However, an interpretation of Moroccan women's presence in urban spaces indicates that women themselves do not fall neatly into these two categories. Small-scale disputes over space reveal how women both engage with and resist competing ideologies that might circumscribe their movement or force them to compromise their sense of morality.

Imbuing public spaces with aspects of the domestic sphere is one tactic by which Fassi women make their presence in urban public spaces more acceptable. But they are also acting in ways that are new and unique, creating a *bricolage* among available rules for conduct and improvising where necessary. The concept of "shame" proves to be socially significant, and Fassis invoke it when situations are muddied by the presence of competing ideologies.[24] "Shame" is a tactic used to control the terms of interactions in new social spaces: the "American-style" exercise club or the nebulous space of the Internet. But shame is also a valued attribute, as the incident with the beggar shows, as do Fassi readings of this woman as having lost her shame. Although some lower- and middle-class Fassis often assume that the upper class follows an imported, Europeanized moral code in their behavior, the conflicts over men's visual access to women in the elite exercise club reveal that this is not always the case. Even at the highest socioeconomic levels, Moroccan women have conflicting ideas about how men and women should occupy a shared space. Similarly, the incident in the cyber café demonstrates how women in cyberspace subvert community controls while simultaneously adhering to local values.

When subject to analysis, situations in which the gendered quality of a space is challenged reveal the current fault lines within Moroccan culture, and the issues that are contested. Controlling the dynamics of women's movement and its meanings is an activity in which disparate groups in Fassi society have multiple political stakes. High levels of unemployment for men, the circulation of new discourses over women's rights and empowerment, and efforts to define the Moroccan relationship to Islam are some of the issues that complicate the presence of women in new, mixed spaces.

As Fassi Moroccans negotiate the terms of their engagement with each other in new public arenas, the loss of "shame" is not the only threat to cultural integrity. People seem uncertain whether signs of the changing position of women in Moroccan society reveal a positive or negative future for the country. Some grumble that educated women take jobs away from men, while others claim that giving women more rights in marriage will lead to an increased divorce rate. Perhaps this is why contestations over women's presence seem so critical. Disagreements about women and space reveal profound uncertainties as to the future of the Moroccan nation-state, and as gendered territories are metaphorically defended or conquered, disputes reveal that more is at stake than simply the matter over which women are arguing. These are not merely debates about the degree of interaction between men and women in an exercise or a cyber club, but arguments over the interpretation of culture, and over conflicting views on how women should behave in an increasingly mixed society. Women in new, mixed spaces are, after all, doing other things besides exercising and searching the Internet. They are making economic contributions to the welfare of their families; receiving university degrees at a rate comparable to that of men; participating in the public sphere through nongovernmental organizations, demonstrations, and even parliament; and demanding to be accepted on their own terms.

Women's tactics shape urban spaces in unique ways, not only affecting the character of the French-built Ville Nouvelle of Fes but also revealing the ways that discourses about the position of women in the Moroccan nation-state are rejected or appropriated by users. Visions of nation are not crafted solely in the media, nor in economic and political capitals, but in provincial cities, towns, and rural areas, where the processes through which individuals define and make use of space are no less significant. Although the gendered character of new urban spaces often remains ambiguous or unresolved, the debates themselves are interesting for what they reveal about local efforts to negotiate competing ideologies in gendering new urban spaces, and by extension, the nation.

Chapter 7
Singing to So Many Audiences

Soumia came late to her old friend Maryam's wedding, just after she finished her last set at the Sheraton. At around one in the morning, when the dancing was in full swing, she arrived in the same outfit she must have worked in, a low-cut black evening dress that plunged dramatically in the front, revealing perhaps a little too much cleavage for the proper Fassi wedding party. She came over to where Maryam sat, perched atop a mountain of embroidered pillows, immobilized in one of the many glittering caftans that she had been dressed in that night. Maryam smiled tentatively beneath the heavy theatrical makeup that had taken several hours for a makeup artist to put on. Her face shining, Soumia took Maryam's hands in hers, which were always cold, even on a hot summer night.

"I want to sing for you," she said. Maryam's husband Karim quickly got up and went over to the leader of the twelve-piece wedding orchestra, requesting they allow Soumia to sing with them. For a few minutes, Soumia discussed songs with the orchestra's leader. The musicians finished the piece they were playing, then struck up the opening bars of a popular Arabic song, 'Amr Diab's "'Amarain" (Two Moons). It was a song Soumia performed on numerous occasions at the hotel bar, and she hoped Maryam would like it.

After a few moments of serenading the newly married couple, all eyes were on her. Soumia's talent with the Arabic songs was stunning, people always said so, her rich voice perfectly capable of the most complex melismas and gravity-defying embellishments. The two hundred or so wedding guests clapped and sang along, and when the band began a more traditional song, Oum Khultoum's "Ghanili shweya shweya" (Sing for Me a Little), Soumia brought the house down. She knew how to work a crowd, her voice in perfect form, her gestures expertly attuned to the audience, who were literally at her feet. An older gentleman in a linen *djellaba* swooned and bent his head to the microphone to sing a line; proper, *hijab*-clad women were moved to dance with abandon, and flashbulbs popped around the room like lightning. One woman had tears in her eyes. Soumia and the orchestra had a good chemistry, playing off one another, improvising and extending the song on and on. But then one of the orchestra's two singers pulled the plug on Soumia's microphone, tired of being upstaged by an interloper. The orchestra, while reputedly one of the best in Fes, still lacked Soumia's charisma. The wedding guests let out a collective moan of disappointment, the band's official singer quickly motioning the musicians to start up a new song. Soumia was a good sport about it; she was used to disappointment.

Soumia's singing was the high point of the wedding, and for months afterward, when family or friends came over to Maryam's mother's house to watch parts of the four-hour video of the wedding (a popular post-wedding practice), they invariably demanded the tape be forwarded to Soumia's performance. Usually these groups were all-female, but occasionally an uncle or a male cousin wandered in to watch for awhile. Observing Soumia prompted extensive reminiscing about the event, as the viewers listed those who had attended; how far they had traveled; and the joys, trials, and disappointments different families had experienced since the last big gathering. Soumia's performance of a classic Egyptian song also conjured up feelings of nostalgia, an enthusiasm for a song that defined the past and a sense of Arab nationalism and unity that had never materialized in any real kind of consensus. Listening to Soumia sing Oum Khultoum, people commented that no songs of the present could ever measure up to what had come before.

Watching the video of their families enjoying the festivities, people announced that this had been a "true Fassi wedding," at which all the good, old families were present. They shook their heads as if this were a disappearing phenomenon, and as if change threatened to make even weddings obsolete. Fassi weddings—with children running around underfoot, women dancing, men smoking outside, and everyone admiring the nuptial couple and the bride's multiple outfit changes—were similar to weddings I had been to in other parts of Morocco, and seemed in no danger of disappearing to me. When I said this, people tsk-tsked and shook their heads.

"On the surface, they might look the same," Fatiha said, gesturing at the television, "but other weddings are not like this."

"All the old Fes families are there," noted Rachid. "The Bennounas, the Ben Jellouns, the Berradas."

"Children grow up," Huriya explained. "A house fills, a house empties."

"There are no jobs," said Habiba, whose forty-five-year-old son was mired in a lifetime of unemployment. "Especially in Fes. People are forced to move to Casablanca, to Europe."

"This is why we never know if we will be together again like this," Huriya added. "Only Allah knows."

No other part of the videocassette elicited so much commentary as Soumia's performance, a moment that summed up the entire event, which was as important for the people it brought together as for the marriage it commemorated. People began to reminisce, not solely about the wedding, but about the past, about the condition of Fes itself and about the world that some felt had passed the city by, ever since the French had moved the capital to Rabat almost a century before. The talk produced by Soumia's performance was not trivial. The festive moment of the song now became an occasion for discussing life's temporality.

But Soumia herself was not forgotten. Inevitably someone commented about the singer herself, who had grown up among residents of the Ville Nouvelle but had fallen on hard times. After all, they said, she had to sing for a living, and we all knew what that meant.

"She has a sadness (*huzun*)," noted Selma, who was around Soumia's age and had recently been divorced by her husband. "I could see it in her eyes."

"She's had a hard life," Maryam affirmed, shaking her head. They were no longer close, Maryam taking the path of propriety while Soumia had gone in another direction.

"I can tell," Selma said sympathetically.

"The best singers have that quality," Fatiha observed. "Pain becomes their well. They draw from it better than anyone else."

"Does she hope to be married?" Selma asked Maryam earnestly.

"Someday," Maryam replied. "If God wants." My mind on another Moroccan woman, a singer I knew well, I decided to ask a question.

"Is it true that as long as she's working as a singer, nobody will marry her?" I was referring to the negative associations of professional female singers with prostitution.

"It's true," Huriya, always wise, shook her head. "If she wants to find a good husband, she has to quit working in that profession. A good husband will never accept her being a singer."

"God help her," somebody said.

Modernity and Recognition

Frederic Jameson has written that "the story of the private individual destiny is always an allegory of the embattled situation of the public . . . culture and society" (1986: 69). Publicly valued yet personally scorned, female singers in Morocco hold an ambiguous position, and the way audiences receive them indicates some of the limits for women in the Moroccan public sphere. During my fieldwork, I came to know one such singer, Layla, very well. In this chapter I consider the social biography of Layla, who sang at various hotels in Fes, as emblematic of the ways Fassi

Moroccans consciously experiment with and implement ideologies of modernity, adapting them to local practices and attempting to use them to prompt a kind of recognition that is often difficult to achieve.[1] The scenes that open this chapter suggest a number of themes that related to Layla's struggle to achieve success as a singer: new means of filtering reality through media, the limits and possibilities for the self-conscious construction of a "modern" identity, and finally, the disjunctures between individual intentions and public recognition.

The concept of "modernity" first arose during the European Enlightenment, positing that science, technology, and rationality would gradually liberate individuals from the supposed constraints of kinship, tradition, religion, and superstition.[2] Closely associated with the rise of capitalism, colonialism, and the modern nation-state, projects of modernity assumed that individuals from what is now called the Global South would be eager to adopt Western forms of rationality in order to become "modern." In recent years, theorists have sharply critiqued the Eurocentric notion of modernity, suggesting that there are multiple ways that people experience modernity, both in the West and elsewhere.[3] "Other modernities" are not simply reactive to "Western" concepts but can respond to ideologies originating from indigenous sources as well (Hodgson 2001: 7). Yet despite acknowledging that modernity often takes its sources not from the West but from indigenous processes, many anthropologists have still proposed modernity as a concrete "rupture" with the past and with tradition.

Rather than considering modernity as an all-encompassing ideology, exemplified by a break or a rupture with tradition, I argue that "modernity" for Fassis carries multiple meanings and represents merely one among many ideologies that can be experienced as hegemonic, depending on the situation. Following Katherine Ewing, I view hegemony as "a control over public discursive space," with room for the experiencing subject to accept, challenge, or subvert different ideologies depending on which is salient in a particular context (Ewing 1997: 5). When individuals do express modernity as a break with the past, this rupture is not located in a single moment (such as the postcolonial one) but rather in a series of ruptures expressed in different idioms depending on the subject. For a group of middle-class Fassis observing a videotape of a wedding, the performance of a particular song might conjure up one of these ruptures, reminding them of a past when their city and their family members were at the center of power and influence. Past configurations of self and the possibility of establishing a stable identity are mourned, but this awareness of loss and temporality is not necessarily specific to the "modern" condition. For many of the "original" male Fassis, modernity meant clinging to social traditions while attempting to

convert former means of livelihood (that of the renowned Fassi merchants of the old *medina*) into the "new" context of life in the Ville Nouvelle. Modernity for many of the women I knew meant maintaining the
appearance of a modern yet modest Muslim woman, and pursuing the
"modern" goals of education and employment while also marrying and
having children. Layla, however, saw modernity as the abandonment of
expected paths to pursue an imaginary lifestyle for which she had no
template. She navigated the territory of a "modern" ideology blind—
without maps.

Constantly reinterpreted and negotiated in local situations, modernity in Fes is not always seen as opposed to "tradition." While Fassis
invoke tradition as a defense against the implementation of new social
practices, it is equally likely that practices can be rejected on other
grounds. Here, I examine tradition and modernity as ideologies that
interpenetrate and inform one another, operating alongside other ideologies in fashioning and negotiating social life. Struggles to define the
Moroccan social body take place at the level of culture, where modernity
competes for primacy with other notions of community and identity.
Just as patriarchal ideologies still hold sway when Fassis debate the mer-
its of changing the personal status code (*mudawana*), Fassis manipulate
ideas of modernity to suit their own attempts to define themselves and
their community. Modernity and patriarchy are not necessarily incommensurable; again, as with everything else, they are used to different
ends depending on the situation.

Rather than being the locus for a repository of past practices, culture
becomes a shifting site in which battles for recognition take place. What
individuals experience as hegemonic depends on the dynamics of a situation, not easily traceable to "modern" or "traditional," but to who (or
what) is determining the terms for engagement. The Hegelian philosophy of recognition at the center of any potentially contentious encounter (and the subsequent possibility of domination) is essential to my
argument here. "Our identity," writes Charles Taylor, "is partly shaped
by recognition or its absence, often by the *mis*recognition of others, and
so a person or group of people can suffer real damage, real distortion,
if the people or society around them mirror back to them a confining or
demeaning or contemptible picture of themselves" (1995: 75). Specific
instances of this quest for recognition must be examined in order to
understand the conflicts at their center. Layla sought recognition of her
humanity from an audience that consistently responded to her performances as signs of prostitution. Complex, long-standing associations of
singing with illicit female sexuality meant that Fassis "recognized" Layla
as a purveyor of potential social chaos (*fitna*). Recognition itself shifts

according to the context and depends on who controls and defines the public sphere at a particular moment.

Gender is significant to the issue of recognition, as "gender serves as one of the central modalities through which modernity is imagined and desired" (Rofel 1999: 19). Never inseparable from power, individuals use gender as a symbol of liberation or oppression, in order to justify, normalize, or change existing relations between men and women. Despite her best intentions, Layla never managed to remove the stigma from her participation in a profession that was not considered appropriate for "good" women. As I have shown in Chapter 6, women's presence in the public sphere is provisional, guided by complex restrictions, resting on the twin threats of shame (*hshuma*) and chaos (*fitna*). "Shame" and "chaos" dictate the comportment of women in certain spheres. The meaning of these terms is unstable, however, and those who appeal to them assume a common frame of reference that is itself contested.

As I have shown, the constraints many women feel in public stem from demands placed on their visibility, whether these demands originate with the Moroccan nation state, Islamist practice, local custom, tradition, or secular discourses. Various factions within society manipulate the image of women to promote their own aims, prescribing a certain disposition their "ideal" Moroccan woman should follow in the public sphere. Each of these discourses attempts to delimit a set of proper "social performances": suitable professions for different social classes or age groups, appropriate religious observances, the type of movement allowed in the streets, behavior toward unrelated males, and marital and reproductive habits. Fassis claim to be able to detect whether a woman or girl successfully follows a particular set of dictates by observing visual cues, namely dress and demeanor. Yet women's social performances are constantly shifting in response to these contradictory demands, and representations of the "Moroccan woman" are therefore highly individualized and fragmented. Identities are not only unstable but also, frequently, deceptive.

In this chapter, I show how Layla's deliberate strategies of self-creation were "read" (or "misread") by her audience, thereby effacing her agency. What James Siegel terms a "fetish of appearances" or "fetish of modernity" results when social actors follow specific conventions of visibility without necessarily intending an internal transformation of identity. Observers perceive surface details (such as dress style or demeanor) as indicative of a transformation, regardless of the intentions of the actors, who are then assumed to embody a particular ideology that they may not in fact possess. Siegel calls this "failed possibility" a "fetish of appearances, a fetish in the Hegelian sense of an orientation to a power which cannot be appropriated but which, nonetheless, one feels one possesses" (Siegel 1997: 10).

Modernity itself becomes a fetish when its manifestations are overemphasized, interpreted by those who have the power to grant recognition. Furthermore, strategies intended to provoke a reading as "modern" are often perceived according to other, competing ideologies. The subsequent misrecognition takes on a life of its own, and failing to achieve recognition on her own terms, the individual becomes caught up in other people's interpretations of who she is. In such instances, we lose sight of the individual subject, and of her intentions and desires. Here I attempt to trace some of those desires in a woman who self-consciously wished to construct an identity that was both modern and culturally specific.

Layla combined available conventions for a proper Moroccan female identity with those she viewed as imported and cosmopolitan, intending to stimulate a certain kind of recognition that ultimately she was unable to attain. Aware of the negative associations of her profession with prostitution, she first tried to renounce her sexuality, eschewing relations with men in the hopes that people would see she was, in her words, "not like other singers." She hoped to craft a self that would be unrecognizable, a self that would escape convention and enable a new "reading," allowing her to maintain a specifically Moroccan notion of honor yet participating fully in an identity she imagined to be "modern." Yet because she constantly altered her practices in an attempt to produce different types of reception (depending on her audience), her sense of identity was constantly in flux. In such situations, identity is never fully achieved; rather, it exists "only at the price of enormous confusions and contradictions," with self-definition requiring an acknowledgment of identity's constantly shifting ambiguities (Siegel 1997: 9).

Layla's story highlights possibilities for the manipulation of notions of modernity in forming identity, and for the representation of modernity as an "elsewhere" fueling the creation of new social possibilities. This chapter focuses primarily on Layla's life and work as a singer, and contains little about her life before, which almost never occupied our discussions but occasionally resurfaced in memories that were obviously difficult for her to recount. Layla lived very much in the present and, I would argue, in the dream world of the future, which, when it arrived, never quite managed to live up to what she had imagined.

An ideal interlocutor for an anthropologist, Layla was able to reflect on her intentions and desires, and to argue with me about theories that I put forth concerning social legitimacy and empowerment. She eloquently articulated the social pressures she felt as a single woman working in a dishonorable profession, and she was explicit in her desire to

distance herself from particular discourses of sexuality that delegiti-
mized her work and objectified her as loose or immoral. She was acutely
conscious that everything depended on her visibility, and that she would
be "read" as a cypher for something she was not, despite her best intentions. Over the course of my fieldwork, I watched Layla struggle against
the public readings provoked by her social performances. Yet ultimately
she found herself enacting the behaviors associated with the stereotypical image of Moroccan female performers that others long thought they
had "recognized" in her.

Layla was passionate about singing for its own sake, and she refused
to engage in activities that would compromise her reputation. She
invented an elaborate framework of rules that she believed would enable
her to remain untouched by the profession's negative associations, and
she was quite cognizant of the fact that in other societies, singing was
not a shameful activity for women. Conversant with discourses of modernity, she constantly spoke of herself as "modern," or "like a European,"
insisting that people would respect her if they only understood that her
philosophy about life was drawn from sources other than the narrow
range of expectations she felt people had for Moroccan women.

"It's not just that I wear these clothes," she told me once, pointing to
her stylishly tailored pants, her high heels, and her fitted V-neck sweater.
"I know that being modern is about more than what you wear. It is a
complete transformation. Many women dress this way but they haven't
changed their mentalities. They still live the way other people want them
to. I live according to how I want. Yet I respect myself, and I think the
people see that."

We often discussed what it meant to be modern, as it was important
for her to sort out her own feelings about the concept. Being modern,
as Layla said, was a "complete transformation," when her interior state
might ideally reflect her outward demeanor. "I know I have arrived
when what I feel on the inside is reflected in how I look and act, but
also in how other people perceive me," she once said. A Eurocentric
modernity was not incompatible with her ideas about Moroccan culture,
which prescribed codes of modesty and sexual propriety that she fully
intended to continue following. Recognition was the final process in her
transformation, when both her appearance and her attitudes would be
accepted by the public. Being modern was also about individualism, and
pursuing her desires despite negative responses from her family or community.

In Fes, the work of a female singer is considered potentially dangerous, involving contact with unrelated men; even more threatening is the
idea that a singer's honor can no longer be vouched for, thus tainting
her marital prospects.

"Singers are not good, because they have no shame," one woman told me. As the previous chapter has shown, being Fassi means defining one's civilization through the attribute of "having shame." Those who have no shame are lost, and being unable to marry because of one's participation in an illicit or shameful profession is tantamount to the same thing. Layla, who was in her early thirties, was conscious of this, but insisted that marriage was not her ultimate goal. She told me:

I guess if I fail at this [singing]—and I've been trying for five years so I'm not sure how much more time to give it—I'd like to be married. But mostly I tell myself no, it would not be worth it, to be married to the only kind of man who would marry you now. Girls my age have to marry older men, or else if they're like me maybe the only one who will have them is somebody with a bad reputation, maybe he drinks, I don't know, but somebody who has something wrong with him. Maybe this is only true in this region of Fes and Meknes. I will see, perhaps, about someone in Rabat or Casa, but no, that's no good either, because the mentality will be the same. They will tell you they're different but deep down they're the same. They want a virgin, they want her to be twenty years old, they want her to know nothing of the world. *And I can never return to that place.* So the best would be for me to marry a foreigner.

Layla was fluent in English, and when she told me this, during one of several recorded interviews we did, I was struck by those words, of the self as a place from which there is no return and no escape, and the past as irrevocable. Georg Lukacs has likened modernity to a condition of "transcendental homelessness," whereby individuals feel alienated from their home communities and value systems, leading them to experience reality as "a prison instead of a parental home" (Lukacs 1971: 61). This, then, seemed to be the price of Layla's modernity: casting off from the familiar, from a path that was once marked out for her, toward an identity unmapped by any clear reference points or guidance. It was not a single fracture or break, but it had happened slowly, over time, until the self she might have been was now closed off to her forever. A series of small ruptures, and then suddenly she was left with a world in which she had too much knowledge and in which no desirable man (except perhaps a foreigner) would accept her.

But here I stop revealing fragments of the story, having set the scene: a city where professional singing and dancing is still associated with illicit sex, despite the visible delight that people display at hearing fine musicianship, and despite the power of the singer to evoke loss, longing, and a fragile solidarity among her listeners. Music is indispensable to life, and herein lies the contradiction, long noted by scholars studying the entertainment profession in the Muslim world: how can something be both indispensable yet marginal and feared at the same time? Layla refused to believe this. She insisted on honor in a dishonorable profession; she wanted, in her own words, "to follow my own path, to do things my way, to not be affected by what other people say about me. I want to respect myself and to have that be enough." Whether or not she was able to succeed at this delicate balancing act remains to be seen.

The Social Biography of a Singer

Layla was not her real name, but even as a performer she went by a pseudonym. You might have seen her performing a popular song on a Moroccan television program dedicated to up-and-coming young musicians, as the fourth act featured between two adolescent rap groups from Meknes. Or maybe she was on your train, and you wondered about the letter she unfolded and reread over and over, her long, auburn hair shielding the words from your view. Perhaps you were a tourist, and you heard her singing, accompanied by a keyboard, in a five-star hotel at a beach resort outside Rabat, or in Agadir, or in Fes. She had worked in many places. You noticed how her voice was perfect for Arabic music, but that she preferred to sing standards: French pop songs, Edith Piaf, the Beatles.

She carried herself like someone who is not afraid to take up space, not afraid to assert her presence in a world of men. At least that was the impression she gave, walking toward me on a bright winter day a few years ago. She looked Spanish in a long, flared skirt, and her white blouse was cut low enough to reveal delicate collarbones. Always Layla was perfectly put together, her makeup and elegant outfits concealing the sadness you could only see when you got up close, when you knew where to look.

She greeted us; she knew the woman I was with, who had been to the hotel where Layla was currently working as a nightclub singer. Popular with large tour groups, Hotel Samir was one of the few Western-style diversions in the Fes Ville Nouvelle, a deluxe four-star hotel where tourists could enjoy a cold beer and a plate of spicy black olives on the terrace overlooking the *medina* in the distance. When you walked into the gleaming marble lobby, its floors piled thick with royal red, Rabati carpets, one of the first things you saw was an easel with an advertisement for Layla's nightly performances. A picture I took of her later ended up there, one in which Layla implores the viewer with wide-eyed earnestness, one arm holding the microphone, the other stretched toward the camera.

I started visiting Layla at the Hotel Samir and at others where she received gigs throughout the course of my fieldwork. The piano bar where she worked was intended as a space for Europeans. Her work was subject to the vagaries of tourism, and long stretches of nights would go by when Layla sang to an empty room. Whenever there were international incidents related to the Muslim world (such as 9/11 or the bombing of a synagogue in Djerba, Tunisia), Moroccan tourism immediately took a hit, and sometimes Layla would be sent home without pay.

Yet it was important to her that people knew she was associated with the *piano* bar and not *the* bar. *The* bar, located on the same floor as the piano bar, featured a two-for-one happy hour in a room filled with smoke and leering businessmen. The *piano* bar was designed to be more sophisticated, a space for the appreciation of music, with more expensive drinks, although, usually later in the night, any number of drunks might stumble in from *the* bar and harass her. She had gotten used to this, and generally her fellow musicians, a guitarist and keyboardist, kept men from bothering her too much.

Layla had been "discovered" by Massoud, the guitarist. Massoud was employed as a music teacher in a local conservatory, where he had been Layla's teacher many years before. He arranged the music and handled the business end of their collaboration—setting up jobs, appearances on television programs, and appointments with recording studios for making cassette demos. He also served as a protector figure for Layla. When he rediscovered Layla by chance several years after she had been his student, he asked if she wanted to work with him and then approached her family for permission, promising to chaperone their daughter and keep other men from bothering her. The moment when Massoud asked her family's permission to lead her in a career as a singer was a turning point in Layla's life, and her description of the incident reminded me of stories of a husband visiting the family of a potential bride. At the time, Layla worked as a receptionist for a car rental company, and her parents were not happy about her proposed employment. But she begged them, and they grudgingly gave her permission.

Massoud was her savior, but in some respects also her jailer. Constrained by his responsibilities to his daytime job and his family, Massoud only sought out long-term gigs close to Fes, and Layla felt that their lack of mobility prevented her from being in contact with influential people who might help her further her career. The keyboardist, Aziz, sometimes worked with local wedding orchestras but was otherwise able to travel freely. In the summers, Massoud would go on hiatus from his teaching job, and the group traveled to work in other cities, but the center of the Moroccan music industry was four hours away in Casablanca, and ideally they needed to be there year-round to make contacts. Layla also depended on Massoud to arrange their work, and she insisted that if she were to strike out on her own, without a male figure mediating her involvement with this world, other men would try to take advantage of her. But Massoud lacked Layla's charisma, and despite his skills as a musician, he was unable to bring out what Layla was capable of when accompanied by a full band or orchestra. At one point when I knew her, she was offered a job as a singer in a prestigious jazz piano bar in Casablanca, with the stipulation that she had to leave her fellow musicians behind.

"I could never do that, after everything Massoud has done for me," she said. "I would feel too guilty." She also hinted that she was scared to work without him, despite the fact that she constantly complained that he was holding her back.

Other Moroccans assumed that Layla had a relationship with one or both men, and she was aware of the rumors, but she insisted that this was not the case. Layla knew that traveling alone with two unrelated men was simply not done by "good" Moroccan women, but she assumed that as long as her intentions were pure, others would eventually recognize this and stop talking. Aziz was not particularly controlling, but Massoud discouraged Layla from pursuing romantic relationships with tourists, despite the fact that one of her goals was to get a visa to Europe (possibly through marriage), where she believed that people would have a greater appreciation for the kind of music she wanted to sing.

A further obstacle to success was the type of music she wanted to sing. Layla preferred to sing a mix of European pop and folk, with a few Middle Eastern songs thrown in for good measure. She did not like indigenous Moroccan music, although there were several different styles she might have performed. *Milhun* and *andalus* music were considered classical Moroccan forms and required highly skilled performers. Because of their historical associations, these types of music achieved an almost sacred quality in people's imaginations. *Shikhat* music, on the other hand, was almost always associated with prostitution. Layla felt this was because the *shikhat* singers also danced, and that moving the body in front of men was highly suggestive of sex. "I don't dance," she insisted, "In my own show, I refuse to dance. Instead, I try to be animated without dancing; I make gestures." Her "gestures" resembled dancing but were not suggestive, and while she might twirl around or toss her long hair, she never shook her hips or performed belly dance. Yet singing, while perhaps slightly less stigmatized than dancing, was still considered shameful, a sign of too much presence for a woman. "Singing, like dancing, laughing, or talking loudly is an exhibition of one's presence and one's sexuality, and a lack of control and 'weight'," writes Willy Jansen about Algeria (1987).

Layla's refusal to dance stemmed not only from the association of bodily movement with sexuality but also from her sense that dancing would distract people from her voice. For Layla, the verbal aspects of performance were not as important as the overall impression she gave, and she stated that her expressiveness lay in "not so much the words I sing but my expressions and gestures, and most of all my voice; I should be showing different emotions and feelings that people will be able to respond to, no matter what language they speak." To her, it was crucial that she bring her audience to "feel" something. She constantly differentiated herself from "folk" performers by emphasizing her education (she had briefly attended university), classical training, and vocal competence. "Each style requires different knowledge [of vocal techniques]," she told me.

Layla often spoke of the Moroccan singer Samira Saïd, who had achieved world renown and now sang in the Egyptian dialect. In Morocco, outside of hotel nightclubs, there was not much of a niche for female singers who performed cover versions of European and Arabic songs.[4] In Fes, her audiences were mixed; early in the night, they were likely to be tourists, but later, more Moroccans arrived for her shows, usually local businessmen who had been drinking at the bar or travelers from other parts of the country. In other regions, her audience would be different, especially when she received summer jobs in Rabat or Casablanca. Then, she said, she had more Moroccan customers, but they were "sophisticated" and "didn't come just to drink." But in Hotel Samir, her repertoire was designed to appeal to the tourists who might want to hear their own music after a long day of being bombarded by Moroccan culture in the *medina.*

"They're far from home; they want to hear something familiar," she said. "The hotel wants to show them that Morocco is modern, and that there are people who know their [the foreigners'] music."

She changed her style depending on the audience and on her level of comfort. With the European music, despite her professed preference for non-Arabic music, her voice was breathy, her movements wooden. With the Arabic repertoire her voice was completely different, strong and sure of itself. This was partly because she had been trained in this genre. As she grew comfortable with her audience and they responded to her, her performances could be stunning. She liked it best, she said, when she had occasion to sing for Moroccan couples, when well-to-do Moroccans from other cities came to stay at Hotel Samir, or when men brought their mistresses to the piano bar to listen to music. Then the men would not bother her, and she could connect with both men and women.

"Sometimes it's hard to know who to look at," she said. "You need to engage your audience but some people will read this the wrong way."

Layla's dream was not to perform only for tourists, but to sing for Moroccans who would appreciate her music, to record compact discs and cassettes, and gradually to take her performances to an international level, where she might be hired to sing concerts throughout the

Middle East or Europe. If that failed, she said, she would go to Europe or America and sing only European pop songs in nightclubs. She was uncertain how to make either of these goals happen. I suggested there were many nightclub singers in Europe who already sang Euro-American music and that she would need to market her unique talents. In my estimation, one of her strengths was in this pastiche of Arabic and European; if she could fuse the two styles, as artists such as the Tunisian singer Amina or the Belgian/Egyptian Natacha Atlas have done, her work would be much more marketable. She agreed, but insisted in one of our recorded interviews that her talent lay in the European songs.

"I met some people from Holland who told me Moroccans sing in bars in Europe, but in Arabic," she said, shaking her head as if she found this idea distasteful. "If I go abroad, maybe I have to sing in Arabic. But I think people would like to hear me sing in English or French. Because many people already sing in Arabic."

"Which people?" I asked. "At nightclubs for North African immigrants?"

"But if I find another style of music, in English or in French, I think people would like it. Like Edith Piaf. If I sing in that style, I think that the people like it. They like a Moroccan who can sing Edith Piaf. Because when I do her songs, everybody tells me that it's very good, and that I must follow that way. I sing many languages, and people tell me this is good. The style is important. I must find a good style."

"But you sound so wonderful when you sing the Arabic songs," I told her.

"Yes, but the songs are not interesting. All those songs have the same rhythm. No variety, not like in foreign music, you have tango, salsa, folk. . . . Arabic is just *tak tak-a-tak*. It doesn't change."

"It's not like that with the classical Arabic music," I said.

"No, but nobody wants to hear that music anymore."

"Why not sing in one of the Moroccan styles?" I asked her. "Like *milhun*?"

"A Moroccan woman who sings *milhun* will find a good path," she agreed. "Because Moroccans like this music and there are many opportunities to sing *milhun* at concerts; they are constantly searching for people to perform. I can sing *milhun*, but I don't enjoy it. I don't find myself in the music, you know? If I sing in *milhun*, I'm confused. I can only find myself in a song that speaks to me. Some nights it's the European music which speaks to me, other nights I feel my soul in the Arabic. But the Moroccan music—I know it, but it's not something special for me."

I asked Slimane, who worked in a recording studio in Casablanca, how a Moroccan performer might become famous. His comments echoed those of others in the music business:

You have to have a catchy song, preferably either an original or a remake of an old Moroccan song, but updated. It can't be a copy of something that's popular now, or a copy of a song that has been really famous in the past few years. If it's a copy it has to be something old that you revive. So you record a short cassette with maybe four songs on it, and one of them will be this catchy tune. Then you go to the television stations and buy an advertising slot during lunch, maybe every day for a week. Thirty seconds, nothing more, and you play a clip of that song, when everyone is home having lunch. They will hear it, but you also have to have enough copies of your cassette that people can get their hands on it. It's best to go through a distributor, to convince them your song will be popular and they will take a risk and produce thousands of cassettes. And publicity is so important. You have to contact the radio and television programs and try to get yourself on them. It helps to have connections.

Layla told me a version of the same process, although she admitted that she lacked original songs to sing. Nonetheless, she recorded a demo tape with Massoud and Aziz. On the demo she sang a mix of European and Arabic cover songs. Massoud ordered a hundred copies, which they sent to various influential people in the Moroccan recording industry in Casablanca. After several months, they had sold only a few cassettes and their efforts had resulted in only one television spot, a two-minute segment on a program that featured Moroccan musicians singing in "new" styles. Most of the other performers on the show were adolescent males who rapped in a mix of Arabic and French. One other performer, a man, wrote and sang his own songs on the keyboard.

In the brief televised appearance, which was not shown during prime-time hours, Layla was nervous and unsure of herself, and she did not come across as particularly telegenic. None of her beauty and charisma were apparent in her performance, and the television studio surrounded her with fog from a smoke machine, which looked silly. For contact purposes Massoud's phone number was printed at the bottom of the television screen, and although the show was aired two more times, they received only one or two phone calls from hotels interested in employing them in the same type of work they already did.

The television appearance was markedly different from Layla's performances in front of an audience. She was heartbroken when their performance received so few responses, and also because she was nearing the end of a contract and needed new work. I wondered why she could not sing at weddings, where the audiences might be mixed.

"Well," she said, "I would enjoy it, but it's not done. Women don't sing at weddings. The *shikhat* do, of course, but not here in Fes, and that is not my style of music anyway. Moroccan wedding orchestras in most of the country are male. They sing music I like, but they wouldn't be interested in me. Also people might think the wrong thing about me if I worked at weddings. Now I sing for tourists, which is different."

But later she changed her mind and wondered if I might ask my husband and his brothers, who made studio recordings for musicians in Fes, to find her a place with a wedding orchestra in Fes.

"Why not?" she said. "I know people would like my singing."

However, when my brother-in-law approached three different orchestras on her behalf, all of them turned him down, stating that they would not work with a female singer. It just wasn't done.

There remained one other obstacle in her path, one which she hoped to circumvent, although she was not aware of any other female singers who had managed to do this. This obstacle was sex. Not only were women in the music business assumed to be on the same level with prostitutes, it was expected that they would trade sexual favors for the opportunity to succeed. Layla was conflicted about this; she wanted desperately for her Moroccan audiences to know she was morally upright, but at the same time, she feared that the only way for a singer to advance her career might be to use sex, somehow. Whenever we sat in cafés together, she was always greeting men who knew her from Hotel Samir, but she pleaded with me to understand that she "respected" herself and kept them at arm's length. When I first met her, I assumed, believing in the stereotypes, that she was a prostitute, but research through a few men I knew in the Ville Nouvelle revealed that after every performance Layla ignored potential suitors and went straight to her room.

"She's not a prostitute," Khaled, a suave nightclub denizen, reported. "I'm not sure what she is, but she's not a prostitute. I know some guys who have tried and got nowhere with her. But nobody is exactly sure about her relationship with the other two musicians. Maybe one of them is her boyfriend."

Layla spoke frequently about the difficulties she had encountered in refusing to sleep with influential men, but she still believed that there were altruistic people who would believe solely in her talent and might help her. She said:

If I am to be a success, I need someone who will help me find my way. Right now, this is Massoud, but he cannot go far because of his life here. I need someone who believes in me and my talent, and who will arrange songs for me that will showcase my voice, original songs. They will pay the *mulahin* (the songwriters), who require a lot of money to write songs for you. I have to be in the right place, and to be successful I have to participate in television. Until now, I have not been lucky. The most important thing is to respect myself, and to do everything with honor. But sometimes I think it is impossible to do this. I knew a girl who started singing at the same time I did. She had "relations" with everyone—the *mulahin*, the producers, the clients—and people wanted to help her. They made her a success. Now she travels to Egypt, Canada, Paris, and she succeeds. Why can I not bring myself to do this? Because I refuse. I would lose self-respect, and it would be like losing . . . I don't know, everything. I know I have talent. If I can participate in television, if I can be lucky, I am sure I will succeed, and I will still respect myself.

She refused to have Moroccan boyfriends because they would not respect her, and in general, she believed she had to avoid relations with men entirely, in order to protect both her reputation and her heart. In theory, she said, she would not mind having a foreign boyfriend, because he might be "more modern than a Moroccan man." But she had had a bad experience with a French boyfriend when she was in her early twenties. The Frenchman had "broken her heart" because he had professed to being in love with her, and she consented to "traveling around with him," but when she introduced him to her family, he "decided that Morocco was primitive and I was, too," and abandoned her. I was stunned by this image—the European lumping together both woman and nation as uncivilized.

"He promised to marry me and instead he left me," she said. She subsequently experienced a nervous breakdown. For months, she could not bring herself to leave her family's house. "I felt ruined," she told me. "I lived through a bad time. This is what happens when you try to have boyfriends like women do in other countries. Nothing I have ever lived through was as bad as that. In my life now, there are difficulties, but of a different kind."

Her family was another aspect of Layla's life that caused her pain. Her father had died a few years before, creating a great gap in Layla's life, as she had been his favorite daughter, and he had allowed her to begin a singing career despite his misgivings about the profession. Her mother was feeble and in ill health, and Layla's income as a singer was her mother's primary means of support, although a brother who worked in a leather shop in the *medina* also contributed. At home with the mother lived two unemployed adult brothers, an aunt, and another sister, who was trying to separate from an abusive husband and maintain custody of her small daughter.

In some way, they all depended on Layla. They were quite proud of her and kept professional photos of her all around the house, telling visitors of the daughter who "had been on television." Because she supported them, they did not expect her to do housework. Most nights, Layla stayed in the hotel, since she sometimes worked until one or two in the morning, returning to her family's house during the day to check on her mother.

She never expressed interest in having a boyfriend or getting married during the first year of our friendship. At one point, a tourist from Switzerland who had stayed in Hotel Samir was interested in her and promised to get her a visa to come there to sing. From Switzerland, he began to telephone her, and their conversations were flirtatious. "But he is a butcher, and he is very fat," Layla confessed. "I don't know what he would want from me if I traveled there." Actually, she knew very well what he wanted, but when he told her he was married, she cut off contact with him. "Thank God nothing happened," she said. "Of course I want to go to Europe, but it should happen honestly, not like this. I forgot myself."

Then in the fall of 2001, a German tourist became enamored with her when he saw her singing one night at Hotel Samir. A plain, balding man in his late thirties who worked in finance, Paul impressed her by not attempting to sleep with her, a tactic, she told me, that "men, often the Italian ones, are always trying." He engaged her in a conversation after her performance and they sat in the lobby of Hotel Samir talking until dawn. The next night, they talked again, and he told her he was fascinated by her, although he was leaving the next morning and would not be coming back to Fes. He made her promise she would write to him, and they struck up a correspondence.

Their relationship developed through letters, which they wrote in English, as Layla spoke no German and Paul knew no French. Occasionally she asked me to help her compose them, if she had a particular sentiment she wanted to express and was unsure how to word it. At other times, she wanted me to analyze his words, if something was ambiguous. Over the months, the courtship grew more intimate, with Paul planning a visit to Morocco in the spring, and in his letters there was no shortage of declarations of his undying love.

At first Layla said she was not sure how she felt, as she had not been attracted to him, although she thought he was a nice person. But she found the earnestness of his letters endearing and decided to begin imagining a future with him. He seemed stable and serious about her. He bought books about Islam "to better understand her culture," which made Layla laugh, as she was not very religious. During Ramadan he fasted for a few days to demonstrate his solidarity with her. He insisted that he was serious about the relationship, and mentioned that he would like them to live together in the future. "We cannot know for sure if our relationship will work until we try living together," he wrote. To this she replied that in her culture this was not done, and that she hoped he understood that she would be taking a big risk by displaying their relationship to others. At the very least, it would be better for her to pretend they were engaged during his upcoming visit.

Arranging Paul's visit occupied her imagination for several months, and turned out to be a major undertaking. Layla rented a furnished apartment close to the hotel, where they could stay together for a week.

This was done through a neighborhood "big man," a person who could procure anything and to whom people (usually men) went if they needed a place for illicit rendezvous, especially with prostitutes. Paul had insisted on the apartment, saying that he wanted to experiment with living together, and to experience everyday life with her. Uncomfortable with this, she said to me sarcastically, "Easy enough for him to come here whenever he wants and order me around. It is never the other way around, with Moroccans telling Europeans we want to see what their lives are like. We can't even get visas to travel there." When she told Paul that she did not think they should stay together, he threatened not to come at all. Insensitive to her attempts to "explain Moroccan culture" to him, he did not understand that she was risking her reputation by staying in the same apartment with him, since Fes was small enough that people in her circle would definitely be aware of what was going on.

Layla was also terrified that the police would arrest her for soliciting a tourist for prostitution, which occasionally happened with Moroccan women and foreign men (but not the other way around, as Moroccan men were welcome to do whatever they wanted with foreign visitors). She even went so far as to get a special permit that indicated he was a friend and that she had permission to show him around. And finally, she asked if my husband and I could spend time with them "so that Paul will see you're in a mixed marriage and that it is possible for Moroccans and foreigners to live together happily, because he has his doubts."

She grew more anxious and manic as the day of his arrival approached. The entire time I knew her, Layla battled with insomnia and depression, which she "took pills for," and her state of mind reflected itself in her appearance. Although she always dressed nicely, in periods of depression she quickly put on weight, and she attempted to conceal the circles under her eyes with too much makeup, which only had the effect of making her look more haggard. Singing for hours, night after night, took its toll on her voice, and she occasionally had bouts of laryngitis when she could barely talk at all. "I'm sick," was a refrain I frequently heard from her, and while this did often manifest itself in physical symptoms—a backache preventing her from singing, for example—it seemed also to be the idiom in which she expressed depression.

When she was happy and relaxed, which was rare, she could be beautiful. There were too many stressors in her life—her ambitions and disappointments as a singer, her entire family leaning on her for support, and the thoughts that kept her awake at night. She often felt like she was utterly alone in her society, and that she had drifted so far away from all other human beings that she could no longer connect with anyone. I was her best friend, she told me, because I was a foreigner, as she had "problems" being friends with middle-class Moroccan women—either they were married and respectable and refused to associate with her, or else they were women she knew from Hotel Samir who were known prostitutes, and she did not want to be associated with them.

"There are only two ways for a woman to be in the eyes of Moroccans," she explained once, "good or bad. And I'm neither." She admitted that she felt constrained by expectations that women should take delight in activities like cooking and housecleaning. "I hate doing that," she said. "I help my mother sometimes, of course, because she's in bad health, but I'm so bored with women who have nothing else going on in their lives except for their houses." Feeling misunderstood by her own culture, she insisted that she would have been better off in Europe where people had "a modern mentality." She constantly returned to this refrain, as if the elusive qualities of modernity she sought might be the cure for all her ills.

When Paul arrived, her manic state had reached new levels. The three of us met for coffee, and she was in a self-deprecating mood, apologizing to him for every detail that wasn't perfect. She brought him over to my apartment to have dinner and see a "mixed marriage," an important element in the Morocco she wanted to display to him. She drank too much wine, which was not like her, and it made her even more anxious. As for Paul, he seemed staid and slightly dull, wanting to have long discussions about whether Islam and Christianity were irreconcilable, especially when two people came together from these different worlds. I tried to explain that he was missing the point, and that people were not reducible to their religions, especially not Layla, whose issues were much more complex than that. "Show him that we're modern!" she pleaded with me in the kitchen, out of Paul's hearing. "This is so important to me."

There was another drama unfolding, related to Layla's work at Hotel Samir. Paul wanted to take a trip to Agadir for a few days, but Hotel Samir told Layla that if she missed any more work (she had recently missed several days due to illness), they would fire her. Massoud, who was not happy about the new visitor, had also given her an ultimatum. If she went to Agadir, she would not only lose her job, but Massoud as well, as he was "finished" with her, and this situation with Paul revealed that she was "silly." "You've lost your reason," Massoud told her. "You're destroying your career."

Layla was torn, and asked Paul if he could go to Agadir by himself, and she would join him after putting in a few more days of work. But he refused, asking her to choose between her work and him. She went to Agadir, and for awhile I heard nothing from her.

In Agadir, everything fell apart. They stayed together in a five-star hotel, which he insisted on splitting fifty-fifty, and Layla used up most of her savings to pay for it. Because she believed he would marry her, she agreed to sleep with him, but when he asked her if she was taking any form of birth control, she lied that she was. Now she wondered if this had been a mistake, but she had just wanted to make him happy, she told me. It had been ten years since she had had "relations" with anyone, she said, and she was not sure how to handle the issue. But the whole trip had been strange. Every night he wanted to take her to the bars and the casinos and get her drunk, which seemed odd, but she gave in.

They had encountered a Moroccan tourist guide Paul knew from his previous trip. The guide told Paul that good Moroccan girls did not have boyfriends, drink alcohol, or stay in hotels with foreign men, which Layla had also tried to explain, but in a different way. Over the past several months, she had tried to tell Paul that she was serious about him and would marry him if he asked, and that it was not acceptable for her to have a boyfriend unless his intentions were also serious. Now the guide was telling Paul that this woman he had traveled so far to see was no better than a prostitute, and Paul believed him. Layla felt that Paul was using the vacation to "test" her, to find out if she would refuse the activities which the guide had told him were "signs" of whether or not she was a bad person. To her these activities signified modernity, and she had done whatever he told her because she imagined he would judge her as a European.

On their last day in Agadir, the taxi driver who took them to the airport accused Layla of stealing his wallet and subjected her to the embarrassment of a police search in front of Paul. The police found nothing, but the damage was done, as the taxi driver then accused Layla (in French so that her foreign companion might understand) of being a whore, a *putain*. Layla was devastated and started to cry, as the whole trip had been too much for her psyche, but Paul was acting cold and distant. He returned to Germany and stopped calling her or sending letters. She was unable to reach him until almost two weeks later, when he told her he had been busy with work and had not had time to speak to her.

"This is history repeating itself," she told me, recalling her French boyfriend. "I think he did not like what he saw. He didn't like my culture, and if you don't like my culture, you don't like Layla. It's too much; I feel like my heart is going to split in two. I invested everything I had in this relationship." To make matters worse, she suspected she might be pregnant. She tried to call Paul and see how he would respond to the idea, still holding out the irrational hope that he might marry her, but he told her that if she were pregnant, it was her problem because she had lied to him. The following week, she received a letter from him, which she showed to me. In the formal breakup letter, such a change from the flood of romantic missives he had sent in the previous months, he told her that "it's not a good time in the world for a Muslim and a Christian to be together, especially not since September 11, as there is too great a distance between our worlds."

Layla discovered that she was pregnant, and one of the women she knew from Hotel Samir, who "knew about these things," helped her to get an abortion. She cried when she told me about it. Massoud and Aziz agreed to continue working with her, and Massoud almost seemed smug when he learned that the German had abandoned her. He had been correct all along; the relationship was a bad idea. But Hotel Samir had already hired another act for the piano bar. Massoud began to search for summer employment, and Layla stayed home with her mother. For a while she was unreachable, her phone constantly turned off. Then there was some good news. She and Massoud had been hired to perform at a gala dinner for the internationally ranked Moroccan tennis player Younes Aynaoui. Possibly the king's brother or sisters would be in attendance. She thought this might be her big break.

But then the government canceled the gala dinner to demonstrate solidarity with the Palestinians, after the situation in the occupied territories had become insupportable. Layla sank back into her depression and disappeared again. In June before I returned home, I finally managed to track her down. She was working again, this time in a beach town near Rabat, at a hotel frequented by Saudi tourists who, she said, harassed her much more than her countrymen ever had. "Every night is like a battle," she sighed. "But it's closer to Rabat and Casablanca, so maybe I will meet someone important there." It was all, she said, a matter of luck.

Layla seemed to have internalized Moroccan attitudes toward her profession. I had one final conversation with her before I returned to the United States, when she came to Fes to say goodbye. She was very tan but otherwise looked drawn and unhappy. The abortion and failed relationship were tormenting her, and she continued to dwell on Paul's comment that their worlds were incompatible. "What does that mean?" she said. "It's like he never saw me for who I am. So what if he read books about Islam and tried to prepare a *tagine*? Is that how he can know me? He listened to what the guide said about Morocco and decided I was a bad person. I thought I was modern to him but then he learned how other Moroccans saw me." She wondered now if she had given in too easily to him. Maybe she should have refused to share a room with him. If only, if only, she continued, but it was too late.

"People have told me, the life of a singer goes nowhere," she said. "I didn't believe them. I wanted to prove them wrong. But look at me. I

Figure 7. A Moroccan fashion show for caftans.

can't even find myself in the music anymore. Or remember why I wanted this life so badly."

"Because you love the music," I reminded her. "Because you respect yourself. Because you have big dreams about making a career as a singer. You've done that, it's your work."

"My dream . . ." Layla said, trailing off with a sigh. "It was big at first but it has become small. You know why? Because I think that it is too difficult to have a dream, a big one, especially after everything that has happened. Too many of us in this country have dreams and no hope of realizing them. Because no one helps us out. There is no one to follow. Nothing changes. So now, I want to follow my way, and I keep my dreams small. I will try to sing one of my own songs. I must do my own songs. That's my only goal. And then I will continue to follow my way. I won't look too far ahead."

Female Singers: Context and Recognition

Ludwig Ammann suggests that as public space is transformed in Islamic societies, "figurations of body and space matter more than Jürgen Habermas's logocentric theory of the bourgeois public sphere indicates" (Ammann 2002: 277). As a singer, Layla was not exempt from the careful scrutiny of women's behavior in the public space, and because of the venues in which she performed, her visibility was heightened. The contexts of performance alone were enough to damage her reputation, and thus her complex strategies for recognition failed, not because Fassis were not modern, but because already a number of other, more powerful ideologies affected how a woman singing in public would be received.

To comprehend Layla's strategies, it is necessary to understand what lies behind Fassi perceptions of her work. To begin with, the sites in which she performed are not considered legitimate. This is not, I suggest, because of some recourse to age-old "tradition" which might someday be swept away by "modern" ideas, but because of a cultural stigma that is unlikely to change as long as venues for female performers remain so limited, and as long as the close association between sexuality/prostitution and singing/dancing remains substantiated by experience.

Many middle-class Fassis I knew would differentiate between what Moroccan women can do within Morocco and what is appropriate behavior elsewhere. For instance, working in a hotel abroad was acceptable for Moroccan women. Yet in Morocco, some said, it would be frowned on. Certain dispositions become morally problematic within Morocco that are acceptable abroad, and this is not interpreted by Fassis as a failure of modernity in Morocco but as an unchanging constant related to societal judgment, male control over women's mobility, and religion. The locus for change is always perceived as being elsewhere; although individuals rarely wanted to align themselves with ideologies that judge women's behavior too harshly, many simply shrugged and said fatalistically that "other" Moroccans would always enforce these standards of behavior. Yet Fassis who were aware of Layla's career—that is, those with the power to grant recognition—refused to accept her despite her insistence that she was able to maintain her honor. Even her European boyfriend was influenced by the same codes that judged Layla's behavior so harshly. His rejection of her threw her completely off balance, for she had believed she was finally asserting her modernity and living like a European, only to find that a "modern" Moroccan was not what he saw either.

Illegitimate Professions

Tourists visiting Morocco will frequently meet men working in tourism who have had extensive contact with foreigners, speak several languages, and seem well adapted to other lifestyles. The media, especially since the rise of satellite television in Morocco in the 1990s, is one of the widest purveyors of ideas about Europe and America: in movies, news, documentaries, and most notably, music. But those who work in tourism have often spent years observing foreigners first hand and thinking about what will please them. Layla was no exception.

In her demeanor, Layla reminded me of these men, as she spoke several languages with fluency, presented a façade of sophistication and worldliness, and had ambitions to go abroad by herself to make a living as a singer. She did not have a university degree, but preferred to speak English with me, simply because she was proud of her linguistic abilities and thought that speaking foreign languages made her cosmopolitan. In Fes, she was fairly unique. Tourism, in most contexts, is considered an inappropriate profession for women. Middle-class families in Fes are not inclined to allow their daughters or wives to work in positions where they will have extensive contact with foreigners. One conversation I had was telling.

"To work in tourism for a girl? In Morocco? Doing what, working in a hotel or as a tour guide?" said Abdelkader, the father of two young daughters. "It's shameful. There's no telling what kind of ideas they would be exposed to, and if they were tour guide leaders, they would be moving around all the time, away from their families. It's better for girls to stay at home until they get married. They can work, but they should be with their parents."

"What about women who go to school to study tourism?" I asked, knowing of the programs that trained Moroccans to manage hotels abroad.

"That's different," Abdelkader said. "That's like going to university, and maybe it will help them to get a job in a five-star hotel in America or Europe when there aren't good jobs here at home. But it's different."

"Different if it's the same kind of work?" I asked. At a few of the five-star hotels in Fes, there were female desk clerks and receptionists.

"It isn't," he insisted. "Going to hotel school gives you skilled employment. It's like studying to be a doctor or a pharmacist. Here, what you will find is not of the same level at all. What work could a woman do in a hotel here? The maids are very poor, and they have no choice but to do that kind of work. But any other woman working with tourists, well, she's probably not the kind of woman you would want to know," he said euphemistically. "They are not good women," he emphasized.

The Fassi university professor, Driss, made a further distinction: "Outside Morocco, it is normal for women to be working in hotels. People think nothing of it. Here, it has a different meaning. It is even against the law for women to work at night. So you can send your daughter outside, and it's a good opportunity for her; she will probably make good money. But here, to have her unsupervised in a hotel, people would bother her. And judge her," he added.

"And judge her family as well?" I asked.

"They might ask why her family would let her work in this job. They might assume she didn't have a family, or that the family didn't care. But the issue is not judging the family but judging the daughter. She's the one who will be hurt if people start to say things about her, and then she won't find a husband."

I found it interesting that Driss phrased his concerns in this manner, placing more emphasis on the daughter's chances for marriage than on the potential threat to the family's honor. The possibility that a profession would interfere with a girl's marital prospects was the most frequent concern people expressed. Most middle- and lower-class Fassis of my acquaintance still consider marriage to be a woman's most important goal in life. Layla's ambivalence in this respect is unusual, but she was not the only woman I knew who felt this way.

Watching the video of another Moroccan singer performing at a wedding with my Fassi in-laws also gave me some clues as to how Layla was perceived. At the time, I was impressed by their perceptiveness in knowing of Soumia's "difficult life," but later I wondered whether the uniformity of these responses did not have a different meaning. Singers like Layla and Soumia fit into a preconceived notion Fassis have about female entertainers, one that has not been altered by experiences to the contrary. Singers represent chaos, *fitna*, the threat of social disintegration that might result from a society of unattached women. Following popular stereotypes, people assumed Soumia had been cut off from her family, that her career was not her choice, and that she had illicit relations with men. ("The woman who belongs to no one belongs to everyone," one man commented.) They juxtaposed her (lack of) attachments with their own, exemplified by the video: all the best Fassis assembled together, forming a cohesive group.

Singers could be valued for their performance—Soumia's rendition of an old song served as a foil for a fragile, illusory solidarity. Her performance on the cassette produced talk, not only of the wedding event as a moment in which a Fassi identity was produced and experienced as stable, but contradictorily, a sense that this identity—and by extension social life—was temporal. The skills of professional singers could clearly delight an audience, yet people felt compelled to comment on the women's personal lives as well. Inevitably when I spoke to other middle-class Fassis about my friendship with Layla, they would always pronounce her to be *meskeen*, or someone to be pitied. The misrecognition Layla elicited was a far cry from what she had envisioned in self-consciously adopting the attributes of a "modern" woman: cosmopolitanism, freedom of movement, open-mindedness, and independence. That others experienced this as a failure is telling.

The Cultural Contexts of Female Performance

The work Layla did as a singer was not a new type of employment for women, but singing and dancing are careers that people widely associate with prostitution. Yet as with everything gender-related, context is crucial. For amateurs, performing in the presence of family members is perfectly acceptable. Even among professionals, those who perform for all-female audiences are less stigmatized than those who sing when men are present.

Contact with unrelated males, particularly in situations involving alcohol, further suggests the shameful attributes of the singing profession. As Karin van Nieuwkerk writes euphemistically in her book *A Trade like Any Other: Female Singers and Dancers in Egypt*, "Female entertainers are still supposed to make long-lasting contacts with customers, but, in contrast to the past, mainly after instead of during working hours. They are expected to have their own customers and bring them to the club" (van Nieuwkerk 1995: 88). In Morocco, singing is considered a dishonorable professional for women, and in the history of Islam, singing and music in general have had an ambivalent status. A popular *hadith* proclaims that "the voice of a woman is shameful" (*sawt al-mar'a 'awra*) (van Nieuwkerk 1995: 12).

Women's voices are said to be capable not only of seduction but also of distracting the listener from his religious duties, as eleventh-century Muslim scholar al-Ghazâli noted. The ethnomusicologist al-Faruqi has shown how religious opinion over the centuries created a generally agreed-on hierarchy of permissible and forbidden forms of music, ranging from Qur'anic recitation at the top, to religious music and chanting, to songs sung in the context of work and family celebration, and at the bottom, music performed in association with forbidden activities such as drinking and prostitution (al-Faruqi 1985: 9). Al-Ghazâli and others also asserted that time, place, and audience were significant factors in judging whether or not a musical performance was acceptable. Performances might be licit in one context, forbidden in another.

Recent anthropological work on this topic has demonstrated that the negative stigma attached to women who work as singers and dancers has remained to this day.[5] In my own research, I interviewed Fassis from different social classes for their opinions of the status of women who work in music and entertainment. In asking them to rank the degree of shame associated with entertainment professions, I found that as with al-Ghazali and the opinions of Muslim scholars throughout history, context is still crucial. Newer forms of media are highly regarded. Thus, women who work in film or television are accorded the highest status, with theater slightly below, followed by women who have achieved fame throughout the Middle East (such as the legendary Umm Khultoum or the local favorite, Samira Saïd), then female singers who sing for women-only audiences, and below them, women who sing in the presence of unrelated men, and still a notch beneath that, women who also dance. Layla's attempt to separate herself from other entertainers by refusing to dance had a basis in reality, yet already the situations in which she performed lowered her status.

Pressing for clarification, I asked people to explain the difference between famous performers and those who worked in nightclubs, like Layla. Do not the famous ones have to start out somewhere? "Yes, but," was a common refrain. Fassis consider well-known artists to be beyond the basic standards of Moroccan society, and as one woman, Fatima, explained of Samira Saïd, "It's like she's not even Moroccan anymore. She doesn't live here, she doesn't sing in our language, she's not one of us." Success and wealth can elevate an artist beyond the moral judgment accrued by local, less famous performers. It was this perception of Samira Saïd as being beyond the basic moral standards of Moroccan society that Layla hoped to emulate.[6] Were not performers like Layla, then, "one of us"?

"Yes," Fatima continued. "That's why they have such a hard time. If they have a lot of money, they can live in Europe or Casablanca and no one can talk to them. Also we think if they are famous, they must have been talented. But the women who do this kind of work around here, why did they start in the first place? We wonder what else they have to do in their circumstances."

I asked my friends if singing for tourists was less blameworthy than singing for Moroccan men, because this was another one of Layla's assertions. Habiba, who was fairly religious, said, "It's shameful to sing for Nasranis (Christians). A Muslim woman and a Christian man are forbidden by the Qur'an and if she sings for them, and it leads to something, it would be a sin against the religion."

Most middle-class Fassis I talked to believe that a local woman would not sing for a living unless she had nobody else to support her. Singing is a last resort, a profession for women who have been abandoned by their husbands or families. When I explained that Layla sang "just because she wanted to," they told me assuredly that I must have misunderstood her, and that "nobody would do that kind of work if they didn't have to." Among the few upper-class or highly educated people whom I solicited for opinions, there was some understanding of the pursuit of a singing career merely for the love of singing, but middle- and lower-class Fassis insisted that such a goal was impossible. "Maybe it's like that in America," they told me, "but not here."

Layla dismissed such responses as the opinions of the unenlightened.

Constantly invoking the image of a world beyond Morocco, she scoffed, "They don't understand because they know nothing of the world outside their families. Some people do not realize that there's more to life than the house, the market, and the public bath (*hammam*)." Such a pointed critique was aimed primarily at women, who she felt had snubbed her. Occasionally, she stated that Moroccan men were "more worldly, more cosmopolitan" than women, but at other times, she said that they did not understand her either.

Despite their disapproval of singing as a career, Fassis love music and consider it an essential form of entertainment. The observation that a performance can be culturally valued while the performer is socially stigmatized has been made by numerous writers.[7] As Ingrid Monson has written, "public performance seems to be an arena where culturally expected gender and cultural ideals may be transgressed" (Monson 1997: 29). This is the argument Kapchan makes for *shikhat* performances in Morocco. Willie Jansen points out that in Algeria, female singers and musicians adopt bodily dispositions and habits of men. Layla was aware of the transgressive behavior usually associated with female singers, but disagreed with the idea that their actions challenged traditional notions of appropriate behavior for a gender.

"What does it challenge?" she argued. "It just makes them the lowest of the low, so everyone else can look down on them. Is there power in that?" She felt it was more of a transgression to pursue singing without exploiting her sexuality. "Because people expect me to sleep with men," she said, "and when I surprise them by showing that I respect myself, I am changing minds, little by little."

As Lila Abu-Lughod has noted, one strategy for Middle Eastern women to attain respect is through "distancing themselves from sexuality and its antisocial associations" (1986: 165). Layla attempted to accomplish this in her bodily disposition, by refusing to dance or engage in sexual activity with customers, but the basic requirements of her profession—staying in hotels every night unchaperoned by a male relative, and singing in the presence of unrelated men, non-Muslims, and alcohol—contradicted her best efforts.

Kapchan argues that in the case of *shikhat*, expressing sexuality is "an assertion of power that has no place in social hierarchy" (Kapchan 1994: 90). In an argument similar to that set forth in Lila Abu-Lughod's *Veiled Sentiments*, where she suggests that poetry provides an outlet for sentiments not considered appropriate for expression in everyday discourse, Kapchan asserts that *shikhat* "turn the social gaze upon aspects of female expression that are taboo except in the context of performance" (1994: 90). In their personal lives, most *shikhat* live up to their reputations for having sexual relations outside the context of marriage, and consuming wine and hashish. In their performances, their melancholy lyrics deal with topics such as unrequited love, social approbation, and abandonment. With *shikhat*, private lives bleed into public ones, such that most Moroccans cannot imagine a "morally upstanding" *shikhat*. As one man from Khenifra, a fan of *shikhat*, told me, "There's no such thing [as a *shikhat* with a good reputation]. A bad reputation and *shikhat* go hand-in-hand. If they didn't live these lives, they would have nothing to sing about. They sing because they can do nothing else."

Layla's own strategy, confirming Abu-Lughod's view, was deliberate: she hoped not only to perform a type of music that was not indigenous to Morocco, but also to renounce her sexuality and thus elevate the profession. She made bargains with herself, wearing tight clothes but refusing to dance, since in her eyes this was an invisible line which, if crossed, indicated sexual availability. "It's important for people to see that I respect myself," she said. "I respect myself and the people will respect me, it's simple. I am accountable for what I do offstage, so I do nothing."

Much of her imagination was consumed with trying to control her reputation. As Mary Steedly has written, "while imagination may exceed the bounds of nation-state control, this does not mean that bodily experience does" (Steedly 2000: 813). While Layla worked in completely different contexts from *shikhat* dancers, from performance to reception, she was nonetheless Moroccan and subject to the same moral codes that judge *shikhat* performers so harshly. There are no prescribed roles to follow for those who want to make a career as a singer without sexuality being prominently featured. And singing in hotels automatically stigmatized her. But Layla wanted to be a nightclub singer, to perhaps branch off into jazz, or to have someone "discover" her and give her original music—Arabic or European—that would catapult her to fame. In creating what she hoped would be a valid identity for herself, she attempted to separate her public self, which as a singer, was by definition sexually charged—from her private one. In Moroccan social imaginaries, this was impossible.

Layla had made a point of distancing herself from acts such as drinking alcohol or engaging in sexual activity with customers who came to hear her sing. But she began to make exceptions when she was with foreigners, because, she said, "Inside, I have a European mentality, too. I can only express it when I am around foreigners." She "never drank with Moroccans," but would drink only when she was not in public and there were no Moroccans present. She had set rules for herself, such as never flirting with customers and always going back to her room immediately after her performances, but when she began to entertain the idea of having a German boyfriend, she stated that "I am taking a risk and abandoning my principles. Hopefully, I will be lucky, and then what people think won't matter, because I'll be gone." One day she told me she had spent New Year's Eve drinking at the Hotel Samir nightclub, dancing with tourists until the early hours of the morning.

"They did not know I was Moroccan," she said excitedly. "They thought I was Spanish. An Italian tried to talk to me, but I told him I was not available."

"What about the Moroccans?" I asked her. "You always said you didn't want them to see you drinking."

"Now that everyone knows I have a fiancé, I don't care what people think anymore." She had begun referring to Paul as her fiancé, even though he had ignored her request to pretend for social reasons that they were engaged. She expressed some reservations just before his actual visit, because "everyone will know we're staying together. So this has to work, it has to, it has to lead to something serious. Otherwise, I'm ruined."

Layla identified herself with modernity and with an elsewhere beyond Morocco, using her "European mentality" as a defense whenever her behavior went against what was sanctioned by the Moroccan social body. Initially she did not deliberately flaunt Moroccan moral codes. In fact, she emphasized her participation in them, stating that during the five years she had worked as a singer, she refused sexual contact with all men. To both sing and engage in illicit sex would confirm societal opinions of singers, which she wanted desperately to change. Yet one of her possible "paths," going to Europe, could not be achieved without falling in love with a European, since she was beginning to abandon the hope that she might be "discovered" by a talent scout who would help her get a visa to work in the nightclubs of Europe. When Paul began to pursue her, she decided to make a further break with her culture, knowing that visibly acknowledging a romantic relationship with a tourist would damage her reputation.

Conclusion: Imagining an Audience

In Fes, the subject of modernity is constantly under discussion, as people argue over whether or not their city, and by extension, their nation, will be able to fully attain the status of "modern." The issue here is not whether Fassis are "modern" by a single standard (since multiple modernities can easily be said to exist), but how modernity as an ideology is imagined and constructed in Fes, and which parts of the Eurocentric discourse Fassis consciously accept or reject.

Layla envisioned a neutral public sphere where her performances would not be judged as a sign of sexual impropriety, a place where men and women could freely interact. In this, she was not far from the opinions of some Fassis who see the liberation imagined by modernity in political terms. Many Fassis imagine modernity as a free space, à la Habermas, in which individuals participate in "democracy" and express themselves, unconstrained by differences of gender or income.

But some Fassis believe that "modernity" must be tailored to fit Moroccan cultural practices, and the aspect of modernity that provokes the most discussion is the status of women. With its different forms constantly under debate, "modernity" is not simply a discourse enacted in imitation of the West. As Nilufer Göle has written, "the encounter between the two cultural codes leads not to a simple logic of emulation or rejection but to improvisations in social practices and cultural meanings. Studying the public sphere as a social imaginary may offer new clues to map out these improvisations in a non-Western context" (Göle 175).

Fassis express the impossibility of engaging fully with forms of modernity in spatial terms: as "meeting a wall" of bureaucracy, as being "hemmed in" by social disapproval, or being "imprisoned" by economic lack. As a singer, Layla did not consider herself to be "marginal" to some imagined centrality. Rather, in choosing to structure her life according to what she believed were "modern" principles, she had drifted beyond the script for available female experience, taking a different path with no clear destination. Center and margins did not apply; rather, at low points she perceived herself as alone and alienated, rejected by her fellow countrymen and women, and beyond Moroccan social life entirely. Having ventured into an unknown space, she was irrevocably separated from the (nonmodern) self she had rejected.

Modernity existed for Layla as an imagined elsewhere, an ideal space located outside the Moroccan nation-state, where she would be liberated by capitalism and the freedom of the public spheres of Europe or America. Our constant discussions about what life was like in other places failed to convince her that elsewhere she still might not be on neutral territory. Modernity as she envisioned it was an ideal world in which individuals were not perceived through the prism of gender and could make choices unconstrained by custom or the weight of "tradition." To her, music was representative of her own struggle, exemplified by her ideological preference for music from other places, since she believed that the music of her own culture was too fraught with relations of inequality.

For some Fassis like Layla, modernity is an all-consuming pursuit, and they interpret their personal defeats in life as a failure of national character, or as an inability to measure up to the standards of more advanced countries. As Dipesh Chakrabarty has argued, modernity constructs itself in terms of difference and opposition, excluding non-Western "others" from achieving a Euro-American subjectivity (1992). The consequences of this "failure" for women are especially severe. Layla internalized her inability to achieve the imagined liberation, blaming herself or, at other times, her Moroccanness, for holding her back from her goals. And in this way, her struggles demonstrate instances when modernity is experienced as hegemonic, used as a yardstick to measure the relative progress (or lack thereof) of society.

Katherine Ewing has written that "the individual is a complex site of conflicting desires and multiple subjective modalities . . . whose experience of wholeness is illusory and contextually specific. This contextual subject is not constituted solely out of the gaze of the Other . . . but out of multiple others that form through different types of relationships or subjective modalities" (Ewing 1997: 35). Depending on her interlocutor, Layla was capable of engaging with various discourses in a way which initially seemed productive. Yet ultimately she reached an impasse, unable to believe in any of the selves she had created. Ironically, it was after the European, through his discussion with the Moroccan guide, recognized not the "modern" Layla but the Moroccan image of singer-as-prostitute, that Layla reached her lowest point. In the encounter with the European other, she had gambled on finally being recognized for the modernity she had carefully cultivated, but instead found herself being judged by Moroccan standards of propriety.

As for Soumia's performance at Maryam's wedding, subsequently revisited so many times on video, the Fassis who watched her were not interested in Soumia as an individual. Her performance highlighted a sense of loss, of mourning and melancholy for a Fes that is no more, which is a constant theme in Fassi narratives. It was no coincidence that she sang a song by Umm Khultoum, whose popularity among Arab audiences and whose links with Arab nationalism of the 1950s still resonate with audiences as far away as Morocco. Fassis of different generations appreciate Umm Khultoum's music, whereas other types of music are more limited in their appeal (for example, Nas el-Ghiwane to Moroccans who came of age in the 1970s, popular Western music to Moroccans under thirty, and *milhun* to Fassis over fifty).

Appadurai has pointed out the problematic notion of modernity as a sudden break, a single dramatic moment in which there is an irrevocable break between past and present. Following Mary Steedly, I view modernity not as an original "break" with the past but as a series of ruptures, which can be held as collective representations or individual ones, and which are constantly repeated and experienced as iconic. "It is through the preservation of a moment of loss," Mary Steedly writes, "that a modern sensibility anchors itself most firmly in social consciousness" (Steedly 2000: 817). Soumia's song on the wedding cassette prompted Fassis to reflect on these ruptures, with the wedding ritual serving as a symbol of social cohesiveness that seems more and more fragile with time.

Meanwhile, Layla continued to flounder, confused about how she might succeed as a singer. "Electronic media," writes Appadurai, "are resources for experiments with self-making in all sorts of societies, for all sorts of persons" (Appadurai 2000: 3). Conscious of this basic need to engage with media, Layla arranged to record cassettes, yet she failed to include original songs. She appeared on television but then had no idea how to interact with a camera and not a live audience. Part of this confusion resulted from her uncertainty as to which "path" she should follow, and the relative lack of role models for female singers in Morocco. But also, in constructing an image of an ideal audience, Layla was filled with indecision. If she only knew for whom she was singing, but her audience constantly changed—depending on the venue, she might find herself singing to a Fassi businessman, a Saudi prince, a European tourist, or an American anthropologist. After she appeared on the television program, she confessed to feeling overwhelmed about how to face the cameras, but also in imagining who was out there.

"I was paralyzed," she said. "I didn't know which song to sing. I didn't know who might be watching. I am always singing to so many audiences." This, then, was the crux of the problem of modernity for Layla. Modernity envisions an audience, envisions provoking a particular kind of reception, yet the other who grants recognition is always beyond reach, beyond imagining. Misrecognition is all too easy when multiple imagined versions of modernity exist. There was no clear audience to receive what Layla proposed becoming, neither in Europe nor in Morocco, and subsequently her self-creation was unstable. Just as, in other realms (in matters of technology, culture, religion, or human rights, for example), Moroccans feel pressured to prove themselves to those who have the power to recognize their "progress," these imagined audiences shift, their locus constantly changing. Everything is done in response to audiences too numerous and varied to be agreed on. Or perhaps, as Layla was gradually learning, those "ideal" audiences are themselves imaginary, and they do not exist at all.

Chapter 8
Conclusion: Community, Chaos, and Continuity

Since I moved away from Fes in July 2002, Morocco has become an else-where for me. Unlike Morocco's would-be migrants who lack visas to travel to Europe, I can return any time I want, which I do at least once a year, but it is not the same as living there. I observe the country at a distance, fighting my desire to romanticize it each time I read an optimistic travel article: about a restored Fes medina house, for example, that is now a bed-and-breakfast, where guests can sleep like pashas, their pillows dusted with rose petals. A campaign to bring ten million tourists to Morocco by 2010 is in full swing, and with investment from the Arabian Gulf, luxury ports are under construction in several coastal cities. Then there are the articles that make me worry: a recent feature on a neighborhood breeding ground for suicide bombers in the city of Tetouan,[1] for example, or reports on the increase of sex tourism, particularly in cities like Marrakech. What price will women pay in the great push for economic development?

Through friends and family living in Morocco, and through the new forms of electronic media that allow us to have virtual conversations on our computer screens, I try to keep up with what is going on in Fes. It is a poor substitute for fieldwork, and for the sense of being immersed in the conversations that drift through everyday life. But it is clear that change continues to happen rapidly. I visited Fes the month after Morocco experienced the worst terrorist attacks in its history on May 16, 2003, in Casablanca.

"You ask if there will be chaos? Here there is chaos," an old friend told me. "At least now that things have fallen apart, the government can no longer ignore that there are problems."

That October, King Mohammed VI presented a revised *mudawana* before Parliament, which was subsequently approved three months later.[2] My friends at the Najia Belghazi Center say it is too soon to tell the long-term effects the revisions will have for women. Because men are now required to support their ex-wives with alimony, however, there have been reports of a decrease in the number of divorces.[3]

One of the main Moroccan television networks, 2M, now broadcasts an *American Idol*-style singing contest, full of fresh-faced young Moroccan contestants who earnestly cover Arabic, French, and English songs. Too late for Layla, who would be too old to qualify. During my visits back to Morocco I have seen her as well, still singing at various hotel bars, looking a few years older, a few years further away from her dreams. Understandably, she has lost much of her optimism, and of the sense that she was somehow breaking new ground. When I watch 2M by satellite, I note the channel's carefully composed audiences, not a headscarf in their midst, which does not reflect what I see when I am in Morocco. I am impressed, though, by many of the campaigns the network reports on: cervical cancer vaccination drives; a stronger push toward educating girls in the countryside; and the new, state-trained and appointed female *murshidat* or religious guides, whose duty is to travel around the countryside ensuring that the version of Islam propagated in local mosques is moderate and textually accurate. There are critics (Nadia Yassine among them) who claim that this is all so much secular window dressing: a regime searching for a way to maintain its hegemony while feigning the outward appearance of freedom and modernity. As Abdeslam Maghraoui has argued, the specter of economic development is often used by the Moroccan government as a stand-in for true reform, the public sphere depoliticized as questions of sovereignty come to be replaced by economic liberalization (Maghraoui 2002: 24).

It is clear that much is new, yet among the middle-class Fassis I knew so well, a sense of the continuity of traditional forms of community remains. Partha Chatterjee has written that "community marks a limit to the realm of disciplinary power" (1993: 237). Beyond the ideologies created by the "other," whether displayed through narratives of nation, civil society, or Islam, a new form of community asserts itself, and rejects being entirely defined by any one discourse. The vision of community for middle-class Fassis is one in which the city and not the nation is the operative term, and one in which local power is, paradoxically, defined by the ability to hold on to representations of the past and convince others that those representations are still valid. As Stuart Hall has written, "Identities are the names we give to the different ways we are positioned by, and position ourselves within, the narratives of the past" (1994: 394).

In defining the relationship of local communities to the nation-state, Yael Navaro-Yashin examines "cynicism" as a process through which ordinary citizens conceive of their relationship to power, while Lawrence Rosen calls for an investigation into "ambivalence" toward power (Navaro-Yashin 2002, Rosen 2002). Both "cynicism" and "ambivalence" could be said to characterize the relationship of Fassis to the state. Despite this ambivalence, Fassis are conscious of themselves as citizens of Morocco at the same time that local, religious, regional, and ethnic factors also influence this sense of "Moroccanness." Identity is produced and remade through talk about local events, affected tangentially by events occurring on the national stage. Local forms of sociability interact seamlessly with national and even transnational sensibilities, as Fassis do not move and dwell in Fes alone. Yet these "national sensibilities" are more about a Moroccan cultural identity than a political one. Identity is characterized by the interplay of movement and rootedness, as every family has its *muhajirin* (emigrants), its daughters who have married Moroccans in France, brothers who work in Saudi Arabia and send money home, cousins who have won the visa lottery to the United States, and neighbors who have stowed away on fishing boats to Spain.

Identity is also characterized by tension between the often contradictory desires of the individual versus those of the family, which become visible in arguments over the role of these two sides in planning marriages. However, personal struggles for autonomy have not advanced to the point of complete detachment by the individual who relies on the family for survival. A few find the incessant chafing of family demands unbearable, and for these people, "these situations of dependency grow into irreconcilable tensions" (Bennani-Chraïbi 1994: 180). Elsewhere, or "ailleurs," is often considered the only escape (180). But while some young people desire only to leave the country, the majority of the middle-class Fassis I knew simply stay put, waiting for something to change.

I have sought to explore how individuals create and maintain a distinctive sense of local culture despite pressures from external ideologies, particularly those ideologies that concern gender. As de Certeau says, culture "articulates conflicts and alternately legitimizes, displaces, or controls the superior force. It develops in an atmosphere of tensions, and often of violence . . . The tactics of consumption, the ingenious ways in which the weak make use of the strong, thus lend a political dimension to everyday practices" (1984: xvii). The conversations I heard about everyday practices, particularly for women, reveal cleavages within society, while simultaneously producing a unique Fassi Moroccan identity, one that remains outside the narratives of the nation. To evoke solidarity with other Fassis is to tell stories, to dispute or discuss the meaning of "Fassiness," or at the very least, to conjure up the sense of power inherent in a name.

Clifford Geertz once commented that "men do not float as bounded psychic entities, detached from their backgrounds and singularly named . . . their identity is an attribute they borrow from their setting" (1974: 41). Yet outside local settings, particularly in the case of Fassi Moroccans who have migrated in search of economic livelihood, some have experienced the loss of this contextualized identity. In an era of globalization, when some middle-class Fassis with prominent social origins have been unable to translate their family connections into the type of wealth and capital that extends beyond the city itself, names become even more significant in local contexts. With the increase in migration and the accompanying meaninglessness that names (and local identities) carry in transnational situations, *nisba* becomes even more significant on the local stage, both for those who return and for those who remain behind. If these characteristics of contextualized personhood, represented by *nisba*, are "supposedly immanent," representing "speech, blood, faith, provenance, and the rest" (42), when the conditions of modernity and globalization remove this context and Others cease to recognize the Fassi, what happens to Fassi selfhood, personhood, and identity?

Middle-class Fassis continue to insist on their distinctiveness: to be an "original" Fassi is to possess an identity inextricably tied up in kinship, in history, and in the past glories of the nation-state. Yet some of these attributes are exactly the types of obstacles that block different agendas. On the one hand, this book can be seen as a study of the way individuals maintain a strong sense of local culture despite large-scale global transformations. But on the other hand, what some may see as resilience may appear to others as stubbornness, accompanied by entrenched social networks and an insistence on remaining rooted in traditions that obstruct the aspirations of those not in the social grouping of "original" Fassis. For Scheherezade, for Layla, and for the women of the Najia Belghazi Center, Fassi culture might be said to serve as a direct obstacle to their goals as and for women: to be able to live an independent existence without being judged, to seek justice and equity across social classes, and to succeed in a system that consistently attempted to resist difference, ambition and ingenuity in favor of old ties and old ways of being.

The issue of *mudawana* reform, which was for many the most pressing topic involving women from 2000 to 2003, provides an interesting window into the issues facing women in Moroccan society. The stances Fassis took on the *mudawana* often revealed less about their sense of Islam and more about what the social group to which they belonged stood to lose or gain from the reforms. The differential access to resources according to social class is one of the most pressing problems facing Moroccan society. Among my friends who did not consider themselves "original" Fassis, most felt they had worked hard, in both education and employment, to attain middle-class status. When they were restricted in some situation where they felt an "original Fassi" had called on privilege to gain the upper hand, they railed against entrenched hierarchies and corruption in Moroccan society. Yet many of these "original" Fassis had the sense that they were losing their influence, and my sense was that there were many Fassis who were economically middle-class and had fallen from a higher status due to the vagaries of postcolonial economic reforms. If the idea of a strong middle class is measured by the ability to pass on wealth to the next generation, or for children do as well or better in life than their parents, then the continuity of this class remains uncertain. Indeed, some among the Moroccan upper classes have consolidated their resources and passed on tremendous wealth and advantages to their children. But the inheritances of the middle-class Fassis I knew continued to be diluted among heirs with each passing generation. While I witnessed small business owners eking out a modest living for themselves and their families, and while it was not uncommon to see a child being groomed for a parent's position at a bank or a local administrative office, some traditionally "Fassi" bourgeois occupations were growing increasingly marginal, and it seemed uncertain whether the next generation would be in a position to do better.

A sense of the part the nation-state has played in leaving some of its citizens behind came out in Fassi narratives. The Moroccan nation, in failing to create a space for all of its citizens, is constantly under scrutiny by Fassis whose critiques surface in unexpected places: in the rumors that point to the government's inability to unify its citizens, or in the creation of NGOs for interactions among women of different classes whose concerns have gone unaddressed by the government. The vision of community that surfaces in rumor is one that emphasizes the strength of local identities and resources, both beyond and prior to that offered by the nation state. For women at the Najia Belghazi Center, community and solidarity are to be found when women recognize their own common interests; yet again, the problem of social class rears its head in the failure of the NGO to gain widespread local acceptance.

An examination of the way middle-class women in Fes conceptualize identity, class, and gendered public and private spaces is useful not only for an understanding of the power of ideologies but also for how categories of gender are altered to adapt to new forms of social life. Moroccan women, without a doubt, are taking on new roles in society, and their active presence in the public sphere gives lie to the stereotypes of Muslim women as passive and oppressed. At times, these "new" roles mirror what has existed before, while at other moments, they diverge significantly.

Ideologies often originate in the metropoles, and those that affect women come from the loci of government as well as from centers of media and capital. To study only the origins of these processes in global cities, therefore, is to ignore the dispersal of ideologies into the hinterlands, where what women appropriate, fashion, and reject from those ideologies is sometimes much more interesting. The condition of the middle class in Fes, a city struggling with its own identity and position in the future of Morocco is, I argue, similar to that of the middle class in other urban areas around the world whose roles in transforming society are bypassed by studies that favor global cities. In cases where the nation-state has failed to provide a substantive plan to integrate all its citizens, the residents of Fes, rather than seeking global fulfillment, look to the city itself for identity and continuity. The middle class of Fes is not aimless, nor do they lack a sense of coherent identity or connectedness. Rather, a study of this group reveals that kinship and family are still paramount, and that being "Fassi" provides one with a sense of identity and rootedness.

Even here, in a city said to be among the most conservative in Morocco, women are present in a range of new occupations and activities within the public sphere. In the struggles recounted here of women seeking recognition and respect, it would seem the ones who had the most success were those who managed to operate within accepted cultural practices, transforming those practices to new ends. Huriya, for example, gained respect because she successfully managed property, a salary, and her family, while also forming social networks characterized by patron-client relations that extended beyond the family. Others who were less successful, like Layla, faced obstacles for other reasons: they lacked access to resources or family reputation, and they tried to manipulate problematic discourses of sexuality. For the many divorced and abandoned women who came to the Najia Belghazi Center, the traditional safeguards of patriarchy had fallen away, and the *mudawana* was of no help to them. Women truly without men were threatening, their perceived unmoored sexuality representing chaos (*fitna*).[4] The women who have the most success in forging new identities in the public sphere are those who, as Lila Abu-Lughod has noted for Bedouin women, deny the negative associations of sexuality with social chaos (1986).

But *fitna* is a productive space as well. The gendering of new urban spaces, or the commentary on the chaos of social life and the nation-state found in rumors, indicates that it is through this space of chaos that culture is challenged and transformed. *Fitna* provides a means of expression through which Fassis can critique social practices and contest strategies of power, whether that power emanates from an "other" social group, the government, or patriarchal interests. Similarly, rejecting others' attempts to read a situation as productive of chaos is also a strategy by which individuals refuse to consider their own behavior as negative.

Stefania Pandolfo calls *fitna* "a flirtation with the unknown, with the insecurity of novel paths, that taste for dissent, dispute, and hazardous games" (Pandolfo 1997: 332). The term may also be associated with "'temptation,' 'fascination,' 'commotion' or 'disbelief'" (Rosen 2002: 208). *Fitna* is necessarily present in social life, as an acknowledgment of the duality of life, in which chaos and order exist alongside each other and are complementary rather than mutually exclusive.

Yet *fitna* is also frequently linked to how different groups perceive the position of women. The notion of "woman" is a prime site in the contradictory process of defining Moroccan modernity and community. The "imagining" of a community (to quote Benedict Anderson), whether it is on the style of the nation or on that of the Muslim *umma*, or "community of believers," is contingent on specified relations between men and women (1991). Thus the imaginary boundary of "public" and "private" is constantly disputed, produced anew in each situation, and often provocatively linked to *fitna*. For the government, the veiled and cloaked Islamist woman, her voice capable of transmitting shame, is a threat to the Moroccan nation insofar as Islamists call into question the legitimacy of the state. For the Islamists, too much freedom for women threatens the end of religiously legislated divisions between men and women, signaling that Moroccan society has become irrevocably corrupt. For both sides, the presence and absence of women, whether through voice or visibility, are read as signs of the current state of Moroccan society. In the highly suggestive words of one Casablancan judge, "civil society is chaos itself because the frontier between private and public spaces vanishes. If women cross the line to the public space and start speaking as if their opinion matters, it is the end of the *hudud*, the sacred boundaries of authority. If women do not obey authority, no one will. As a judge, I call that chaos; in the West, they call it civil society" (Hegasy 1997: 135).

At this particular moment, when Moroccans seem intensely concerned with defining a future for their country, conversations often focus on how men and women will relate to each other in this imagined, ideal Morocco. Morocco is a country of multiple contexts, often extremes— between rural and urban, poor and wealthy, religious and secular, provincial and cosmopolitan, Berber and Arab—and there are just as many identities between those ranges, which are intended here as guides and not binaries. Conflicting ideologies set forth particular guides for a singular Moroccan, female identity, but the country's diversity is evidence that there is not solely one ideology that holds sway. From the dusty market *suqs* of rural Morocco to the sleek and gleaming cafés of Casablanca, it is impossible to see Morocco as one unified country, or to hear it speak with one unified voice. Even within a city there are multiple ways to imagine modernity. Whether commenting on the proper place for women in an exercise club or in a marriage, Fassis are, simultaneously, commenting on the state of the nation, the world, and their places within these. An ethnography of Morocco, like that of any nation, should therefore be an attempt to engage with many voices, to embrace both synthesis and dissonance, and to tease out the disparate strands that are woven into the haphazard tapestry that comprises the Moroccan nation.

Glossary

'arubi – people of rural origin, sometimes used disparagingly
asl – origin
djellaba – robelike garment worn in public by men and women
hadith – sayings of the Prophet Muhammad
halal – permissible by Islam
haqq – rights, justice
hammam – public bath
haram – forbidden by Islam
hshuma – shameful
huquq al-insan – human rights
huquq al-mar'a – women's rights
in sha'llah – God willing
klam dyal nas – gossip, people's talk
medina – literally "city"; the name given in Morocco to the original Moroccan-
    built cities prior to French occupation
mudawana – personal status codes covering a woman's rights in marriage and
    divorce
al-Qarawiyin – Fes mosque and university built in the ninth century
shemker – "glue sniffers"; derogatory term given to runaways and orphaned
    street children
tagine – stew of meat and vegetables traditionally cooked in conical clay pot
taqalid – tradition
talaq – divorce
ville nouvelle – new cities constructed in Morocco during the French protectorate
    usually alongside the existing Arab *medinas.*
wali – male guardian who gives bride away under Maliki law
wili-wili – exclamation

Notes

Chapter 1. Introduction: Women of Fes and the Territories of Ideology

1. A "Fassi" is a resident of Fes.
2. For a particularly insightful and relevant commentary on the colonial underpinnings of the discourse of "saving the oppressed," see L. Abu-Lughod 2002.
3. See, for example, van Nieuwkerk, 1995.
4. The CEDAW argues that men and women have full equality under the law, equal rights when entering or dissolving a marriage, and the same rights over property in the event of a divorce. Discrimination is defined as any impairment that prohibits women from enjoying full human rights to the same degree as men. For the full text, see http://www.un.org/womenwatch/daw/cedaw/text/econvention.htm, accessed October 8, 2007.
5. I discuss these debates more extensively in Chapter 3.
6. This is less true for blue-collar positions, in which women as primary income earners represent only 10 percent of the total population, although these statistics do not take into account the numerous unaccounted-for occupations of women.
7. For a collection of interdisciplinary essays exploring the limits of women's participation in public life, the effects of class and gender on identity, and the relationship between power and gender in everyday life, see Göcek and Balaghi 1994. An account of women's power relations in a rural Moroccan village can be found in Davis 1982, and in an urban context, Rassam 1980.
8. See Butler 1997 for more on the idea of power as an object lost, and the subsequent condition of melancholy, which Cohen (2003, 2005) draws on in describing the creation of a detached, global middle class in Casablanca.
9. In this way, my first exposure to Morocco mirrored that of the many thousands whose experience of the Muslim world came through exhibitions. For more on the relationship of the Western gaze, imperialism, and the developing world as seen through World's Fairs and other exhibitions, see Rydell 1984; Mitchell 1988; Çelik and Kinney 1990; Çelik 1992; Coombs 1994; Hoffenberg 2001.
10. A number of pioneering anthropological studies of women's lives in Morocco have influenced the present one. Willy Jansen's *Women Without Men* (1987), an excellent portrayal of women's lives, resources, and social networks in Algeria of the 1970s, was an important text that guided my initial thinking about women's encounters with the public sphere, unmediated by men. Deborah Kapchan's *Gender on the Market* (1996), which explores the effect of women's participation in the labor market on verbal expressive genres that have traditionally been reserved for men, also enhanced my interest in the new roles women play in Moroccan public space. Moroccan sociologist Fatima Mernissi's theoreti-

cal contribution to the understanding of gender dynamics in Muslim societies was foundational in my early thinking about these topics. Vanessa Maher also authored a pioneering work that examined the types of networks that women form outside the market economy, particularly within the realm of kinship and simulated kinship (Maher 1974a). For a useful characterization of representations of men and women, particularly in folklore, see Dwyer 1978. On the effect of shame on female sexuality, see Guessous 1984. On the anomie experienced by urban youth, Bennani-Chraibi 1994 is illuminating. For an excellent ethnography concerning women's life cycles, networks, identity formation, and gender segregation, see Evers Rosander 1991.

11. There is an extensive literature exploring the links between women/gender and nationalism in the Muslim world. See, for example, Kandiyoti 1991, 2001; Mohanty, Russo, and Torres 1991; Yeganeh 1993; Badran 1995; Joseph 2000; Timmerman 2000; Charrad 2001; Baron 2007.

12. Place of origin is still very important to Moroccans, many of whom feel intense loyalty to their natal region. The principle of *nisba*, discussed in more detail in Chapter 5, is a linguistic strategy that identifies family origins and the group to which one belongs according to last name; see Geertz 1979; Rosen 1984. In Morocco, much more so than in the United States, a surname frequently contains significant clues that can identify a person's origin, social status, profession, or membership in a religious order.

13. After 808, Arabs and Berbers settled on either half of the river Oued Fes, and in 814, Muslims fleeing Cordoba in Andalusia settled the eastern half of the city, comprising what is still called the Andalusian quarter. Tunisians from the city of Qarawiyin came several years later, lending their name to the now famous center of Islamic learning, built in 857. Throughout the history of Morocco, Fes served as the capital under various dynasties, including the Merinid and the Saadian eras. Under the Merinid dynasty in the thirteenth century, a new city, Fes El Jdid, was constructed, and waves of Muslim and Jewish immigrants expelled from Muslim Spain came in the fifteenth century.

14. Geoffrey Porter notes that the claim to Islamic knowledge is no longer distinctive to Fes. The recent revival of the Qarawiyin has not restored the importance of Fes as a "city of knowledge," but rather has brought an influx of rural students into the city (2002b: 127).

15. A more complete bibliography on the Islamic City can be found in J. Abu-Lughod 1987. See Hourani and Stern 1970 and Hanedi and Miura 1994 for more on the academic history of the "Islamic City." Two recent reexaminations of the concept can be found in Gottreich 2007 and Wheatley 2001.

16. For a survey of French colonial architectural practices, see Wright 1991. On how French colonizers sought to transform colonial spaces into an image of French modernity and to represent reality in spatial terms, see Rabinow 1989.

17. What Silverstein calls "structural nostalgia"—nostalgia for disappearing institutions, reflected in attitudes toward domestic space—could be evident here. See Silverstein 2004 for more on colonial objectification and the nostalgia for "traditional" spaces such as the Kabyle home, enshrined as the epitome of Algerian Kabyle culture by sociologist Pierre Bourdieu (1977).

18. "Social class" is a problematic term with meanings ranging from a group's objective relation to the means of production (Marx) to a group of people who share the same economically shaped life chances (Weber). Ideas of class are further complicated by the fact that theories about social class cannot be applied uniformly to every society, since a variety of other "cultural" factors

both affect and are intertwined with social position. Thus, I use "middle class" here with full acknowledgment of the complex associations of this term. In terms of property, Weber characterizes the middle class as lying between the "positively privileged property classes" and the "negatively privileged property classes" (1978: 303). The "positively privileged property classes" are distinguished not only by their ability to acquire luxury goods but also by their monopolization over such resources as land, capital, creditors, and the labor of others (303). "Negatively privileged property classes" have no property or capital and seldom the means to acquire more than the basics necessary for survival. Between those two, the "various 'middle classes'" possess some property or skills but may be employed in a range of positions (entrepreneur, official, or craftsman) (303). "Original" Fassis can also be said to constitute a status group, following Weber, insofar as they were a stratified group "in terms of honor and styles of life" (936) whose claim to prominent family names and Fassi origins lifted their status well above their material resources. Because of the differences of status and origin, middle-class Fassis did not constitute a group that recognized itself as a community. Thus, while "middle class" defined solely in economic terms might encompass a much wider set of people, the claim of Fassi origins distinguished the differential statuses of members of the middle class and led to an implicit stratification. The middle-class Fassis in this study were owners of property and small businesses, were politically conservative, and shared a sense of nostalgia for an idealized past when Fes was the most prominent city in Morocco.

19. In addition to the classic work by Halpern 1963, see also LeTourneau 1956, Adam 1968.

20. "Tradition" is a constructed category, because it does not refer to an unchanging past but in fact is formed in relation to current discourses. Often the imagined, essentialized past is produced anew in narratives, as Fassis draw on their knowledge of the city's history and reputation, using it to support particular positions in arguments or debate, to make statements about gender or class, but above all, to produce an essentialized Fassi identity. This identity is somewhat defensive and responds very much to the demands of the present. Efforts to define a historic, unchanging Fassi self or identity are particularly ironic, considering the fact that the majority of the "original" Fassis no longer live in the ancient medina. For more on this process of the construction of tradition, see the collection of essays in Hobsbawm and Ranger 1992.

21. Interestingly, outside of academic circles, few of the Fassis I knew specifically blamed colonialism for societal woes, and one man in his forties even expressed the subversive idea that "it would be good if the French would come back, because at least they knew how to make trains run on time."

22. This attitude was everywhere in evidence after the terrorist attacks on Casablanca on May 16, 2003, by a group loosely affiliated with al-Qaeda. Twelve suicide bombers killed themselves and thirty-three other people. For more on the contexts and fallout from this attack, see Howe 2005.

23. For further anthropological work on the topic of the history of Sufism in Morocco, see Gellner 1969, 1981; Eickelman 1976; Mernissi 1977; Dwyer 1978; Crapanzano 1981; Joffé 1997; Cornell 1998.

24. The term "Salafi," meaning "predecessors" or "ancestors," has been associated both with Muhammad ibn ʿAbd al-Wahhab (1703–92), a theologian from the Saudi peninsula, and, for its popular revival in the nineteenth century, Muhammad Abduh (1849–1905). See Laroui 1992, Burgat and Dowell 1993;

Ruedy 1994; Shahin 1997; Tozy 1999; Layachi 2000, for more on Salafism and Islamism in Morocco.

25. For a thorough examination of the history of Islamic discourses on women, see Ahmed 1992.

26. www.mincom.gov.ma/english/generalities/woman/moroccan.htm. The section on women, with versions in Arabic, French, and English, was visible from 1999 until the fall of 2003, when it was removed from the Moroccan government website.

27. A section on women in Moroccan history highlights the contributions of women to history, including the creation of the Qarawiyin University in the eighth century, which marks "the period of islamization and arabization." It is interesting that the site uses these terms, as "arabization" as a state practice did not become commonplace until the 1980s, and Morocco had some difficulty convincing the Arab league that they even qualified as an Arab country. Mention of the significant Berber population (estimated at 40 percent, see Lacoste 1991; Brett and Fentress 1996) is effaced by ideologies of arabization, exemplified by a post-independence declaration that Morocco is, first and foremost, an Arab Muslim nation.

28. Despite their presence in the labor force, Moroccan women have failed to reach top positions at managerial levels. In all the countries of the Middle East and North Africa (MENA), working women "are heavily concentrated in lower-level white-collar jobs, and underrepresented in managerial and professional positions, and the MENA region compares unfavorably with other developing areas in this regard" (Doumato and Posusney 2003: 13).

29. Although the government itself had originally promoted *mudawana* reform, it was unclear between 2000 and 2003 how the king would rule on the controversial issue. Many privately speculated that King Mohammed VI's hands were tied, and that he was cowed by the Islamists, who presented too much of a threat to be challenged. Subsequent events, most notably the suicide bombings in Casablanca in May 2003, led to a backlash against Islamism, which may have contributed to a sense that the time was ripe to push through some of the reforms.

Speculations aside, the king finally stepped in to end the stalemate, reflecting a long-standing pattern of monarchical conflict resolution. Abdellah Hammoudi has suggested that the state manipulates divisions between social groups, noting that even in colonial times, "particularisms" or differences "were highlighted and used as avenues of hyper-centralization" (Hammoudi 2001: 158). Authoritarian strategy has always been concerned with producing "a specific Morocco based on cleavage, difference, hierarchy, and so on" (Hammoudi 1997: 174). This strategy encourages oppositions (Islamist/secularist) that enforce a boundary and declare the two positions to be incommensurable, with no room for common ground in the debates. With *mudawana* reform, the state initially refused to get involved in the quagmire that it had, perhaps, created by its encouragement of both positions, as evidenced by the government website (woman as traditional, woman as modern). Divisions fracture the community; subsequent mediations assert the strength of the monarchy and the unity of the Moroccan nation.

Chapter 2. Rumors: Constructing Fes

Epigraph: Khaled Mattawa, "Letter to Ibrahim" (Mattawa 1997: 67).

1. For more on the possibilities for narrative to generate multiple partial

selves, particularly in public and private contexts, see Ochs and Capps 1996; Haviland 1977; Goffman 1974, 1959.

2. "Jmel ma tayshufsh hdibtu, tayshuf ghayr hdibit nas."

3. For an overview of current Moroccan attitudes toward the management of spirits, see Spadola 2004.

4. On the shaping of narrative for a particular audience, see Bauman 1986.

5. See Kapchan 1996 for an excellent discussion of the gendered nature of talk (*l'hdra*) and gossip in Moroccan society. Her description of gossip as a "*forum for* speech rather than a *forum of* speech," and as a genre containing other oral genres including proverbs, jokes, or stories, "from lies to truth and legend," is broad enough to encompass rumor as a form of *l-hdra*.

6. See, for example, Shryock 1997; Kapchan 1996; Caton 1991; Lavie 1990; L. Abu-Lughod 1986.

7. Writing of Fes and Meknes in the 1970s, Amal Rassam says that "unmarried women defer to married ones and, in company, they tend to keep silent. A forty-year-old unmarried woman is still considered a girl (*bint*), without much social status or relevance" (1980: 174).

8. In Fes, I attended a number of middle-class weddings over the course of my fieldwork where the bride's average age was twenty, the groom's age thirty-five or more.

9. A detailed overview of the history, contexts, and destinations of migration can be found in de Haas 2005.

10. See Kapchan 1996 for more on class-based talk (*l-hadra*) concerning maids who represent these discourses of contagion. On discourses of contagion in urban spaces, see Stallybrass and White 1996, and more generally, Mary Douglas's classic work of 1966.

11. For more on the effect of structural adjustment policies in North Africa, see Pfeifer 1999.

12. This fear, as it turned out, was a legitimate one. On May 16, 2003, several small-scale attacks were carried out in the city of Casablanca, killing nineteen people.

13. In this incident, a general strike called for by opposition parties and labor unions on December 14, 1990, turned into rioting and looting, particularly by unemployed youth (Bennani-Chraïbi 2000: 53). The rioters targeted not only symbols of government but also businesses, factories, and wealthy villas on the Rue d'Immouzer.

14. Susan Slyomovics's excellent work, *The Performance of Human Rights in Morocco* (2005) offers a detailed examination of the control over political discourse, and the interaction between the speech of the people and the government's official silences. The subject of her book is the new emphasis on public recounting of the "years of lead"—the period during the regime of King Hassan II when many political opponents were imprisoned, tortured, or disappeared.

15. In fact, Moroccan legal codes are mostly derived from European ones, with the exception of the *mudawana* personal status codes or family law, which do come from *shari'a*. See Chapters 3 and 4 for more on this subject.

16. See Cohen 2004 and Bennani-Chraïbi 2000 for more on the problem of integrating educated youth into Moroccan society.

17. Unemployment for university graduates is extremely high, around 33 percent, which leads many young Moroccans to look for other avenues of technical training that might lead to work. For all Moroccans aged 19–24, unemployment figures are around 35 percent (De Haas 2005: 21).

Chapter 3. Mudawana *Reform and the Persistence of Patriarchy*

1. Henna is the plant-derived dye used to decorate women's hands with elaborate designs prior to marriage celebrations.
2. See Ziba Mir-Hosseini 1993 for a useful comparison of Moroccan and Iranian family law. A collection of articles focusing on the history of gender relations, family, and divorce in Muslim societies can be found in Sonbol 1996. Mounira Charrad 2001 provides essential background into the principles underlying the laws' codifications after Moroccan independence.
3. Sharabi argues that modernization has transformed patriarchy into "neo-patriarchy," still authoritarian whether taking the form of religious, secular, nationalist, or leftist ideologies. Yet Hammoudi notes that the usage of the term "neo-patriarchy," perpetuates dualisms (such as tradition/modernity) that imply a discontinuity with past forms of authoritarianism, thus obscuring the long, unbroken history of patriarchal authoritarianism in North Africa (Hammoudi 1997: 155).
4. For more on the intersection of gender and patriarchy in the greater Middle East, see Joseph 2000. On Islam's formation under patriarchal conditions, see Karmi 1996.
5. See Khodja 1985 and Zerdoumi 1970 for a discussion of patriarchy within the family in a North African context.
6. For more on this dynamic, see Rassam 1980 and LaCoste-Dujardin 1985.
7. Lawrence Rosen suggests that it is potentially risky to attribute a cultural model that explains the workings of power in society to one source. Power may be drawn from multiple sources, and there are numerous subtle ways that power might be exercised in social life. Acknowledged ambivalence about power does not necessarily signify an intent to usurp the position of the master, but may instead be necessary to the stability of Moroccan social life (Rosen 2002).
8. On the political patronage system, see Hammoudi 1997, Claisse 1987, Brown 1977, Leveau 1976, Waterbury 1973.
9. It is nonetheless important to point out, as Lawrence Rosen does in *The Justice of Islam* (2002), that despite the laws' origins in European legal codes, actual courtroom procedures are not simply Europeanized, but take on a distinctly Moroccan form.
10. The *mudawana* has its origins in the Maliki school of Islamic law (*shari'a*), which is derived from four sources: the Qur'an, *hadiths* (sayings and recorded behavior of the Prophet), *qiyas*, and *ijma*. The final two are legal interpretations of the Qur'an and the *hadiths*—the first, *qiyas*, through analogy, the second, *ijma*, through community consensus. From the first to the fourth centuries since Islam's foundation (seventh–eleventh centuries), Islamic scholars created the versions of *shari'a* practiced today. Muslim countries follow four schools of jurisprudence with slightly different interpretations of *shari'a*: Maliki, Hanafi, Hanbali, and Shafi'i.
11. The changes to the *mudawana* in 1993 were preceded by a two-year campaign by Moroccan feminist organization Union de l'Action Féminine to gather one million signatures in support of reforming the laws according to international standards of human rights. Islamist opponents immediately attacked the campaign as an act of apostasy aimed at completely westernizing Moroccan society (Brand 1998). King Hassan II authorized only minor changes to the laws, including the requirement that two witnesses and the wife had to be present for a husband to initiate a divorce, that a woman could choose her own marital

guardian (*wali*), and that a woman had to be informed if her husband took another wife. Some feminists perceived these reforms as significant evidence of a new willingness on the part of the monarchy to consider previously taboo topics, while others felt that the reforms were cosmetic changes only and had not gone far enough. For more on these reforms, see Buskens 2003 or Brand 1998.

12. Jamila Bargach's excellent book, *Orphans of Islam: Family, Abandonment, and Secret Adoption in Morocco* (2002), examines the implications for illegitimate children when Moroccan emphasis on ties of lineage (*nasab*) prevent adoption or the children's full participation in society.

13. On the establishment of alliances through marriage in another Moroccan context, see Brown 1976.

14. Moroccan courts have echoed this sentiment on the importance of virginity in their rulings on divorce settlements. Ziba Mir-Hosseini has shown how judges often reduced husbands' consolation payments in divorce cases where the marriage was a woman's second, accepting the argument that "the second divorce could not be considered as causing serious harm," and therefore reflecting the "premium placed on virginity" (Mir-Hosseini 1993: 91).

15. See, for example, Maher 1974a, b.

16. The fact that director Tazi places his protagonist in the *medina*, locus of Moroccan tradition, is no coincidence. As Roy Armes notes, in North African cinema, the *medina* frequently serves as "a focal point of contemporary contradiction of the locus of nostalgia for lost or threatened values" (2006: 14).

17. However, if the wife refuses her husband's request to take another wife, he still reserves the option of divorce.

18. See Barron 1957, Ziai 1997. A study of 1,000 Casablanca households in 1953 revealed that 2 percent were polygamous. According to Ziai, official statistics are currently around 3 percent, although actual numbers could be higher.

19. Historically, polygamy enabled levirate marriages, in which a man marries his brother's widow in order that she might keep her children (who might otherwise be taken by the husband's kin group); Charrad 2001: 39. But this type of levirate marriage is no longer common, and in the case of widowhood or divorce, many women prefer not to remarry at all, in order to maintain custody of their children.

20. Literally "age of desperation." Khadija's belief that menopausal women were unable to have sex was not necessarily shared by other educated middle-class Fassis. I did not gather enough data on this topic to conclude that this opinion was representative.

21. On North African women's cynicism over male fidelity, see Dwyer 1978 and Jansen 1987.

22. This was a popular means of picking up prostitutes.

23. For more on the struggles lower class Moroccan women face in supporting themselves and their families, see Mernissi 1989.

24. For more on the stigma associated with divorce in North Africa, see Jansen 1987.

25. See *Journal hebdomadaire* 129 (October 11–17, 2003) and 130 (October 18–24, 2003) for a survey of reactions.

Chapter 4. Solidarity with Distinctions: The Limits of Intervention at a Fassi Nongovernmental Organization

1. UNESCO reports an illiteracy rate of 60 percent for women from the years 2000–2004. See http://www.unicef.org/infobycountry/morocco_statistics.html, accessed October 26, 2007.

2. See Chomiak 2002 for more on the conflicts between criminal laws dealing with violence against women and the comparative absence of laws against spousal rape at a similar NGO in Rabat.

3. Judges, especially in rural areas, still frequently disregarded the 1993 revisions. Although this fieldwork was conducted prior to the *mudawana* reforms proposed by King Mohammed VI in 2003 and legalized in 2004, many Fassi activists feared that judges would continue to ignore the more recent changes.

4. The headquarters were named after a Moroccan activist for Amnesty International who was killed in a car accident.

5. One of the 2004 revisions to the *mudawana* gives partial ownership of the marital household to the wife, so that the husband can no longer demand that she leave.

6. "Casa" is short for "Casablanca," the bustling business center of the country. As I explain in Chapter 5, in disputes between spouses of different regions, "original" Fassis frequently draw on regional stereotypes to explain the source of the problems.

7. *Sdaq* or *mahr* is the money given by the husband to the wife that he does not have the right to take from her after marriage. Sometimes part of the *sdaq* is deferred and unclaimed by the woman until the event of a divorce, where she had the right to demand the husband pay it, unless she forfeits this right as a condition of the husband agreeing to a divorce he does not want.

8. For legal case studies concerning Moroccan marital disputes that have crossed international borders, see Rosen 2002.

9. This was made illegal in the revisions to the code proposed by King Mohammed VI in 2003 and approved by Parliament in February 2004.

10. This has been a common strategy of the women's movement in Morocco since the 1980s, since early efforts to politicize women's issues were suppressed by elites. Instead, women's associations have sought to become part of the domain of civil society while quietly working to draw attention to the state's duplicity in asserting its progressive aims while continuing to appease patriarchal interests in practice; see Naciri 1998: 1.

11. See, for example, Ong 1996 and Spivak 1996

12. In Fes, people spoke more Arabic than French, across social classes and educational levels. (This was not the case among educated professionals and academics in Rabat or Casablanca, where more French was spoken.) Even though most of the literature and training manuals used at the Center were in French, the volunteers still spoke Moroccan Arabic (*darija*) to one another, occasionally peppering the conversation with French terms related to psychological counseling, volunteering, human rights, and nongovernmental activities.

13. See, for example, Guehenno 1995; Ohmae 1996.

14. Lawrence Rosen notes that in the past, metal workers from Morocco's Jewish community also doubled as plumbers. With most Jews having left the country, there is a demand for this type of skilled labor (personal communication, November 18, 2003).

Chapter 5. Kinship: Seeking Sanctuary in the City

1. For the possibility of the client inverting the ties of patronage to his or her own advantage, see Smith 2002.

2. See, for example, Early 1993; J. White 1994; Singerman 1995; Singerman and Hoodfar 1996; Hoodfar 1997; Holmes-Eber 2003.

3. See, for example, Royaume du Maroc 1996; Guerraoui 1996; Stevenson (1997; L. Abu Lughod 1986.

4. Vanessa Maher authored a pioneering work that examined the types of networks that women formed outside the market economy, particularly within the realm of kinship and simulated kinship (Maher 1974a).

5. Although older and larger than Sefrou, Fes offers useful possibilities for comparison to Geertz's Sefrou, since they are located in the same region and share similar cultural features, including strains of conservatism and traditionalism that differentiate them from other urban centers such as Casablanca or Marrakech.

6. Lawrence Rosen has observed that households headed by women were more numerous in the past than scholars were asserting at the time, a fact which is echoed in the censuses in *Meaning and Order in Moroccan Society* (Rosen, personal communication, May 2003).

7. This is less true for blue collar positions, in which women as primary income earners represent only 10 percent of the total population, although these statistics do not take into account the numerous unaccounted-for occupations of women.

8. All the names in this chapter have been changed to pseudonyms. My focus is on my husband's maternal kin, and Moroccan women generally keep their names at marriage.

9. I have been asked over the years whether my in-laws "accepted" me despite my different nationality, religion, and culture, and my answer has always been an unqualified yes. If anything, my observations of Moroccans in mixed marriages, which are fairly common, indicate that Moroccan in-laws are frequently more welcoming of the "Other" spouse than Westerners are.

10. My husband, for example, has taught me volumes about Moroccan social life, but he has been very clear that he does not wish to become an "informant."

11. Six of the nine Tazi children living in the building were women. Two (Huriya and Habiba) had been widowed, one (Fatiha) divorced, two (Bouchra and Khadija) were unmarried, and one was married and living with her husband (Mounia). All the women who had been married had lived part of their married lives in the building, with the exception of Huriya. Of the three sons of Si Mohammed Tazi, one had been married several times (Ahmed), the other (Rachid) only once, and the third (Abdel) never.

12. I discuss the significance of the *nisba* principle for Moroccanist anthropology later in this chapter. For more on the significance of proper names in Islamic history, see Sublet 1991.

13. A discussion of the anthropological literature on patron-clientage in Morocco can be found in Smith 2002. In particular, see Cherifi 1983; Hammoudi 1997, 1999.

14. Comments such as these demonstrated the prejudice Ville Nouvelle dwellers often expressed toward rural-urban migrants living in the *medina.*

15. For more on middle-class responses to the dangers and possible social contagion presented by maids, see Kapchan 1996.

16. These names include Berrada, Sqalli, Tazi, Bennani, Bennouna, Ben Chekroun, Alami, Bel Khiyat, Tajmouati, Sebti, Gnoun, and Chraibi.

17. Three hundred dirhams equalled about thirty U.S. dollars in 2001.

Chapter 6. Occupying the Public: New Forms of Gendered Urban Space

Epigraphs: "Alli da mrato li jamaa, taytlaq-ha" and "Ma t-tshuf min al-sma ghayr duz al-halqa." These two proverbs were known to older Fassis, although most of the younger generation were unfamiliar with them.

1. I use the term "public space" cognizant of its meaning as a place of free assembly where individuals do not have to pay to gain admission. Because access to the exercise club and cyber cafe is restricted to those who can pay, this limits participation in these spaces to middle- and upper-class Fassis. "Public space" is distinguished from "public sphere," for which I follow Habermas's definition of a public sphere as a space "where private people come together as a public" (1991: 27) to form opinions and mediate between family and state. Debates about the Eurocentrism of Habermas's theories are too numerous to go into here.

2. The public/private dichotomy remains a much-debated framework of analysis in both anthropology and Middle East Studies, criticized for being more of a reflection of Euro-American constructs than the societies anthropologists study. See, for example Lamphere 1993; Nelson 1974; Pateman 1983; Afsaruddin 1999; Bekkar 1997; L. Abu-Lughod 1986.

3. A website published by the Moroccan government of 2000–2003 best represents the government's position. Slightly altered since the revision of the personal status codes governing a woman's rights in marriage and divorce, the website nonetheless continues to promote the same ideologies concerning the ideal Moroccan woman.

For the opposing religious discourse, see for example Benkirane 2002.

4. Name given to residents of the city of Fes.

5. "Ville Nouvelle" is the term used to refer to those districts of the city built by the French Protectorate (1912–56) and since. Although numerous studies have been conducted in the ancient *medina* (founded 808), little attention has been given to the ways that Fassis interact with the French-built environment and build over and around the original buildings constructed by the French.

6. See, for example, Early 1993; Ossman 1994; Singerman and Hoodfar 1996; Hoodfar 1997; Ghannam 2002; Salamandra 2004; L. Abu-Lughod 2005.

7. See, for example, Ossman 1994; Kapchan 1996; Cohen 2005.

8. See Buitelaar 1993 for more on Moroccan women during Ramadan.

9. The work of Moroccan sociologist Fatima Mernissi (1987) is the most notable example.

10. Eickelman 1976 thus categorizes the home/street dichotomy for Morocco of the 1970s.

11. See footnote above, also Göle 1997. An SSRC working bibliography on public spheres in comparative context contains a number of recent contributions to the literature on Islam, women, and public space; Bier 2006.

12. Rural women did not experience as many restrictions on their movement, as Mernissi 1994 has shown.

13. Deborah Kapchan (1996) in particular has explored the emergence of transgressive expressive genres as a result of women's movement into the public sphere for economic reasons.

14. A few women spoke of not wanting to be taken for a "prostitute," but this did not literally mean being confused for someone who might accept money for sex. Rather, this term was used along with a few others loosely meant to imply a woman who engages in illicit sexual activity.

15. Regular socializing outside the home for the middle-class Ville Nouvelle women who did not spend time in cafés took place in the public bath (*hammam*). In the neighborhood of Cinema Lux where I conducted my fieldwork, women of all ages go to the *hammam* once a week and stay for hours. But many younger professional women have foregone this practice and do not like the *hammam* because it "takes too much time" and is too "traditional," an activity they associate with their mothers' generation. For more on the changing meanings of the *hammam* in the Moroccan context, see Buitelaar 1998.

16. Although I never witnessed any actual occurrences of this, Fassis told me that marriages sometimes begin this way.

17. Literally, a "girl of the people" or good girl.

18. I thank an anonymous reviewer for offering the latter observation. Veiling has been the subject of books and articles too numerous to go into extensively here. For more on this topic, see Chebel 1988; El Guindi 1999; Hessini 1994; MacLeod 1991; Mernissi 1987; and Zuhur 1992.

19. "Fundamentalist" was used disparagingly by the young professional women at the exercise club. I am certain that the women who wore *hijab* would have objected to being called "*ikhwaniyin*," as it had certain class (rural migrants who had come to the city and fallen into extremist groups) and cultural (the Egyptian brotherhood, the Taliban) connotations and was a term that most religious Fassis I knew did not wish to be identified with.

20. According to Islamic law, a Muslim man may marry a Christian or Jewish woman, but a Muslim woman cannot marry outside of the faith unless her partner agrees to convert. Thus, it is rare that Moroccan women marry foreigners, while relationships between foreign women and Moroccan men are widely accepted.

21. For more on the role of women in North Africa in defining and participating in Internet technologies, see Skalli 2006.

22. My own ethnocentrism is also visible here, as I was not accustomed to seeing women breastfeeding in public spaces such as the street, so in choosing to highlight this incident, I was also unconsciously translating my own cultural framework to a different circumstance.

23. Women's honor lies in how successfully they demonstrate these cultural attributes. As Bourquia has noted, honor separates men from women, functioning in a space both relational and hierarchical (Bourquia 1996: 28). Men's honor partially depends on their certainty that "their" women are obeying the proper codes of conduct. There is an extensive literature about "honor" and "shame" in the anthropology of the Middle East. Yet the concepts of "honor" salient in these contexts are not spoken of in exactly the same manner by Fassi Moroccans, as Rosen has also pointed out for Sefrou (1984: 132). However, "shame" is a large part of everyday discussions, and is culturally valued. "Having shame" means respecting one's family, religion, and culture by displaying the ideal demeanor for one's gender and stage of life. An excellent study of the negative effects of shame on Moroccan women's sexuality can be found in Guessous 1984.

24. See Guessous (1984) for more on shame in the Moroccan context.

Chapter 7. Singing to So Many Audiences

1. I have borrowed the term "social biography" from Dale Eickelman. The term acknowledges the mutual presence of both the author's and subject's voices throughout the text.

2. Habermas 1983; Harvey 1989; and Berman 1982 have all traced these processes in great detail.

3. See Hodgson 2001 and Miller 1995 for anthropological essays that offer alternative conceptualizations of modernity.

4. This would change a few years after I left Morocco, when *Studio 2M*, a Moroccan television show that mimicked the format of *American Idol*, became hugely popular. Most of the contestants were in their late teens and early twenties, and they were judged on their abilities to sing both Western-style and Middle Eastern popular songs. In the minds of many of the middle-class Fassis I have spoken with, there is nothing shameful about a girl performing on this show. Rather, the controlled and televised setting keeps young women from being in contact with men in a live audience.

5. See, for example, Jansen 1987, van Nieuwkirk 1995, Kapchan 1996, Schade-Poulsen 1999.

6. Despite this sense that famous stars are beyond judgment, male Fassis often mentioned the rumor that Samira Saïd had appeared in low-budget porn films before becoming famous.

7. See, for example, Kapchan 1996; Weiss 1993; Lavie 1990; L. Abu-Lughod 1986.

Chapter 8. Conclusion: Community, Chaos, and Continuity

1. *New York Times Magazine*, November 25, 2007.

2. Many Moroccans commented that the ease in finally passing the *mudawana* reforms related in part to the backlash against Islamists after the May 16 attacks.

3. My Fassi friends have mentioned this to me anecdotally, but at a conference in 2005 the Moroccan government pressed this argument. It has been disputed by women's activist organizations (U.S. Department of State 2006).

4. For more on the ambivalence of *fitna*, see Pandolfo 1997.

Bibliography

Abu-Lughod, Janet. 1987. "The Islamic City—Historic Myth, Islamic Essence, and Contemporary Relevance." *International Journal of Middle East Studies* 19: 155–76.

———. 1981. *Rabat: Urban Apartheid*. Princeton, N.J.: Princeton University Press.

Abu-Lughod, Lila. 2005. *Dramas of Nationhood: The Politics of Television in Egypt*. Chicago: University of Chicago Press.

———. 2002. "Do Muslim Women Really Need Saving? Anthropological Reflections on Cultural Relativism and Its Others." *American Anthropologist* 104, 4: 783–90.

———. 1986. *Veiled Sentiments: Honor and Poetry in a Bedouin Society*. Berkeley: University of California Press.

Adam, André. 1968. *Casablanca: Essai sur la transformation de la société marocaine au contact de l'occident*. Paris: CNRS.

Afsaruddin, Asma, ed. 1999. *Hermeneutics and Honor: Negotiating Female "Public" Space in Islamic/ate Societies*. Cambridge, Mass.: Harvard University Press for Middle Eastern Monographs.

Ahmed, Leila. 1992. *Women and Gender in Islam: Historical Roots of Modern Debate*. New Haven, Conn.: Yale University Press.

Ahmida, Ali Abdullatif, ed. 2000. *Beyond Colonialism and Nationalism in the Maghrib: History, Culture, and Politics*. New York: Palgrave.

al-Fasi, Allal. 1963. *Maqasid al-shari'a al-islamiyya*. Casablanca.

al-Marouri, Abderazzak. 1989. "Regards sur la question de la femme: Sur le concept de la relation." *Risalat al-Ousra* 1: 5.

Altavista Maroc. 2003. Portail web Marocain. "Plan d'intégration de la femme au développement." http://avmaroc.com/dossiers.php?op=printpage&artid=98.

Ammann, Ludwig. 2002. "Islam in Public Space." *Public Culture* 14, 1: 277–80.

Anderson, Benedict. 1991. *Imagined Communities: Reflections on the Origin and Spread of Nationalism*. London: Verso.

Antoun, Richard T. 2000. "Civil Society, Tribal Process, and Change in Jordan: An Anthropological View." *International Journal of Middle East Studies* 2, 4: 441–63.

Appadurai, Arjun. 2000. "Grassroots Globalization and the Research Imagination." *Public Culture* 12, 1: 1–19.

———. 1996. *Modernity at Large: Cultural Dimensions of Globalization*. Minneapolis: University of Minnesota Press.

Arabic News.com. 2003. "Over 20,000 Violence Acts Against Women." http://www.arabicnews.com/ansub/Daily/Day/981113/1998111340.html; accessed April 15, 2007.

Armes, Roy. 2006. *African Filmmaking: North and South of the Sahara*. Bloomington: Indiana University Press.

Baker, Alison. 1998. *Voices of Resistance: Oral Histories of Moroccan Women*. Albany: SUNY Press.

Bakhtin, Mikhail Mikhailovich. 1986. *Speech Genres and Other Late Essays*. Trans. Vern W. McGee, ed. Caryl Emerson and Michael Holquist. Austin: University of Texas Press.

Badran, Margot. 1995. *Feminists, Islam, and Nation: Women and the Making of Modern Egypt*. Princeton, N.J.: Princeton University Press.

Bargach, Jamila. 2002. *Orphans of Islam: Family, Abandonment, and Secret Adoption in Morocco*. Lanham, Md.: Rowman and Littlefield.

Barlas, Asma. 2000. "Sex, Texts and States: A Critique of North African Discourses on Islam." In *The Arab-African and Islamic Worlds: Interdisciplinary Studies*, ed. R. Kevin Lacey and Ralph Coury. New York: Peter Lang. 97–116.

Baron, Beth. 2007. *Egypt as a Woman: Nationalism, Gender, and Politics*. Berkeley: University of California Press.

Barron, A. M. 1953. "Mariage et divorce à Casablanca." *Hesperis* 40, 3: 419–40.

Bauman, Richard. 1986. *Story, Performance, and Event: Contextual Studies of Oral Narrative*. Cambridge: Cambridge University Press.

Bekkar, Rabia. 1997. "Statut social des femmes, accès a l'espace et à la parole publique." In *Espaces publics, paroles publiques au Maghreb et au Machrek*, ed. Hannah Davis Taïeb, Rabia Bekkar, and Jean-Claude David. Paris: Harmattan.

Belarbi, Aïcha. 1992. "Mouvements des femmes au Maroc." In *La société civile au Maroc*, ed. Noureddine El Ayoufi. Rabat: Imprimerie El Maârif Al Jadida. 186–96.

Bendahman, Hussain. 1984. *Personnalité maghrébine et fonction paternelle au Maghreb*. Paris: Pensée universelle.

Benkirane, Abdelilah. 2002. Interview. *Femmes du Maroc* 83 (November).

Bennani-Chraïbi, Mounia. 2000. "Youth in Morocco: An Indicator of a Changing Society." In *Alienation or Integration of Arab Youth: Between Family, State, and Street*, ed. Roel Meijer. Oxford: Routledge. 143–60.

———. 1994. *Soumis et rebelles: Les jeunes au Maroc*. Casablanca: Éditions le Fennec.

Berque, Jacques. 1958. "Medinas, villeneuves, et bidonvilles." *Cahiers de Tunisie* 21/22: 5–42.

Berman, Marshall. 1988. *All That Is Solid Melts into Air: The Experience of Modernity*. New York: Penguin.

Berrada, Mohammed. 1996. *The Game of Forgetting*. Austin: University of Texas Press.

Bessis, Sophie and Sohayr Belhassen. 1992. *Femmes du Maghreb: L'enjeu*. Casablanca: Editions Eddif.

Bhabha, Homi, ed. 1990. *Nation and Narration*. London: Routledge.

Bier, Laura. 2006. "A Working Bibliography of Public Spheres in Comparative Context." www.ssrc.org/programs/mena/publications/ Public_Spheres_Bibliography.pdf; accessed June 12, 2006.

Blanc, François-Paul and Rabha Zeidguy, ed. 2000. *Moudawana: Code de statut personnel et des successions*. Casablanca: Sochepress-Université.

Bloch, Maurice and Jean Bloch. 1980. "Women and the Dialectics of Nature in Eighteenth-Century French Thought." In *Nature, Culture and Gender*, ed. Carol MacCormack and Marilyn Strathern. Cambridge: Cambridge University Press. 25–41.

Borrmans, Maurice. 1977. *Statut personnel et famille au Maghreb: De 1940 à nos jours*. Paris: Mouton.

Boudhiba, Abdelwahab. 1985. *Sexuality in Islam*. London: Routledge and Kegan Paul.

Bouraoui, Soukeïna. 1987. "Order masculin et fait féminin." In *Tunisie au present: Une modérnite au-dessus de tout soupçon?* ed. Michel Camau. Paris: CNRS. 343–71.

Bourdieu, Pierre. 1977. *Outline of a theory of Practice*. New York: Cambridge University Press.

———. 1966. "The Sentiment of Honour in Kabyle Society." In *Honour and Shame: The Values of Mediterranean Society*, ed. John Perstiany. London: Weidenfeld and Nicholson. 191–241.

Bourquia, Rahma. 1996. "Habitat, femmes et honneur." In *Femmes, culture et société au Maghreb*, vol. 1, *Culture, femmes et famille*, ed. Rahma Bourquia, Mounira Charrad, and Nancy Elizabeth Gallagher. Casablanca: Afrique-Orient. 15–36.

Brand, Laurie. 1998. *Women, the State, and Political Liberalization: Middle Eastern and North African Experiences*. New York: Columbia University Press.

Brenner, Suzanne. "Reconstructing Self and Society: Javanese Muslim Women and 'the Veil.'" *American Ethnologist* 23, 4: 673–97.

Brett, Michael and Elizabeth Fentress. 1996. *The Berbers*. Oxford: Blackwell.

Brown, Kenneth. 1977. "Changing Forms of Patronage in a Moroccan City." In *Patrons and Clients in Mediterranean Societies*, ed. Ernest Gellner and John Waterbury. London: Duckworth.

———. 1976. *People of Salé: Tradition and Change in a Moroccan City, 1830–1930*. Cambridge, Mass.: Harvard University Press.

Brunvand, Jan Harold. 2001. *Encyclopedia of Urban Legends*. Santa Barbara, Calif.: ABL-CIO.

Buitelaar, Marjo. 1998. "Public Baths as Private Places." In *Women and Islamization: Contemporary Dimensions of Discourse on Gender Relations*, ed. Karin Ask and Marit Tjomsland, Oxford: Berg. 103–23.

———. 1993. *Fasting and Feasting in Morocco: Women's Participation in Ramadan*. Oxford: Berg.

Burckhardt, Titus. 1992. *Fez: City of Islam*. Cambridge: Islamic Texts Society.

Burgat, François and William Dowell. 1993. *The Islamic Movement in North Africa*. Austin: Center for Middle Eastern Studies, University of Texas.

Burke, Edmund, III. 2000. "Theorizing the Histories of Colonialism and Nationalism in the Arab Maghrib." In *Beyond Colonialism and Nationalism in the Maghrib: History, Culture, and Politics*, ed. Ali Abdullatif Ahmida. New York: Palgrave. 17–34.

———. 1976. *Prelude to Protectorate in Morocco: Precolonial Protest and Resistance, 1860–1912*. Chicago: University of Chicago Press.

Burke, Kenneth. 1969. *A Grammar of Motives and a Rhetoric of Motives*. Berkeley: University of California Press.

Buskens, Leon. 2003. "Recent Debates on Family Law Reform in Morocco: Islamic Law and Politics in an Emerging Public Sphere." *Islamic Law and Society Journal* 10, 1: 70–131.

Butler, Judith. 1997. *The Psychic Life of Power*. Stanford, Calif.: Stanford University Press.

———.1990. *Gender Trouble: Feminism and the Subversion of Identity*. New York: Routledge.

Caton, Stephen. 1991. *The Peaks of Yemen I Summon: Poetry as Cultural Practice in a North Yemeni Tribe*. Berkeley: University of California Press.

Çelik, Zeynep. 1992. *Displaying the Orient: Architecture of Islam at Nineteenth Century World's Fairs.*. Berkeley: University of California Press.

Çelik, Zeynep and Laura Kinney. 1990. "Ethnography and Exhibitions at the Expositions Universelles." *Assemblages* 13: 35–59.

Centre d'Etudes et de Recherches Démographiques. 1988. *Situation démographique régionale au Maroc: Analyses comparatives.* Rabat: In Fre.

Chakrabarty, Dipesh. 1992. "Postcoloniality and the Artifice of History: Who Speaks for 'Indian' Pasts?" *Representations* 37: 1026.

Charrad, Mounira. 2001. *States and Women's Rights: The Making of Postcolonial Tunisia, Algeria, and Morocco.* Berkeley: University of California Press.

Chatterjee, Partha. 2000. "Two Poets and a Death: On Civil and Political Society in the Non-Christian World." In *Questions of Modernity,* ed. Timothy Mitchell. Minneapolis: University of Minnesota Press.

———. 1993. *The Nation and Its Fragments.* Princeton, N.J.: Princeton University Press.

Chebel, Malek. 1988. *L'esprit de serail: Perversions et marginalités sexuelles au Maghreb.* Casablanca: Lieu Commun.

Cherifi, Rachida. 1983. *Le Makhzen politique au Maroc: Hier et aujourd'hui.* Casablanca: Afrique Orient.

Chomiak, Laryssa. 2002. "Civil Society in Transition: The Experiences of Centres for Abused Women in Morocco." *Journal of North African Studies* 7, 4: 55–82.

Claisse, Alain. 1987. "Makhzen Traditions and Administrative Channels." In *The Political Economy of Morocco,* ed. I. W. Zartman. New York: Praeger. 34–58.

Clancy-Smith, Julia. 1999. "A Woman Without Her Distaff: Gender, Work, and Handicraft Production in Colonial North Africa." In *Social History of Women and Gender in the Modern Middle East,* ed. Margaret Meriwether and Judith Tucker. Boulder, Colo.: Westview Press. 25–62

Cohen, Shana. 2004. *Searching for a Different Future: The Rise of a Global Middle Class in Morocco.* Durham, N.C.: Duke University Press.

———. 2003. "Alienation and Globalization in Morocco: Addressing the Social and Political Impact of Market Integration." *Comparative Studies of Society and History* 45, 1 (January): 168–89.

Colonna, Fanny and Zakya Daoud, eds. 1993. *Être marginal au Maghreb.* Paris: CNRS.

Combs-Schilling, M. E. 1989. *Sacred Performances: Islam, Sexuality, and Sacrifice.* New York: Columbia University Press.

Coombes, Annie. 1994. *Reinventing Africa: Museums, Material Culture, and Popular Imagination in Late Victorian and Edwardian England.* New Haven, Conn.: Yale University Press.

Cornell, Vincent J. 1998. *Realm of the Saint: Power and Authority in Moroccan Islam.* Austin: University of Texas Press.

Coury, Ralph M. 2000. "Introduction." In *The Arab-African and Islamic Worlds,* ed. R. Kevin Lacey and Ralph M. Coury. New York: Peter Lang.

Crapanzano, Vincent. 1981. *The Hamadsha: A Study in Moroccan Ethnopsychiatry.* Berkeley: University of California Press.

Crawford, David. 2001. "Work and Identity in the Moroccan High Atlas." Ph.D. dissertation, Department of Anthropology, University of California, Santa Barbara.

Creed, Gerald. 2000. "'Family Values' and Domestic Economies." *Annual Review of Anthropology* 29: 329–55.

Davis, Susan Schaefer. 1982. *Patience and Power: Women's Lives in a Moroccan Village.* Cambridge, Mass.: Schenkman.
de Certeau, Michel. 1984. *The Practice of Everyday Life.* Berkeley: University of California Press.
De Haas, Hein. 2005. "Morocco's Migration Transition: Trends, Determinants, and Future Scenarios." Global Migration Perspectives 28. Geneva: Global Commission on International Migration.
de Man, Paul. *Allegories of Reading: Figural Language in Rousseau, Nietzsche, Rilke, and Proust.* New Haven, Conn.: Yale University Press, 1979.
Deeb, Lara. 2006. *An Enchanted Modern: Gender and Public Piety in Shi'i Lebanon.* Princeton: Princeton University Press.
Direction de la Statistique. 2000. *Activité, emploi, et chomage 2000: Rapport de synthèse.* Rabat.
———. 1971. *Le Maroc en chiffres.* Rabat.
Djebar, Assia. 1993. *Fantasia: An Algerian Cavalcade.* Portsmouth, N.H.: Heinemann.
Douglas, Mary. 1966. *Purity and Danger.* London: Routledge and Kegan Paul.
Doumato, Eleanor Abdella and Marsha Pripstein Posusney. 2003. "Introduction." In *Women and Globalization in the Arab Middle East: Gender, Economy, and Society,* ed. Doumato, Abdella, and Posusney. Boulder, Colo.: Lynne Rienner. 1–24.
Dwyer, Daisy Hilse. 1978. *Images and Self-Images: Male and Female in Morocco.* New York: Columbia University Press, 1978.
Early, Evelyn. 1993. *Baladi Women of Cairo: Playing with an Egg and a Stone.* Boulder, Colo.: Lynne Rienner.
Eickelman, Dale. 2001. "Islam and modernity." In *Identity, Culture and Globalization,* ed. E. Ben-Rafael and Y. Sternberg. Leiden: International Institute of Sociology. 93–104.
———. 1985. *Knowledge and Power in Morocco: The Education of a Twentieth-Century Notable.* Princeton, N.J.: Princeton University Press.
———.1976. *Moroccan Islam: Tradition and Society in a Pilgrimage Center.* Austin: University of Texas Press.
El Aoufi, Noureddine and Mohammed Bensaïd. 2005. *Chômage et employabilité des jeunes au Maroc.* Rabat: Cahiers de la stratégie de l'emploi.
El Aoufi, Noureddine, ed. 1992. *La société civile au Maroc.* Rabat: Imprimerie El Maârif Al Jadida.
El Guindi, Fadwa. 1999. *Veil: Modesty, Privacy, and Resistance.* Oxford: Berg.
El Mansour, Mohamed. 1994. "Salafists and Modernists in the Moroccan Nationalist Movement." In *Islamism and Secularism in North Africa,* ed. John Ruedy. New York: St. Martin's Press. 53–72.
Ennaji, Moha and Fatima Sadiqi. 2006. "The Feminization of Public Space: Women's Activism, the Family Law, and Social Change in Morocco." *Journal of Middle East Women's Studies* 2, 2: 86–107.
Ertürk, Yakin. 1991. "Convergence and Divergence in the Status of Muslim Women: The Cases of Turkey and Saudi Arabia." *International Sociology* 6, 1: 307–20.
Esposito, John L. 1982. *Women in Muslim Family Law.* Syracuse, N.Y.: Syracuse University Press.
Evers Rosander, Eva. 1991. *Women in a Borderland: Managing Muslim Identity where Morocco meets Spain.* Stockholm: Studies in Social Anthropology.
Ewing, Katherine. 1997. *Arguing Sainthood: Modernity, Psychoanalysis, and Islam.* Durham, N.C.: Duke University Press.

Faruqi, Lois Ibsen al-. 1985. "Music, Musicians and Muslim Law." *Asian Music* 17, 1:3–37.

Fayad, Mona. 2000. "Cartographies of Identity: Writing Maghribi Women as Postcolonial Subjects." In *Beyond Colonialism and Nationalism in the Maghrib: History, Culture, Politics*, ed. Ali Abdullatif Ahmida. New York: Palgrave Press. 85–108.

Fineman, Joel. 1981. "The Structure of Allegorical Desire." In *Allegory and Representation*, ed. Stephen J. Greenblatt. Baltimore: Johns Hopkins University Press. 26–60.

Fisher, William F. 1997. "Doing Good? The Politics and Antipolitics of NGO Practices." *Annual Review of Anthropology* 26: 439–64.

Foucault, Michel. 1980. *Power/Knowledge: Selected Interviews and Other Writings*. Ed. C. Gordon. New York: Pantheon.

Fox, Richard G., ed. 1990. *Nationalist Ideologies and the Production of National Cultures*. Washington, D.C.: American Anthropological Association.

Geertz, Clifford. 1974. " 'From the Native's Point of View': On the Nature of Anthropological Understanding." *Bulletin of the American Academy of Arts and Sciences* 28, 1: 26–45.

Geertz, Clifford, Hildred Geertz, and Lawrence Rosen. 1979. *Meaning and Order in Moroccan Society: Three Essays in Cultural Analysis*. Cambridge: Cambridge University Press.

Geertz, Hildred. 1979. "The Meanings of Family Ties." In *Meaning and Order in Moroccan Society*, ed. Clifford Geertz, Hildred Geertz, and Lawrence Rosen. Cambridge: Cambridge University Press. 315–407.

Gellner, Ernest. 1983. *Nations and Nationalism*. Ithaca, N.Y.: Cornell University Press.

———. 1981. *Muslim Society*. Cambridge: Cambridge University Press.

———. 1969. *Saints of the Atlas*. Chicago: University of Chicago Press.

Ghannam, Farha. 2002. *Remaking the Modern: Space, Relocation, and the Politics of Identity in a Global Cairo*. Berkeley: University of California Press.

Göcek, Fatma Müge and Shiva Balaghi, eds. 1994. *Reconstructing Gender in the Middle East: Tradition, Identity, Power*. New York: Columbia University Press.

Goffman, Erving. 1974. *Frame Analysis: An Essay on the Organization of Experience*. New York: Harper and Row.

———. 1959. *The Presentation of Self in Everyday Life*. Garden City, N.Y.: Doubleday.

Gold, John R. and Margaret M. 2003. "Representing Culloden: Social Memory, Battlefield Heritage, and Landscapes of Regret." In *Mapping Tourism*, ed. Stephen P. Hanna and Vincent J. Del Casino, Jr. Minneapolis: University of Minnesota Press. 108–31.

Göle, Nilufer. 2002. "Islam in Public: New Visibilities and New Imaginaries." *Public Culture* 14, 1: 173–90.

———. 1997. "The Gendered Nature of the Public Sphere." Public Culture: 10, 1: 61–81.

Gottreich, Emily. 2007. *The Mellah of Marrakech: Jewish and Muslim Space in Morocco's Red City*. Bloomington: Indiana University Press.

Greenblatt, Stephen J. "Preface." In *Allegory and Representation*, ed. Stephen J. Greenblatt. Baltimore: Johns Hopkins University Press, 1981. vii–xiii.

Guehenno, Jean. 1995. *The End of the Nation State*. Minneapolis: University of Minnesota Press.

Guerraoui, Driss. 1996. "Famille et développement à Fès." In *Femmes, culture et société au Maghreb*, vol. 1, *Culture, femmes et famille*, ed. Rahma Bourquia, Mounira Charrad, and Nancy Elizabeth Gallagher. Casablanca: Afrique-Orient. 157–78.

Guessous, Soumaya Naamane. 1984. *Au-delà de toute pudeur.* Casablanca: Éditions Eddif.

Gupta, Akhil and James Ferguson, eds. 1997. *Culture, Power, Place: Explorations in Critical Anthropology.* Durham, N.C.: Duke University Press.

Habermas, Jürgen. 1991. *The Structural Transformation of the Public Sphere.* Cambridge, Mass.: MIT Press.

———. "Modernity: An Incomplete Project." In *The Anti-Aesthetic: Essays on Postmodern Culture*, ed. Hal Foster. Port Townsend, Wash.: Bay Press. 3–15.

Haddad, Lahcen. "Women Singers (Shikhat) and the Notion of 'Nashat' in Moroccan Popular Culture." Unpublished paper, 2001.

Haddad, Yvonne Yazbeck and John L. Esposito, eds. 1998. *Islam, Gender and Social Change.* New York: Oxford University Press.

Hall, Stuart, "Cultural Identity and Diaspora." 1994. In *Colonial Discourse and Post-Colonial Theory: A Reader*, ed. Patrick Williams and Laura Chrisman. New York: Columbia University Press. 392–403.

Halpern, Manfred. 1963. *The Politics of Social Change in the Middle East and North Africa.* Princeton, N.J.: Princeton University Press.

Hammoudi, Abdellah. 2001. "From Recognition to Political Nationalization: The Tribal, the Ethnic and Their Relation to the Moroccan State." In *State Formation and Ethnic Relations in the Middle East*, ed. Usuki Akira. JCAS Symposium Series 5. Osaka: Japan Center for Area Studies. 143–62.

———. 1999. "The Re-invention of *Dar al-mulk*: The Moroccan Political System and Its Legitimation." In *In the Shadow of the Sultan: Culture, Power, and Politics in Morocco*, ed. Rahma Bourquia and Susan Gilson Miller. Cambridge, Mass.: Harvard University Press for Center for Middle Eastern Studies. 129–75.

———. 1997. *Master and Disciple: The Cultural Foundations of Moroccan Authoritarianism.* Chicago: University of Chicago Press.

———. 1993. *The Victim and Its Masks: An Essay on Sacrifice and Masquerade in the Maghreb.* Chicago: University of Chicago Press.

Hanedi, Masashi and Toru Miura, eds. 1994. *Islamic Urban Studies.* London: Kegan Paul.

Harvey, David. 1992. *The Condition of Postmodernity: An Enquiry into the Origins of Cultural Change.* New York: Wiley.

Haviland, John Beard. 1977. *Gossip, Reputation, and Knowledge in Zinacantan.* Chicago: University of Chicago Press.

Hegasy, Sonja. 1997. *Staat, Öffentlichkeit und Zivilgesellschaft in Marokko: Die Potentiale der sozio-kulturellen Opposition.* Politik, Wirtschaft und Gesellschaft des Vorderen Orients. Hamburg: Deutsches Orient-Institute.

Hegel, G. W. F. 1967. *The Phenomenology of Mind.* Trans. J. B. Baillie. New York: Harper TorchBooks.

Hessini, Leila. 1994. "Wearing the *Hijab* in Contemporary Morocco." In *Reconstructing Gender in the Middle East: Tradition, Identity, Power*, ed. Gösek, Fatma Müge, and Shiva Balaghi. New York: Columbia University Press. 40–56.

Herzfeld, Michael. 1986. "Within and Without: The Category of 'Female' in the Ethnography of Modern Greece." In *Gender and Power in Rural Greece*, ed. Jill Dubisch. Princeton, N.J.: Princeton University Press. 215–33.

Hodgson, Dorothy, ed. 2001. *Gendered Modernities: Ethnographic Perspectives.* New York: Palgrave.

Hoffenberg, Peter. 2001. *An Empire on Display: English, Indian, and Australian Exhibitions from the Crystal Palace to the Great War.* Berkeley: University of California Press.

Hobsbawm, Eric and Terence Ranger, eds. 1992. *The Invention of Tradition.* Cambridge: Cambridge University Press.

Holmes-Eber, Paula. 2003. *Daughters of Tunis: Women, Family, and Networks in a Muslim City.* Boulder, Colo.: Westview Press.

Hoodfar, Homa. 1997. *Between Marriage and the Market: Intimate Politics, and Survival in Cairo.* Berkeley: University of California Press.

Hourani, Albert and S. M. Stern, eds. 1970. *The Islamic City.* Philadelphia: University of Pennsylvania Press.

Hourani, George. 1985. *Reason and Tradition in Islamic Ethics.* Cambridge: Cambridge University Press.

Howe, Marvine. 2005. *Morocco: The Islamist Awakening and Other Challenges.* Oxford: Oxford University Press.

Jacobs, Jane. 1993. "The City Unbound: Qualitative Approaches to the City." *Urban Studies* 30: 827–48.

Jameson, Fredric. 1986. "Third-World Literature in the Era of Multinational Capitalism." *Social Text* 15: 65–88.

Jansen, Willy. 1987. *Women Without Men: Gender and Marginality in an Algerian Town.* Leiden: E.J. Brill.

Joffé, George. 1997. "Maghrebi Islam and Islam in the Maghreb." In *African Islam and Islam in Africa: Encounters Between Sufis and Islamists,* ed. Eva Evers Rosander and David Westerlund. Athens: Ohio University Press.

Joseph, Suad. 2000. "Introduction." In *Citizenship and Gender in the Middle East,* ed. Suad Joseph. Syracuse, N.Y.: Syracuse University Press. 3–32.

———. 1996. "Gender and Citizenship in Middle Eastern States." *Middle East Report* 198: 4–10.

Joseph, Suad and Susan Slyomovics. 2001. "Introduction." In *Women and Power in the Middle East,* ed. Suad Joseph and Susan Slyomovics. Philadelphia: University of Pennsylvania Press. 1–14.

Kandiyoti, Deniz. 2001. "The Politics of Gender and the Conundrums of Citizenship." In *Women and Power in the Middle East,* ed. Suad Joseph and Susan Slyomovics. Philadelphia: University of Pennsylvania Press. 52–58.

———. 1991. "Islam and Patriarchy: A Comparative Perspective." In *Women in Middle Eastern History: Shifting Boundaries in Sex and Gender,* ed. Nikki R. Keddie and Beth Barron. New Haven, Conn.: Yale University Press. 219–35.

———, ed. 1991. *Women, Islam, and the State.* Philadelphia: Temple University Press.

Kapchan, Deborah. 1996. *Gender on the Market: Moroccan Women and the Revoicing of Tradition.* Philadelphia: University of Pennsylvania Press.

———. 1994. "Moroccan Female Performers Defining the Social Body." *Journal of American Folklore* 107, 423: 82–105.

Kapferer, Jean-Noel. 1990. *Rumors: Uses, Interpretations, and Images.* New Brunswick, N.J.: Transaction Press.

Karmi, Ghada. 1996. "Women, Islam, and Patriarchy." In *Feminism and Islam: Legal and Literary Perspectives,* ed. Mai Yamani. Berkshire: Ithaca Press for University of London. 69–85.

Keck, Margaret and Kathryn Sikkink. 1998. *Activists Beyond Borders: Advocacy Networks in International Politics.* Ithaca, N.Y.: Cornell University Press.

Kilito, Abdelfettah. 1995. *La querelle des images.* Casablanca: Eddif.

Keesing, Roger. 1972. "Simple Models of Complexity: The Lure of Kinship." In *Kinship Studies in the Morgan Centennial Year*, ed. Priscilla Reining. Washington, D.C.: Anthropological Society of Washington. 17–31.

Khodja, Souad. 1985. *Les algériennes du quotidien.* Algiers: Enterprise nationale du livre.

Kleinman, Arthur, Veena Das, and Margaret Lock. 1997. *Social Suffering.* Berkeley: University of California Press.

Kozma, Liaf. 2003. "Moroccan Women's Narratives of Liberation: A Passive Revolution?" *Journal of North African Studies* 8, 1:112–30.

Kristeva, Julia. 1974. "La femme, ce n'est jamais ça." *Tel Quel* 59 (Fall): 19–26.

LaCoste-Dujardin, Camille. 1985. *Des mères contre les femmes: Maternité et patriarcat au Maghreb.* Paris: Éditions de la Découverte.

Lacoste, Yves. 1991. "Peuplements et organisation sociale." In *L'état du Maghreb*, ed. Camille Lacoste and Yves Lacoste. Tunis: Cérès Productions. 229–34.

Lamphere, Louise. 1993. "Domestic Sphere of Women and the Public World of Men: The Strengths and Limitations of an Anthropological Dichotomy." In *Gender in Cross Cultural Perspective*, ed. Caroline Bretell and Carolyn Fishel Sargent. Englewood Cliffs, N.J.: Prentice-Hall. 86–95.

Laroui, Abdallah. 1992. *Esquisses historiques.* Casablanca: Centre Cultural Arabe.

———. 1967. *L'idéologie arabe contemporaine.* Paris: Maspero.

Lavie, Smadar. 1990. *The Poetics of Military Occupation: Mzeina Allegories of Bedouin Identity Under Israeli and Egyptian Rule.* Berkeley: University of California Press.

Layachi, Azzedine. 2000. "Islamism in Algeria, Morocco, and Tunisia and the Struggle for Change." In *The Arab-African and Islamic Worlds: Interdisciplinary Studies*, ed. R. Kevin Lacey and Ralph M. Coury. New York: Peter Lang. 23–47.

LeTourneau, Roger. 1956. "Le développement d'une classe moyenne en Afrique du Nord." In *Development of a Middle Class in Tropical and Sub-Tropical Countries, Record of the XXIX Session Held in London from 13–16 September 1955.* Brussels: International Institute of Differing Civilizations. 106–10.

———. 1949. *Fés avant le protectorat: Étude économique et sociale d'une ville de l'occident musulman.* Casablanca: SMLE.

Leach, Edmund. 1970. *Claude Lévi-Strauss.* New York: Viking.

Leis, Nancy. 1974. "Women in Groups: Ijaw Women's Associations." In *Woman, Culture, and Society*, ed. Michelle Rosaldo and Louise Lamphere. Stanford, Calif.: Stanford University Press. 223–42.

Lemon, Alaina. 2000. *Between Two Fires: Gypsy Performance and Romani Memory from Pushkin to Postsocialism.* Durham, N.C.: Duke University Press.

Leveau, Rémy. 1976. *Le fellah marocain: Défenseur du trône.* Paris: Presses de la Fondation Nationale des Sciences Politiques.

Lévi-Strauss, Claude. 1969. *The Elementary Structures of Kinship.* Boston: Beacon Press.

Lukacs, Georg. 1971. *The Theory of the Novel.* Cambridge, Mass.: MIT Press.

MacCormack, Carol P. 1980. "Nature, Culture and Gender: A Critique." In *Nature, Culture and Gender*, ed. Carol MacCormack and Marilyn Strathern. Cambridge: Cambridge University Press. 1–24.

Macleod, Arlene. 1991. *Accommodating Protest: Working Women, the New Veiling, and Change in Cairo.* New York: Columbia University Press.

Maghraoui, Abdeslam. 2002. "Depoliticization in Morocco." *Journal of Democracy* 13, 4: 24–32.

Maher, Vanessa. 1978. "Women and Social Change in Morocco." In *Women in the Muslim World*, ed. Lois Beck and Nikki Keddie. Cambridge, Mass.: Harvard University Press. 100–23.

————. 1974a. *Women and Property in Morocco: Their Changing Relation to the Process of Social Stratification in the Middle Atlas.* Cambridge: Cambridge University Press.

————. 1974b. "Divorce and Property in the Middle Atlas of Morocco." *Man* n.s. 9, 1: 103–22.

Malti-Douglas, Fedwa. 1991. *Women's Body, Women's Word: Gender and Discourse in Arabo-Islamic Writing.* Princeton, N.J.: Princeton University Press.

Mattawa, Khaled. 1997. *Ismailia Eclipse: Poems.* Riverdale-on-Hudson, N.Y.: Sheep Meadow Press.

Mauss, Marcel. 2002 (1954). *The Gift: The Form and Reason for Exchange in Archaic Societies.* Abingdon: England.

Megzari, M. 1984. *La dédensification de la médina de Fès: Cadre et moyens juridiques.* Rabat: Mémoire INAU.

Merini, Rafik. 2000. "A Socio-Literary Perspective of Women in the Maghreb: Morocco, Algeria, and Tunisia." In *The Arab-African and Islamic Worlds,* ed. R. Kevin Lacey and Ralph M. Coury. New York: Peter Lang. 153–65.

Mernissi, Fatima. 1994. *The Harem Within: Tales of a Moroccan Girlhood.* London: Bantam.

————. 1991. *The Veil and the Male Elite: A Feminist Interpretation of Women's Rights in Islam.* Perseus.

————. 1989. *Doing Daily Battle: Interviews with Moroccan Women.* New Brunswick, N.J.: Rutgers University Press.

————. 1987. *Beyond the Veil: Male-Female Dynamics in Modern Muslim Society.* Cambridge, Mass.: Schenkman.

————. 1977. "Women, Saints, and Sanctuaries." *Signs* 3, 1: 101–12.

Miller, Daniel. 1995. *Worlds Apart: Modernity Through the Prism of the Local.* New York: Routledge.

Miller, Susan Gilson and Rahma Bourquia. 1999. "Introduction." In *In the Shadow of the Sultan: Culture, Power, and Politics in Morocco,* ed. Susan Gilson Miller and Rahma Bourquia. Cambridge, Mass.: Harvard University Press. 1–16.

Mir-Hosseini, Ziba. 1993. *Marriage on Trial: A Study of Islamic Family Law: Iran and Morocco Compared.* New York: Taurus.

Mitchell, Timothy. 1988. *Colonising Egypt.* Berkeley: University of California Press.

Moghadam, Valentine M. 1993. *Modernizing Women: Gender and Social Change in the Middle East.* Boulder, Colo.: Lynne Rienner.

Mohanty, Chandra Talpade, Ann Russo, and Lourdes Torres, eds. 1991. *Third World Women and the Politics of Feminism.* Bloomington: Indiana University Press.

Monson, Ingrid. 1997. "Music and the Anthropology of Gender and Cultural Identity." *Women & Music* 1, 1: 24–32.

Naciri, Rabéa. 1998. "The Women's Movement and Political Discourse in Morocco." Occasional Paper 8. New York: United Nations Research Institute for Social Development, March.

Navaro-Yashin, Yael. 2002. *Faces of the State: Secularism and Public Life in Turkey.* Princeton, N.J.: Princeton University Press.

Navez-Bouchanine, Françoise. 1990. "L'espace limitrophe, entre le privé et le public, un no man's land?" *Espaces et Sociétés* 199: 135–59.

Nelson, Cynthia. 1974. "Public and Private Politics: Women in the Middle Eastern World." *American Ethnologist* 1, 3: 551–63.

Ochs, Elinor and Lisa Capps. 1996. "Narrating the Self." *Annual Review of Anthropology* 25: 19–43.

Ohmae, Kenichi. 1996. *End of the Nation State: The Rise of Regional Economies.* New York: Touchstone.

Ong, Aihwa. 1996. "Strategic Sisterhood or Sisters in Solidarity? Questions of Communitarianism and Citizenship in Asia." *Indiana Journal of Global Legal Studies* 4, 1: 107–35.

Ormond, Meghann. 2000. "Beyond Public and Private: Cyberspace as a New Space for Young Moroccans." http://7mares.terravista.pt/meghannormond /morocco/internet.html; accessed February 29, 2004.

Ortner, Sherry. 1974. "Is Female to Male as Nature Is to Culture?" In *Woman, Culture, and Society,* ed. Michelle Rosaldo and Louise Lamphere. Stanford, Calif.: Stanford University Press. 67–87.

Ossman, Susan. 1994. *Picturing Casablanca: Portraits of Power in a Modern City.* Berkeley: University of California Press.

Pandolfo, Stefania. 1997. *Impasse of the Angels: Scenes from a Moroccan Space of Memory.* Chicago: University of Chicago Press.

Pateman, Carol. 1983. "Feminist Critiques of the Public/Private Dichotomy." In *Public and Private in Social Life,* ed. S. I. Benn and Gerald F. Gaus. London: Croom Helm. 281–303.

Pennell, C. R. 2000. *Morocco Since 1830: A History.* New York: New York University Press.

Pfeifer, Karen. 1999. "How Tunisia, Morocco, Jordan and Even Egypt Became IMF 'Success Stories' in the 1990s." *Middle East Report* 210: 23–27.

Porter, Geoffrey D. 2002. "At the Pillar's Base: Islam, Morocco and Education in the Qarawiyin Mosque, 1912–2000." Ph.D. dissertation, New York University.

———. 2002b. "Unwitting Actors: The Preservation of Fez's Cultural Heritage." *Radical History Review* 86: 123–48.

Pyle, Jean. 1990. "Export-Led Development and the Underdevelopment of Women: The Impact of Discriminatory Development Policy in the Republic of Ireland." In *Women Workers and Global Restructuring,* ed. Kathryn Wood. Ithaca, N.Y.: ILR Press. 85–112.

The Qur'an. 1990. Trans. N. J. Dawood. London: Penguin.

Rabinow, Paul. 1989. *French Modern: Norms and Forms of the Social Environment.* Chicago: University of Chicago Press.

Rassam, Amal. 1980. "Women and Domestic Power in Morocco." *International Journal of Middle East Studies* 12 (September 1980): 171–79.

Rchid, Abderrazak Moulay. 1996. "La Mudawwana en question." In *Femmes, culture, et société au Maghreb,* vol. 2, *Femmes, pouvoir politique et développment,* ed. Rahma Bourqia, Mounira Charrad, and Nancy Gallagher. Casablanca: Afrique Orient.

Reiter, Rayna. 1975. "Men and Women in the South of France: Public and Private Domains." In *Toward an Anthropology of Women,* ed. Rayna Reiter. New York: Monthly Review Press. 252–82.

Rofel, Lisa. 1999. *Other Modernities: Gendered Yearnings in China After Socialism.* Berkeley: University of California Press.

Rosaldo, Michelle Zimbalist. 1974. "Women, Culture, and Society: A Theoretical Overview." In *Woman, Culture, and Society,* ed. Michelle Rosaldo and Louise Lamphere. Stanford, Calif.: Stanford University Press. 281–99.

Rosen, Lawrence. 2002. *The Culture of Islam: Changing Aspects of Contemporary Muslim Life.* Chicago: University of Chicago Press.

————. 2000. *The Justice of Islam: Comparative Perspectives on Islamic Law and Society*. Oxford: Oxford University Press.

————. 1984. *Bargaining for Reality: The Construction of Social Relations in a Muslim Community*. Chicago: University of Chicago Press.

————. 1970. "I Divorce Thee." *Transactions* 7, 8: 35.

Rotenberg, Robert and Gary McDonogh, eds. 1993. *The Cultural Meaning of Urban Space*. Westport, Conn: Bergin & Garvey.

Royaume du Maroc. 1996. *Famille au Maroc: Les reseaux de solidarité familiale*. Rabat: Centre d'Etudes et de Récherches Demographiques.

Ruedy, John. 1994. "Introduction." *Islamism and Secularism in North Africa*, ed. John Ruedy. New York: St. Martin's Press. xxiii–xxi.

Rydell, Robert. 1984. *All the World's a Fair: Visions of America at American International Exhibitions, 1876–1916*. Chicago: University of Chicago Press.

Saad, Stephanie. 2000. "Interpreting Ethnic Quiescence: A Brief History of the Berbers of Morocco." In *The Arab-African and Islamic Worlds*, ed. R. Kevin Lacey and Ralph M. Coury. New York: Peter Lang. 167–81.

Saaf, Abdallah. 1992. "L'hypothèse de la société civile au Maroc." In *La société civile au Maroc*, ed. Noureddine El Ayoufi. Rabat: El Maârif Al Jadida. 11–31.

Sabbah, Fatna. 1984. *Woman in the Muslim Unconscious*. New York: Pergamon.

Said, Edward. 1989. "Representing the Colonized: Anthropology's Interlocutors." *Critical Inquiry* 15, 2: 205–25.

————. 1978. *Orientalism*. New York: Vintage Books.

Salahdine, Mohamed. 1992. "Les organisations internationales non gouvernementales au Maroc." In *La société civile au Maroc*, ed. Noureddine El Ayoufi. Rabat: Imprimerie El Maârif Al Jadida. 229–45.

Salamandra, Christa. 2004. *A New Old Damascus: Authenticity and Distinction in Urban Syria*. Bloomington: Indiana University Press.

Sapir, Edward. 1924. "Culture, Genuine and Spurious." *American Journal of Sociology* 29: 401–29.

Sassen, Saskia. 2000. "Spatialities and Temporalities of the Global: Elements for a Theorization." *Public Culture* 12, 1: 215–32.

Sater, James. 2002. "The Dynamics of State and Civil Society in Morocco." *Journal of North African Studies* 7, 3: 101–18.

Schade-Poulsen, Marc. 1999. *Men and Popular Music in Algeria: The Social Significance of Rai*. Austin: University of Texas Press.

Schneider, David. 1972. "What Is Kinship All About?" In *Kinship Studies in the Morgan Centennial Year*, ed. Priscilla Reining. Washington, D.C.: Anthropological Society of Washington. 32–63.

Shahin, Emad Eldin. 1997. *Political Ascent: Contemporary Islamic Movements in North Africa*. Boulder, Colo.: Westview Press.

Shibutani, Tamotsu. 1966. *Improvised News: A Sociological Study of Rumor*. Indianapolis: Bobbs-Merrill.

Shirabi, Hisham. 1988. *Neopatriarchy: A Theory of Distorted Change in Arab Society*. New York: Oxford University Press.

Shryock, Andrew. 1997. *Nationalism and the Genealogical Imagination*. Berkeley: University of California Press.

Siegel, James. 1997. *Fetish, Recognition, Revolution*. Princeton, N.J.: Princeton University Press.

Silverstein, Paul. 2004. *Algeria in France: Transpolitics, Race, and Nation*. Bloomington: Indiana University Press.

Singerman, Diane. 1995. *Avenues of Participation: Family, Politics and Networks in Urban Quarters of Cairo*. Princeton, N.J.: Princeton University Press.

Singerman, Diane and Homa Hoodfar. 1996. *Development, Change and Gender in Cairo: A View from the Household.* Bloomington: Indiana University Press.

Skalli, Loubna. 2006. "Communicating Gender in the Public Sphere: Women and Information Technologies in the MENA Region." *Journal of Middle East Women's Studies* 2, 2: 35–59.

Slyomovics, Susan. 2005. *The Performance of Human Rights in Morocco.* Philadelphia: University of Pennsylvania Press.

Smith, Andrew R. 2002. "Sedq in Morocco: On Comunicability, Partonage, and Partial Truth." *Cultural Critique* 51, 2: 101–42.

Sonbol, Amira El Azhary, ed. 1996. *Women, the Family and Divorce Laws in Islamic History.* Syracuse, N.Y.: Syracuse University Press, 1996.

———. 1994. "Changing Perceptions of Feminine Beauty in Islamic Society," in *Ideals of Feminine Beauty: Philosophical, Social and Cultural Dimensions,* ed. Karen A. Callaghan. Westport, Conn.: Greenwood Press. 53–68.

Spadola, Emilio. 2004. "Jinn, Islam, and Media in Morocco." In *Yearbook of the Sociology of Islam,* ed. Georg Stauth and Armando Salvatore. Piscataway, N.J.: Transaction. 142–72.

Spivak, Gayatri Chakravorty. 1996. "'Woman' as Theatre: United Nations Conference on Women, Beijing 1995." *Radical Philosophy* 75 (January–February): 2–4.

Stallybrass, Peter and Illon White. 1986. *The Politics and Poetics of Transgression.* Ithaca, N.Y.: Cornell University Press.

Steedly, Mary Margaret. 2000. "Modernity and the Work of the Memory Artist." *Comparative Studies in Society and History* 42, 4: 811–46.

Stevenson, Thomas. 1997. "Migration, Family and Household in Highland Yemen: The Impact of Socio-economic and Political Change and Cultural Ideas on Domestic Organization." *Journal of Comparative Family Studies* 28, 2: 14–53.

Sublet, Jacqueline. 1991. *Le voile du nom: Essai sur le nom propre arabe.* Paris: Presses Universitaires de France.

Taylor, Charles, 2002. *The Ethics of Authenticity.* Cambridge, Mass.: Harvard University Press.

———. 1995. "The Politics of Recognition." In *Multiculturalism: A Critical Reader,* ed. David Theo Goldberg. New York: Wiley. 75–106.

Taylor, Diana. 1997. *Disappearing Acts: Spectacles of Gender and Nationalism in Argentina's "Dirty War".* Durham, N.C.: Duke University Press.

Tillion, Germaine. 1983. *The Republic of Cousins.* London: Ali Saqi Books.

Timmerman, Christiane. 2000. "Muslim Women and Nationalism: The Power of the Image." *Current Sociology* 48: 15–27.

Tozy, Mohammed. 1999. *Monarchie et Islam politique au Maroc.* Paris: Presses de Sciences Politiques.

Turner, Victor. 1986. *The Anthropology of Performance.* New York: PAJ.

U.S. Department of State. 2006. "International Religious Freedom Report." http://www.state.gov/g/drl/rls/irf/2006/71428.htm; accessed December 3, 2007.

van Nieuwkerk, Karen. 1995. *"A Trade like Any Other": Female Singers and Dancers in Egypt.* Austin: University of Texas Press.

Visweswaran, Kamala. 1994. *Fictions of Feminist Ethnography.* Minneapolis: University of Minnesota Press.

Waltz, Susan E. 1995. *Human Rights and Reform: Changing the Face of North African Politics.* Berkeley: University of California Press.

Waterbury, John. 1973. "Endemic and Planned Corruption in a Monarchical Regime." *World Politics* 25: 533–35.

Weber, Max. [1922] 1978. *Economy and Society.* Ed. Guenther Roth and Claus Wittich. Berkeley: University of California Press.

Weiss, Sarah. 1993. "Gender and Gender: Gender Ideology and the Female Gender Player in Central Java." In *Rediscovering the Muses: Women's Musical Traditions,* ed. Kimberly Marshall. Boston: Northeastern University Press. 21–48.

Wheatley, Paul. 2001. *The Places Where Men Pray Together.* Chicago: University of Chicago Press.

White, Jenny. 1994. *Money Makes Us Relatives: Women's Labor in Urban Turkey.* Austin: University of Texas Press.

White, Luise. 2000. *Speaking with Vampires: Rumor and History in Colonial Africa.* Berkeley: University of California Press.

Wright, Gwendolyn. 1991. *The Politics of Design in French Colonial Urbanism.* Chicago: University of Chicago Press.

Yamani, Mai, ed. 1996. *Feminism and Islam: Legal and Literary Perspectives.* Berkshire: Ithaca Press for University of London.

Yeganeh, Nahid. 1993. "Women, Nationalism and Islam in Contemporary Political Discourse in Iran." *Feminist Review* 44: 3–18.

Ziai, Fati. 1997. "Personal Status Codes and Women's Rights in the Maghreb." In *Muslim Women and the Politics of Participation: Implementing the Beijing Platform,* ed. Mahnaz Afkhami and Erika Friedl. Syracuse, N.Y.: Syracuse University Press. 72–82.

Zerdoumi, Nefissa. 1970. *Enfant d'hier: L'éducation de l'enfant en milieu traditionnel algérien.* Paris: Maspero.

Zghal, Abdelkader. 1971. "L'édification nationale au Maghreb." *Revue Tunisienne de Sciences Sociales* 27: 20.

Zuhur, Sherifa. 1992. *Revealing Reveiling: Islamist Gender Ideology in Contemporary Egypt.* Albany: SUNY Press.

Index

rural judges and implementation problems, 204n.3; and the state's use of authoritarian strategy, 200n.29; and triple divorce formula, 71, 84; and urban-rural dichotomies, 52–53, 64–65
mudawana reforms (and patriarchal social structure), 6, 53, 59–63, 65–78, 81–82; authoritarianism and master/disciple power schema, 61, 202n.7; the basic patriarchal social model, 59–60; and bride price (*sdaq*), 53, 55, 66–71, 91–92; and early marriages, 65; and history of *mudawana* law, 61–62; and Islam/Maliki school of jurisprudence, 70–71; and male legal guardian (*wali*), 55, 56, 62–63, 66–71, 202–3n.11; and middle- and upper-class women, 59; "neo-patriarchy" and authoritarianism, 202n.3; and 1993 changes, 62, 68–69, 202–3n.11; tensions between traditional/modern views of marriage, 68, 70
mudawana reforms (and polygamy), 56, 71–76; abandoned wives and men's failure to support (*nafaqa*), 74–75; and economics, 73–74; illegality in other Middle Eastern nations, 71–72; and Islamic law, 71–72; and levirate marriages, 203n.19; middle-class defenders of, 72–73, 77, 203n.20; popular Fassi views of polygamous marriages, 71–74; and 2003/2004 revisions, 71, 77; and "triple divorce" formula, 71, 84; and women who do not want to divorce, 75–76
mudawana reforms (2003/2004 revisions), 26, 77, 186, 200n.29; challenges in enforcement, 77; and the custom of the *wali*, 69; and divorce, 77, 186, 208n.3; and Islamist political organizations, 77; issues still not addressed, 77; the king's role, 26, 77, 186, 200n.29; and marital property/houses, 204n.5; muted criticisms, 77; and polygamy, 71, 77
music, Moroccan: *milhun* music, 163, 165; and repertoire of Layla (female singer), 163, 164, 165; *shikhat* performers, 163, 180–81; and singing/music in history of Islam, 178. *See also* female singers in Morocco
Muslim Spain, 198n.13

nafaqa (women's legal right to support), 74–75, 91–92

Najia Belghazi Center (women's NGO in Fes), 2, 79–105; and abandoned/unsupported wives, 75, 87–88, 92, 191; attempts to create solidarity, 82, 92–93, 97–102, 103–4, 190; building location of, 84–85; building tour, 84–85; and child support, 80; and clients' invocations of human rights discourse, 86; client-volunteer interactions, 82, 99; complexity of women's problems without quick legal fixes, 81–82; and culturally specific problems/causes of inequality, 98–99; daily operations/typical day, 2, 84–92; difficulties recruiting professional volunteers, 100–102; difficulties related to laws favoring patriarchal authority, 93–94; divorced and abandoned women, 80–81, 87–88, 92, 191; and documentary evidence, 83, 89; domestic violence issues, 52, 85, 88–90, 92; and employment initiatives for women, 85, 104–5, 204n.14; as existing outside "civil society," 92–93; expanding mandate, 85; failures/difficulties in creating solidarity, 82, 92–102, 103–4, 190; and familial/kinship idioms, 77–78; focus on "juridical violence," 98–100; formal sessions/legal consultations, 86; and history of Moroccan women's NGOs, 94–96; Malika's story, 52, 53–56; marital rape cases, 83–84; and Moroccan feminist movement, 94–96; and Moroccan modernization/globalization, 82, 93, 94, 102, 103–4, 109; and *mudawana* reforms, 85, 97, 99, 186; name of headquarters, 204n.4; and new socioeconomic challenges linked to SAPs and globalization, 82, 93, 94, 102–4, 109; and patriarchal structures of Moroccan legal system, 81–82, 93–94; and police, 83, 89; the possibilities/limits for NGO-led intervention in the Moroccan context, 81–82; resistance encountered, 93, 100; and social class differences, 93, 100, 102, 104; success stories, 52; toning down radical discourse, 97, 204n.10; transnational links with other women's NGOs, 98; and transnational marriage disputes, 91–92; and "violence against women" umbrella issue, 97–99; volunteers' characteristics, 84; women's

rumors (continued)
regret," 42, 50; shantytown residents
and discourses about wealth/poverty,
33–36, 38–42; and social context, 32–
34, 51; as social critique of rural migration and unemployment, 40–42; stories
of disenfranchised young men, 33,
46–50; stories of the successful Fassi émigrés, 33, 48–50
rural migration. See migration (rural-to-
urban)

Saadi, Mohamed Said, 97–98
Sadiqi, Fatima, 94, 95
Said, Edward, 14
Saïd, Samira, 164, 179, 208n.6
Salafi Islam, 23, 199n.24
SAPs. See structural adjustment programs
Sassen, Saskia, 103
Schneider, David, 123–24
Sefrou, Morocco, 110–11, 113–14, 122,
123, 205n.5
shame (hshuma): breast-feeding and display-and-concealment, 147–49, 207n.22;
and female beggars, 127–28, 147–49;
and female singers, 157, 160; and fitna
(societal chaos), 157; middle-class ideas
of, 147–49; and women's disputes in
new public spaces, 139, 149–50; and
women's honor, 148, 207n.23; and wom-
en's presence in new urban spaces, 130,
138, 139, 141–42, 147–50, 157
shantytowns/shantytown residents: and
'arubi (people of rural origin), 41–42;
and discourses of 'arubi contagion,
41–42; in large cities of Morocco, 38;
rumors and Fassi discourses of wealth/
poverty, 33–36, 38–42
Sharabi, Hisham, 202n.3
shikhat performers, 163, 180–81
Sidi Mohamed Ben Abdellah University
(Fes), 59
Siegel, James, 157–58
Sikkink, Kathryn, 98
Silverstein, Paul, 198n.17
Slyomovics, Susan, 76, 201n.14
social class: and education, 20; and employ-
ment/occupations possibilities, 20; and
family sizes/family planning, 119; and
Najia Belghazi Center's attempts to create solidarity, 93, 100, 102, 104; and

"original" Fassis, 18–19, 189–90, 198–
99n.18; and stances on mudawana
reforms, 58–59, 189–90
Steedly, Mary, 181, 184–85
streets: idealized orientation of men
toward, 135; and men's demeanor,
140–41; photograph of women outside
Ville Nouvelle newsstand, 141; rules for
women's demeanor, 127, 135, 140–42;
street harassment, 141
structural adjustment programs (SAPs),
19–20, 93, 102–4, 109; and challenges
for women's NGOs, 82, 93, 94, 102–4,
109; and deterioration of extended family structures, 94; and development of
private sector, 19–20; and globalization
in Morocco, 19–20, 82, 102–4; and kinship as middle-class resource, 109; and
rural-to-urban migration, 42, 82; and
unemployment, 19–20, 82, 103, 104, 109
"structural nostalgia," 198n.17

Taliban, 31
Taylor, Charles, 156
Taylor, Diana, 131
Tazi, Abderrahmane, 71, 203n.16
Tazi family of Fes: author's participant-
observation with, 111–14, 205n.9; family
members' employment, 112–13; family
members' marital status, 112, 205n.11;
family members' migration, 125; family
name, 112, 120–22; family origins/his-
torical ties to city of Fes, 112–13; family-
owned apartment building and its
inhabitants, 112–13, 121, 123, 205n.11;
family sizes, 118–19; marriage practices,
116–20, 123; perceptions of patron-client relationships, 114, 116; residential
patterns of married couples, 114, 117,
122–23; unmarried women and public
sphere, 117–18, 122; and woman-cen-
tered patron-client networks, 108–9,
114–16, 123. See also kinship and Moroccan middle class
Taznakht, Morocco, 12–13
territories of ideology, 7–10, 21–26; competing ideologies, 4; and conceptualizations of power, 9; and "everyday
practices," 21–26; and Fassi identity, 9,
199n.20; and female singers, 152–85;
and hegemony, 155; the ideal Moroccan

Acknowledgments

This research was completed with support from Princeton University, a Fulbright Fellowship, and a Cornell grant from Rollins College. In Fes, I would like to thank all the women from the Nawal Belhamr Center. To Jamila Ben Cheqroun and Jamila El Bekkaoui I will be endlessly grateful. The American Language Institute of Fes, ALIF, provided essential instruction in dialectical Arabic that enabled me to switch over from Modern Standard Arabic to better communicate with people. People in Fes at various points in my fieldwork who were instrumental in my thinking through many of these issues include Mara Kronenfeld, Beth Daniel, Karla Sabin, Ben Troutman, Emilio Spadola, Jenny Gillott, Zakia El Ouezzani, Asma El Mehdi, and Fatima Sadiqi.

In Rabat: Abdelhay Moudden and Farah Cherif D'Ouezzan, who first introduced me to Morocco and have continued to be wonderful friends and colleagues.

In Princeton: Abdellah Hammoudi and Larry Rosen, first and foremost, for their guidance in all things scholarly and Moroccan. I was extremely lucky to have been able to apprentice myself to them throughout graduate school. I am also grateful to Rena Lederman, Carolyn Rouse, and Jim Boon, for excellent comments along the way that were helpful in revising this book. I thank Carol Zanca, for supporting not only me but also countless other graduate students who would not have been able to succeed without her. I am lucky to have known Lisa Wynn, who has always been very generous with her time and in blazing a trail before me, and all the other members of the Cyber Writing Group— Alexander Edmonds, Chris Garces, Kristi Latta, Sarah Pinto, Haley Duschinski, Tom Strong, Kirsten Scheid, and Susanna Trnka. Delia Welsh and Yahia Amehraye have also provided years of experience and feedback on all things Moroccan.

For reading and commenting incisively on different chapters, I would like to thank David Crawford, Alexander Edmonds, and Kirsten Scheid.

At Rollins College, Larry Van Sickle, Jenny Cavenaugh, Margaret McLaren, and Nolan Kline provided essential feedback on various parts of the manuscript. The Bad Ones Writing Group, under the able leadership of Julian Chambliss, gave useful commentary on various parts of the manuscript. Many thanks go to Gay Biery-Hamilton, Helen Byrd, Mimi

Fernandez, Carol Lauer, Bob Moore, and Pedro Pequeño for providing a supportive department and a wonderful working environment. I could not ask for better colleagues.

At the University of Pennsylvania Press, I am particularly grateful for the encouragement and guidance of Kirin Narayan, the editor of this series, whose literary sensibilities helped me shape the narratives herein. I thank Peter Agree, editor-in-chief, for reading and supporting this project wholeheartedly. I am also thankful for the editorial guidance of Chris Hu and Alison Anderson. Holly Knowles provided expert assistance with the index. Deborah Kapchan offered a close and careful reading that has been instrumental in the revision process.

I thank Haley Duschinski for introducing me to anthropology in the first place, and for her friendship, comments, and helpful critiques over the years. Mara Kronenfeld has provided essential friendship, moral support, and critical advice on both life and ethnography.

I am most thankful for my husband, Noureddine Bennani, who drew me to Fes in the first place and who has offered incredible insight into Fassi social life. This book would not have been possible without him. And finally, I dedicate this to my parents, Wilburn Newcomb and Lorraine Gorrell. My father's profound curiosity in the human condition helped me to become a better observer of social life. In addition to her unconditional support, my mother has read and provided thoughtful and productive critiques of almost everything I have ever written. She is a model for the kind of scholar, teacher, and mother I would like to be.

Portions of Chapter 2 appeared in an earlier form in "Disorganized Shantytowns, Disorderly Fundamentalists: The 'Other' Sense of Fassi Rumors," *Journal of North African Studies* 9, 4 (Winter 2004), reprinted with permission of Taylor & Francis Ltd (http://www.tandf.co.uk/jour nals). The argument and significant parts of Chapter 5 first appeared in "From the 'Unseen' to the Visible: Transformations in Women's Kinship Practices Among the Urban Middle Class in Fes, Morocco," *Anthropology of the Middle East* 2, 1 (Spring 2007), published by Berghahn Press and appearing with permission of the publisher. Finally, parts of Chapter 6 were derived significantly from "Gendering the City, Gendering the Nation: Contesting Urban Space in Fes, Morocco," *City and Society* 18, 2 (December 2006), reprinted by permission of Blackwell Publishing.